CLIO'S LAWS

Joe R. and Teresa Lozano Long Series in Latin American and Latino Art and Culture

CLIO'S LAWS

ON HISTORY AND LANGUAGE

MAURICIO TENORIO-TRILLO

TRANSLATED BY MARY ELLEN FIEWEGER

University of Texas Press ⟡ Austin

Chapters 1 and 5 were part of *Historia y celebración* (two editions, Mexico City, 2009, and Barcelona, 2010, both published by Tusquets). Different versions of chapters 2, 3, 7, and 9 were published in *Culturas y memoria* (Mexico City: Tusquets, 2012). The author thanks Editorial Tusquets for reverting the rights to both works to him. A preliminary version of chapter 4 was published in the magazine *Letras Libres*; a shorter, different version of chapter 6 was published in *Nexos*; parts of an early version of chapter 8 were published in *Public Culture* (19, no. 3, 2007); and chapter 10 was extracted from *Maldita lengua* (Madrid: La Huerta Grande, 2016).

Requests for permission to reproduce material from this work should be sent to:
   Permissions
   University of Texas Press
   P.O. Box 7819
   Austin, TX 78713-7819
   utpress.utexas.edu/rp-form

♾ The paper used in this book meets the minimum requirements of ANSI/NISO Z39.48-1992 (R1997) (Permanence of Paper).

Library of Congress Cataloging-in-Publication Data

Names: Tenorio-Trillo, Mauricio, 1962–, author. | Fieweger, Mary Ellen, translator.
Title: Clio's laws : on history and language / Mauricio Tenorio-Trillo ; translated by Mary Ellen Fieweger.
Other titles: Joe R. and Teresa Lozano Long series in Latin American and Latino art and culture.
Description: First edition. | Austin : University of Texas Press, 2019. | Series: Joe R. and Teresa Lozano Long series in Latin American and Latino art and culture | Includes bibliographical references.
Identifiers: LCCN 2019012747
   ISBN 978-1-4773-1926-0 (cloth : alk. paper)
   ISBN 978-1-4773-1928-4 (library e-book)
   ISBN 978-1-4773-1929-1 (nonlibrary e-book)
Subjects: LCSH: Historiography. | History--Methodology. | History--Philosophy. | Literature and history. | Language and history.
Classification: LCC D13 .T4545 2019 | DDC 907.2--dc23
LC record available at https://lccn.loc.gov/2019012747

doi:10.7560/319260

CONTENTS

History is a serious matter; language, too, especially dwelling fully within it. After years of toiling in these solemn matters, at times it has seemed that writing and teaching history is like wrecking a riddle: either because the historian, being unable to approach it with all the facts in hand, has to abandon the enigma or because the riddle vanishes when it is explained with method and precision. In order to advance a wise and well-documented study, the historian must put her riddles away in a drawer, for what history can be told by lingering over the many enigmas of each situation, fact, or concept? Then again, if the historian doesn't possess a drawer of doubts and riddles, what history can she tell? In short, a veritable mess; every historian faces it as best she can.

Through the years, along with such serious and professional works as I've been able to write in English and Spanish, I've published "divertimentos," attempting to deal with the riddles that attract me. I've done so in the only tone and language in which I can: in Spanish—the language in which I can experiment and at the same time be experimented on—and in essays at once humorous, historiographic, and literary, blending facts, research, and imagination of the past, present, and future. To be sure, the style of each piece is no accident; I don't know whether I would have been able to explore my riddles without irony and paradox. The style frees me to experiment, true, but it also forces me to explore historical, philosophical, and political riddles deeply and honestly. That rigor limits my prospects of intellectual grandeur, political relevance, or stylistic innovation. Don't get me wrong: I claim neither innocence nor modesty; just like any mainstream professor, I make use of those common, powerful contentions of academic English—*I argue, I submit, I theorize*. I do it with my neck attached to the leash of irony and to those few certainties that I have managed to gain in my role as teacher, researcher, and writer of histories and stories. I hope it is clear that I essay, that is, I try, I criticize, I self-criticize, and I attempt to imagine better futures. Nothing more. If such a task displays a lack or an excess of intellectual vanity, let that be measured by the annoyance, indifference, doubts, and laughter that my essays provoke.

I never thought, however, that my riddles in Spanish would be read in English. Maybe I write essays in such a vernacular due to my inability to feel at home in our current Latin (English), which I learned poorly after language's neurons had hardened. Maybe. But also I have done so to speak to my tribe, which is much more and much less than "Mexico," and thus satisfy my passion for words and ideas. How much of this rusticity is translatable or interesting, beyond the natural confines of my prose in Spanish, remains to be seen. I thank the University of Texas Press for the interest and efforts that have made the translation possible. I am of the opinion, however, that most of what I've written in Spanish, the way I've written it, either is untranslatable or is not of the slightest interest in the Latin of our era. That's why the experiment inspires in me both hope and terror.

The essays deal with two fundamental concerns: on the one hand, history, its what and its how; on the other, words, language, as a craft, as a refuge, and as a jail. These are subjects so vast that my "divertimentos" only add a few riddles, a bit of mocking, and, why not, a bit of irreverence: a voice perhaps mistaken but not more of the same.

I thank the Alexander von Humboldt Stiftung for the Humboldt-Foreschungspreis, and the Friedrich-Meinecke-Institut, Freie Universität, Berlin, for granting me the time and facilities to work on the translation of these essays. I am profoundly grateful to both Mary Ellen Fieweger for the translation of complicated prose and Matico Josephson, *un hombre de palabra*, for his invaluable editorial work in the book's last stages of production.

I want the English rendition of these essays to be my belated statement of gratitude to my friends Judith Coffin, William Forbath, James Sidbury, William Tobin, Kevin Kenny, and Tony, John, Terrie, and Scarlet Nerad.

Mauricio Tenorio-Trillo
Chicago, Berlin, Mexico
Winter 2017–2018

CLIO'S LAWS

I

ON HISTORY

Chapter 1

THE LAWS OF HISTORY

I know neither how nor why, but these laws were entrusted to me and I transcribe them here. They are the laws of history. I hope the reader will forgive the complex prose: the subject requires it.

Herod's Law:[1] In history, everything turns out badly in the long run. In light of the proliferation of happy endings in histories written during the nineteenth century, nowadays the law comes with the "Machado Addendum," which goes like this: "Hoy es siempre todavía" (Today is forever still).[2] From this three axioms follow: (a) evil in history is a matter of time; (b) happiness has already happened; and (c) any good fortune, peace, or happiness in the present, no matter how relative, is a victory that must be defended, at times even against history itself (cf. Universal Law of History's Injustice).

Coda:

"Cualquiera tiempo pasado fue mejor" (Any past time was better): a sentiment expressed by a fifteenth-century poet (Jorge Manrique). For twentieth-century mystic and Marxist philosopher Walter Benjamin, present happiness was only possible via redemption. That is, the image of happiness "is indissolubly bound up with the image of redemption. The same applies to our view of the past, which is the concern of history" ("On the Concept of History," in *Illuminations*, translated by Harry Zohn). Behold Herod's Law defeated by redemption, which, nevertheless, is only possible at some point in the future, neither in the present nor in the past, that shines—the metaphor is Benjamin's: "As flowers turn toward the sun, by dint of a secret heliotropism the past strives to turn toward that sun which is rising in the sky of history." In other words, present happiness is conceivable only as the possibility of future happiness. (For that matter, the Catholic ideas of heaven, purgatory,

3

and hell serve the same purpose.) But, as we know, Benjamin, historical materialism, and God also turned out badly (Herod's Law).

On the other hand, the present can be a more or less acceptable half-heaven or half-hell, as a result of which writing history becomes either a pragmatic resignation or a tabula rasa. Either "this is how we come to a more or less acceptable present, it's neither ideal nor perfect, but it's what there is" or "since every glance at the past only opens more wounds, let's build the present from zero." Neither procedure defeats Herod's Law, but each delays its irrevocable verdict.

Faustian Law of History: This law is difficult to observe because no one has seen the face of either Mephisto or Faust. To understand it, we have to accept two truths. On the one hand, *ars longa, vita brevis*—science (knowledge) is long, life is short. On the other, in any modern "today," time is experienced as acceleration. Given these truths, the historian responds by selling his soul to an odd Mephisto who, in exchange for furnishing him with a bit of erudition, imposes three sentences on the historian (in the voice of Mephisto):

(a) In the face of growing complexity, the lucidity that I grant you will allow you to imagine general and universal abstractions, but they will be unpronounceable without history, that which is past and that which is passing. *Ergo*, *ceteris paribus*, for you there will be no *ceteris paribus* worth a rat's ass.

(b) I will grant you erudition, but you will be unable to narrate it. I thus condemn you to synthesis.

(c) You will manage to intuit as though you were in the past—and that's nothing to be sneezed at—but, so you don't just become another run-of-the-mill prophet, I condemn you to carry a heavier load of the present in the past than of the past in the present.

Generally, these sentences go unnoticed or are even at times confused with "good historiography." Not so. This is merely the historian serving her sentences.

Law of History's Party-Loving Nature: History, in and of itself, doesn't demand celebrations; its concern is with the past. The verb "to celebrate" connotes a charged present tense. For centuries, religious calendars cyclically celebrated the one true history: God (generally throughout the year).

Calendars privileged agricultural, religious, and political cycles. It follows that celebration is to history as Isaac Newton's apple is to the law of universal gravitation. That is, first, the historical celebrations par excellence, the celebrations of national history, are modern phenomena, like Newton's apple. Second, celebration has nothing to do with the past (just as the apple was in no way to blame for Newton's digressions). Third, despite this, celebrations can become evidence of history's relevance and logic—just as the apple, as it fell, was evidence of universal gravitation. It follows that history demands no celebration, but Clio's demands and concerns may take charge once the fete is underway. History can veer into partying and stop being true historical knowledge—stop being a discussion of interpretations of the past, the state of the present, plans for the future. Or it can become a densely historical blowout—that is, a celebration can preserve debates about the past like a time capsule, a mark on the road that leaves proof of past imaginings: of imagined futures at a given moment and public doubts about the past, present, and future. Three essential axioms of historical celebration are derived from this:

(a) The past in the rough doesn't demand celebration.

(b) It is a political decision to celebrate, not a historical or historiographical one. Ergo, when societies celebrate history, they celebrate not past but present.

(c) Historical celebrations fall, like Newton's apple, on their own. Everything depends on the what, how, and why of the celebration.

Universal Law of the Origin of Heroism (also known as Carlyle's Law or Wilde's Law):[3] Heroes are made not by the sword but in bed. And all of them wind up killing, or being killed by, what they love.

Law of the Growing Transitional Tendency, or G-Spot, of the Writing of History: The discipline of history calls every period, phenomenon, moment, or event in which what really happened is not known a "transition." Ergo, unless something else altogether happened, or until proven otherwise, history was transitioning, transitioned, was experienced, or is being experienced as a period of transition. A wise historian has expressed this law with the following metaphor, an astute paraphrase of Heraclitus: "We never step into the same river twice, but it's always the same transition that gets us wet."

Law of History's Null Utility: History serves, in essence, to provide the conditions of existence, real and theoretical, for the irrevocable question: why history? The question is its own answer; anything added is simply proof of history's null utility: *Narrare necesse est.*

Law of the Omnipresence of Oblivion or Funes's Law:[4] History is the science of forgetfulness; what prevails in history is not memory but forgetting, because, on the one hand, before knowing the past all is accidental forgetfulness, and, on the other, to know the past, history works like a selective forgetting that also aspires to a greater oblivion in the form of a great idea or belief made of utmost forgetfulness—such as nations, eras of peace, empires, identities.

> Coda:
> The universe of what has happened in the past, until it is discovered and written down, is forgetfulness. In, for example, the history of the Crusades from the Muslim side, many things are rescued from forgetfulness while others remain forgotten. What's more, once a synthesis of forgetfulness and memory is roughly established, what generally follows, sooner or later, is forgetting. Example: consider the histories told by Pan-Germanism versus the treatment of Germany's past today or the history of the United States up to 1968 versus the new social history of the United States.

Law of Universal Concupiscence: It's the human condition, given the opportunity, for everything and everyone to bed down with everyone and everything, yesterday, today, and tomorrow. The law is also known as genesic appetite: history has the monopoly on promiscuity.

> Coda:
> The myth of Mexican *mestizaje*, for example, is the glorification of this law of history, as though eating and sleeping were the exclusive boast of one people. Where are there no mestizos? Could it have been any other way? Meanwhile, in light of this law of history, the myth of nonmiscegenation in American historiography is absurd. The laws of history have not even forgiven the incorruptible Thomas Jefferson, an aristocrat who fell victim to this implacable law by loving a plebeian black woman. The Law of Universal Concupiscence, which made thousands, like Mr. Jefferson, beget offspring to follow in the footsteps of all the hybrids "que en el mundo han sido" (that have ever existed in the world).[5] Also, the history, for instance, of American pragmatism was the result of a long promiscuity of ideas that made possible: (a) that Charles S.

Pierce could advance an American school of philosophy; and (b) that, say, Antonio Cánovas del Castillo during the Spanish Restoration could be a philosophical pragmatist without ever having read Pierce.

Addendum to the Law of the Triumphant Writing of History: In effect, history is written by the victors . . . if they know how to write history; losers don't write history . . . unless they do know how to do it. In other words: not all those who are able to write history are victors; nor are all victors interested in writing history.

Coda:

Francisco Xavier Clavijero and Lucas Alamán, for example, wrote the first important histories of Mexico but were losers. Hernán Cortés and Spain were the winners, but Cortés did not write the complete victor's history and Spain did not stop contradicting the histories that mocked its victory—those stories that the true victors wrote: the black legend of Spain, which produced more history than Spain's triumphal epic in importance and quantity. Another example: the most solid and influential history of the Spanish Civil War until well into the 1980s was written by the losers: former members of the International Brigades (especially the English), exiles, historians from various non-Spanish universities, all with clear Republican (and sometimes also anarchist and Communist) sympathies. The Francisco Franco regime chose, instead, to silence the subject, and what little history was produced was not well regarded at all, neither then nor now, within Spain or without.

Law of History's State of Nature: In the beginning all was violence and afterward, too. The natural state of history is violence—peace is the exception (cf. Herod's Law).

Law of Universal Exoticism or the General Theorem of Otherness: In history the goodness of the good guys, and the badness of the bad guys, is directly proportional to the temporal, cultural, and spatial distance from which they are viewed. At close range, almost nobody and nothing in history is overwhelmingly bad or absolutely good. Evil exists, certainly, but it's more impure than extraordinary. From this the four basic postulates of the theorem of otherness follow:

(a) By definition, in history, the bad guys are the others. Or . . .

(b) If we are the bad guys, the others won big time.

(c) If the best of the best are the others, it's because we see them from a great distance.

(d) If the worst of the worst are the others, then we aren't paying much attention to ourselves.

Bloch's Law or Law of the Indetermination and Insignificance of the Uncaused Cause (also known as the "go no further" enigma): Behind every historical cause is another cause, and behind that yet another, and so on ad infinitum. The uncaused cause cannot be pointed to because it may be as large, though useless, as God or Class Struggle or as simple and insignificant as a cold, a bad day, or "because they felt like it." From which follows the axiom of historical reason: History wears down our sanity because within it reason lasts as long, determines in like fashion, saves neither more nor less, and explains just as unreason does. Small wonder that generally Bloch's Law is followed by an addendum regarding what is vital in history, which goes like this: "In history, as in life, rational steps tend to be what is important; the vital steps are the irrational ones."

Coda:

To search for the final, essential cause, for example, of capitalism or the French Revolution, can lead to rational absurdities. Therefore, historians tend to take refuge in what, in Mexico, is called the *muégano casuístico*, the casuistic combo which is to affirm that a little bit of everything caused this or that historical phenomenon. What proves impenetrable is the irrational nature of the vital steps: as immoral as it may seem, in 1933, National Socialism presented a rational agenda for the reconstruction of the country after the debacle of the Weimar Republic. It even managed to stop Germany's inflation, unemployment, and loss of prestige. Ergo, what was important was achieved through means that, though immoral, were rational. But reassigning tremendously valuable material and human resources—in the midst of the battle against the Allied powers that required all the trucks, tanks, resources, and men available—to slaughter two million Jewish Poles . . . that was irrational, but it was above all a vital decision without which National Socialism could not live.

Shakespeare's Law:[6] The worst always happens, but as long as we can still say "this is the worst," the worst is never the worst (cf. Herod's Law).

General Law of the Kinematics of Perjury: Betrayal is to history what oxygen is to fire; without betrayal there would be neither history nor any reason to write it. We conclude that loyalty in history either is false or constitutes "the end of history." That history has not ended is the irrefutable proof that treachery is on the loose.

General Law of Hope: Johan Huizinga said that during the decline of the Middle Ages optimism did not exist; hope is the science of history's foster sibling. History, the modern history that we recognize as our real journey from the beginning to today, arises with the possibility of optimism—that is, progress, hope, advancement. In history, hope is essential for the survival of individuals and societies, but hope is neither born nor dies naturally. It is created and destroyed with more or less conscious contrivances: for individuals, as for nations, the mechanisms for the creation of hope are as important as those for its destruction. There is no one who could live without hope, nor anyone who could survive without knowing how to kill hope when the inevitable moment arrives—this final moment frequently mediated by the so-called Pedro Flores Amendment, which goes: "esperanza inútil, flor de desconsuelo . . . ¿por qué no te mueres, por qué no te mueres en mi corazón?" (useless hope, flower of distress . . . why won't you die, why won't you die in my heart?) (cf. Herod's Law).

Juárez Law or Law of History's Permanent Secularization: History is not ruled by divine mandate, but God, though dead, never leaves history's stage. From here comes the sarcasm of a certain philosopher of history, whose name I prefer not to remember, who fawningly stated that Clio was not a *musa* (muse) but a *misa* (mass). It follows that history is the only nondivine and even antireligious art that God does not leave to its own devices.

Coda:
All modern national histories are one or another form of a triumphant narrative of secularization; but, on the one hand, no history can be told, yesterday or today, without the omnipresence of God as a historical factor as important as class contradictions, industrialization, or the Enlightenment. On the other, the history of secularized concepts such as the people, sovereignty, the state, and community has to make a great effort to disregard their religious nature. For Karl Marx as for Auguste Comte, history ran from the excess to the absence of God. More careful historians, like Ernest Renan, knew that "God never dies," that the historian has to write history while recognizing

but evading his shadow. And, very prophetically, Renan left this in writing (*Histoire du peuple d'Israël*) so that we could read it in our time of massacres in the name of Christian, Jewish, and Muslim fundamentalisms:

> It is by no means impossible that the world, tired out by the constant bankruptcy of liberalism, will once more become Jewish and Christian. It will be then that a disinterested history of these two great creeds will be of value; for the period when impartial studies upon the past of humanity are possible to us may not last very long. The taste for history is the most aristocratic of tastes; so it runs some risks.[7]

Dixit Renan, but this is about nothing more than history's Juárez Law.

Law of the Universal Gravitation of History: History is knowledge that levitates over a mass of documented facts, but, first, it is knowledge that neither begins nor ends in pure documents; and, second, the attraction that facts exert on this type of knowledge does not allow it to fly free. Neither is every interpretation valid nor can everything that is said be exchanged for documents.

Law of the Amorphous Nature of History: In its natural state, the past has no top, bottom, or middle. Nor center or periphery. When historians talk about history from the top down, or from bottom up, they are shaping rather than describing the past. From which it follows that, in social terms, it isn't as if there were not, let's say, "those above" and "those below" in the past, but rather that those extremes can only be recovered in a pure state a posteriori, that is, from the historian's point of view. It's possible to do a history of the elites or of workers, but in the past itself it was not possible to be elite without the people or be the people without the elite—and in ways unimaginable for the historian, given the limits of evidence and imagination. It also follows that center and periphery are categories only deducible from the present—when empires and nations take on fixedness and significance—but in the day-to-day life of historical actors, center and periphery were changing or unimaginable categories.

> Coda:
> Jerusalem was imagined to be the center of the world on medieval maps. Metaphors associated with that tiny city proliferated in the writing of the elites and also in popular traditions. Even in New Spain and in the kingdom of Peru in the seventeenth century, indigenous peoples talked about biblical tribes and the Valley of Josaphat. On the other hand, what was the center for the Polish kingdom in the twelfth century? Or for a Lithuanian peasant from

the same period? Years ago, Norman Cohn demonstrated that popular culture in the Middle Ages was much freer and more promiscuous—inwardly and vis-à-vis elite culture—than historians thought. By the same token, the history of dynasties is clearly discernible, but it isn't so easy to crystallize cultural differences between elite and nonelite beginning with the rise of modern times. Because a worker from Manchester might look like a member of the elite compared to an illiterate but property-owning peasant from the south of France, but the illiterate peasant might be a member of the local elite. Hence the attractiveness of the Marxist definition of class, which achieved clear, irrevocable, atemporal criteria to define who was who (according to position in the productive process). That was truly a mold shaping history's amorphous nature.

General Law of Novelty in History: In history, the new is suspect; that which seems radiantly new is either an accumulation of old phenomena or isn't new or isn't really history.

Coda:
The invention of the telephone, for example, was a novelty that synthesized more or less one hundred years of research in various fields. Globalization, by contrast, is nothing new; it has been a historical matter for at least three or four hundred years. The Internet revolution, meanwhile, is not history: we aren't yet far enough away to see it historically.

Universal Law of History's Injustice: For individuals and for societies, history is not just (Herod's Law), but for everybody history is *justiciera* (a bringer of justice). It's inevitable, though, that history's *justiciero* aspect be tempered by its own injustice. In two senses. First, given Herod's Law, history is experienced as injustice that nevertheless can be cured by history itself, if only the true history were to come to pass. But here we must turn to the painful but ruthless logic that something that is intrinsically unjust cannot do justice. Second, history's injustice follows not only from Herod's Law but from history's own temptation to be *justiciero* (to bring justice). It's risky for history, in any present time, to do justice. It's just as likely to create justice, peace, and stability as it is to promote injustice, war, and instability. Remembering is essential; living is even more so. It follows that justice will be done with or in spite of history.

Coda:
It is said that world history is the world's tribunal, that recovering "memories"

is just, that only by writing the true history of events is justice possible in the present, that history condemns or absolves. But history was not just to the Protestants persecuted in France in the seventeenth century, the Christians persecuted by Rome, the Mixtecos defeated by the Spanish, or the Jewish survivors of the Holocaust. And yet, for Justo Sierra and for Ulysses Grant, history brought justice: after the war with Mexico, the United States was plunged into an imbalance of power among the states of the Union, which led to the fateful Civil War that cost more than half a million human lives. He who lives by the sword dies by the sword. Now, if we wanted to do justice today, for example, regarding the policies that discriminate against Mexican immigrants in the United States, we might be tempted to go back to 1847, claiming the justice of the idea of reconquest, for history dictates that the initial theft by the United States was an injustice. This would not produce justice and well-being for the immigrants but instead prolong the injustice and its possibilities. *Justiciero* history (history that brings justice), in this case, is a double absurdity: first, because, according to the logic of "he who lives by the sword dies by the sword," there can be no justifiable reconquest for Mexico, because Mexican history's claim on those territories is simply the right of conquest over their original inhabitants, the indigenous peoples of North America. So the *justiciero* argument in favor of Mexico is not theoretically sustainable. On the other hand, justice for the immigrants will be achieved, as difficult as it may seem, in spite of history: starting with the fact that two nation-states are here to stay, with the same infamies and virtues. And where are we headed from here? History and its derivations in identities and sovereignties get in the way of achieving present and future justice. Another more tragic case: the Israeli-Palestinian conflict, in which there seems to be no doubt about which side is historically righteous. In this case again, history as avenging angel presents theoretical and practical contradictions. If we were to analyze the history of the Middle East and of Europe closely, infamies would appear on all sides; absolute evil and absolute good would not be so crystal clear on either side. Even if we managed to find an absolutely guilty party, peace and justice would not be achieved today, for example, either by destroying the state of Israel or by continuing to expel Palestinians. In this case as well, the question of whether justice is possible will be determined in spite of history. At times the true sentences that history hands down seem to begin with the preamble: "Don't pay me any heed, settle it among yourselves from this point on."

Santayana's Law or José Alfredo's Law:[8] The years teach us nothing, humanity always makes the same mistakes, sometimes because it knows history and sometimes because it doesn't.

Law of History as Gossip: History's raw material is gossip, for gossip it is and unto gossip shall it return.

Law of Truth in History (or History's Uncertainty Principle): Truth in history is never written; it is always rewritten. Hence it can be concluded that truth in history is not, generally, a finding but rather a drawn-out dialogue; ergo, it is never done being said.

> Coda:
> Proving the truth of this law is an extremely drawn-out affair, precisely because a truth in history is always under construction.

Benetton Law or the Multikulti Law of the Historian's Gig: Historians, like clothing, come in distinct and changing styles. Those who go about being liberals, homogenizers, and universalists are as out of date as top hats or greatcoats. At the beginning of the twenty-first century, it's not that members of the first Benetton generation of historians (multi-, post-, anti-, and alter-) know more or less history. It's that they dress differently. And in historiography, as on the street, they treat you according to the way you look. From this two possible cyclical paradigms follow: always wear clothes that are in style or always wear the same clothes because, fashion being cyclical, what you are wearing always comes back into style.

Hempel's Law or the Universal Law of History's Scientific Character:[9] The laws of science are to history what history is to science: a solvent.

> **Postulate 1.** The universal laws governing historical knowledge are the same—in explanatory efficacy, predictability, neutrality, verisimilitude, and exactitude—as the laws governing the physical-mathematical sciences.

> **Postulate 2.** But, unlike decent women (*dixit* Amado Nervo), history's laws have a history.

> **Postulate 3.** Thus, either "history's laws" are divine or no laws govern the history of "history's laws." From this it follows that history obeys universal laws, but universal laws also obey history.

> **Final postulate.** Therefore, history's increasing tendency (which is empirically verifiable) not to obey laws is irrefutable proof of the scientific character of historical knowledge: when history is obedient, it does obey laws, but when it isn't, that is because it's obeying history, which is to say, the law prior to the law. QED.

Chapter 2

POETRY AND HISTORY

Poetry and history? Nothing is farther from the historian than poetry; nothing more foreign to the poet than history, a tedious record of facts and dates. Or so it seems. However, I find it useful for cultural history to consider, if briefly, the way modern poetry and history see one another. After all, it's not as though the two fields have been total adversaries in the past; nor is it so idiotic today to marry them. So I speak of these two kingdoms in unison, not as literary genres or rhetorical styles but as two ways to come to human knowledge. Because in what this apparently so incompatible couple illuminates we discover that history and poetry cast the same shadow: imagination charged with memory.

1

The coupling of poetry and history is ancient; it goes back to the Greek and Roman classics. For centuries, much has been written about history in poetry (from Aristotle to Péter Szondi), though less about poetry in history (from Giambattista Vico to Martin Heidegger). "The poet and the historian," according to Aristotle, "differ not by writing in verse or in prose. . . . The true difference is that one relates what has happened, the other what may happen. Poetry, therefore, is a more philosophical and a higher thing than history: for poetry tends to express the universal, history the particular" (*Poetics*, translated by S. H. Butcher). For Aristotle, the hierarchy was crystal clear. I suspect that this is why intellectual histories in various languages narrate what can be glimpsed from one kingdom to the other (poetry and history); sometimes they declared poetry the victor, the giver of truth, and sometimes history is the guarantor of truth. But, again, I don't want to highlight the affinities or the differences between the *rhetoric* of poetry and of history, but, rather, the interweaving between the two ways of coming to know.

In Germany, Reinhart Koselleck explained, the concepts of history—*Geschichte, Historie*—varied their position within the Aristotelian knowledge hierarchy. History (*Geschichte*), says Koselleck, climbed "to a rank that placed it very close to poetry. It required not only reality but also and primarily the conditions for its possibility" (entry in *Geschichtliche Grundbegriffe: Historisches Lexikon zur politisch-sozialen Sprache in Deutschland*). Through its ability to intuit the possibilities of the real, history was harnessed to poetry. History became, then, the "teacher of life" and poetry the bearer of the essences of heroism, kindness, love; that is, the provider not of parts, not of specificities, but of wholes, of humanly great truths. Thus, in 1820 one of the nineteenth-century's great writers of historical novels, Alessandro Manzoni, wrote to French poet and playwright Victor Chauvet: "If one takes from the poet what distinguishes him from a historian, the right to invent facts, what is left? Poetry; yes, poetry. For what, in the end, does history give us? Events that are known only, so to speak, from the outside, what men have done. But what they have thought, the feelings that have accompanied their decisions and their plans . . . the words by which they have asserted—or tried to assert—their passions and wills on those others . . . by which in a way they have expressed their individuality: all that, more or less, is passed over in silence by history: and all that is the domain of poetry" (Lettre à Monsieur Chauvet, 1820, in Alessandro Manzoni, *On the Historical Novel*, translated by Sandra Bermann). In this way, poetry and history seemed to compete to say something grand that would be trivialized if pronounced solely by history, whereas, if expressed by poetry, that something could be a sublime truth but not practical worldly knowledge.

The domains of poetry and history seemed clearly delimited, though always cohabiting as if by accident, at least until the first half of the nineteenth century. In the twentieth century Martin Heidegger launched one of his tangled questions: "Can the truth occur in some fashion and then be historical?" ("The Origin of the Work of Art"). Professional history, from the end of the nineteenth century, said *no*: all truth is the product of history; there is no ahistorical truth. However, at times history has functioned as though the truth could exist before history, even today, in spite of three decades of all kinds of political and philosophical disappointments. Some ideas, values, and presumptions of the present, it seems to me, cannot be exchanged for concrete facts or documents; they are with or without history and "parasitize" eternity backward (they acquire past) and forward (they make history).

That is, think of any important category of current historical analysis, such as race and nation. Without needing a moment's thought, we would reply that neither is an absolute: both are social constructions, particular histories. So far, so good. But let's go on with the exercise, if only hypothetically. Let's try, then, to imagine any flow of modern historiography without the categories of race and nation organizing the passing of time and events. And, of course, that's nearly impossible, at least today. Might it not be the case that grand historical categories sometimes work like truths that later produce history?

For its part, modern poetry seems to have responded to Heidegger's question with a resounding *yes*: the truths of poetry are not truthful by virtue of being historical. Any poem, great or silly, can become evidence of the culture of the past, but only if we risk attempting to decipher its meanings. And if we do, it's possible that senses, feelings, ideas, intuitions, and knowledge inherent in poetry occur without history, independent of past or present. The historian, for example, can include countless poems as evidence of the notion of peace at the time of the Peace of Westphalia. But, on reading those poems, the historian runs the risk of finding poetry that still powerfully resounds in her own present. Poetry comes about within and in spite of history.

The professional historian, however, doesn't seem to give a damn about the poet's truths. Sure, the modern poet is tormented by the enigmas of how to write history, how to recollect anything more than incoherent bits. Thus, in modern times, poets and historians have gone their separate ways; but, almost by accident, poets embraced history, making it the subject of or the excuse for their verses. They not only took their subjects from history but, in some cases, also absorbed the nineteenth-century passion for how history is written; they made that "how" a constitutive part of poetic creation. In the nineteenth century, for example, Robert Browning made poetry with historical subjects while also poeticizing the strong historical consciousness of that century. Romantics like William Wordsworth disdained the small, inert, naïve truths brought forth by the nineteenth-century's powerful historiography. For the Romantics, historians produced plebeian truths that would never ascend to the aristocracy of the poet's total, universal truths. On contemplating Roman ruins, Wordsworth wrote (in a poem whose title says it all: "At Rome—Regrets—In Allusion to Niebuhr and Other Modern Historians," 1837):

These old credulities, to nature dear,
Shall they no longer bloom upon the stock
of History, stript naked as a rock
'Mid a dry desert?

Indeed, naïveté is what the modern historian produces, at least according to the way some Romantics saw things. But the prodigious historiography produced in the nineteenth century with pretensions of truth lost its guile-lessness when it came up against these questions: How is history written? How do we glean a simultaneous and revealing whole for the present from the smallest bits? Thus, as Mary Ellis Gibson (*History and the Prism of Art*) demonstrated, Browning, Wordsworth's successor in English poetic fame, made poetry out of the historian's dubious ingenuousness. A friend of Thomas Carlyle and the son of an amateur historian, Browning stitched poetic knowledge to the historical and ended up by transcribing in poetry not the product but the anguish of the historian (*Sordello*):

I feel, am what I feel, know what I feel;
So much is truth to me. What Is, then? Since
One object, viewed diversely, may evince
Beauty and ugliness—this way attract,
That way repel,—why gloze upon the fact?
Why must a single of the sides be right?
What bids choose this and leave the opposite?
Where's abstract Right for me?

To be sure, in the historiographical century par excellence, the nine-teenth, even the poets were philosophers of history. Then, in the twen-tieth, Octavio Paz believed that the poem was "a fabric of perfectly datable words and an act that precedes every date: the original act with which all social or individual history begins; the expression of a society and, simul-taneously, the foundation of that society, the condition of its existence" (*El arco y la lira*, translated as *The Bow and the Lyre* by Ruth L. C. Simms). This sounds good, but it's just a poet's opinion. There is, however, something here to be explored without falling into the conviction displayed by Paz—who also, of course, tried to write history (for example, *Sor Juana Inés de la Cruz o las trampas de la fe*).

In effect, these modern interweavings between poetry and history can be traced quite far back, and I leave you with just a few samples of the poet's lessons for the historian: Borges (*El aleph*) said that reality, past or present, is simultaneous, while writing is consecutive. He learned it from Carlyle ("On History"): "The most gifted man can observe, still more can record, only the series of his own impressions: his observation, therefore, to say nothing of its other imperfections, must be successive while things done were simultaneous." Carlyle believed that when the true history of poetry was written, it would include the historian, that frustrated poet whose most important struggle, in which she is never victorious, derives from the fact that the past happens simultaneously: "narrative is linear, action solid" ("On History"). Carlo Ginzburg (personal communication, 2017) believes that Carlyle learned it from Dante Alighieri. I trust Ginzburg, but I have no way of proving his hypothesis. For his part, Browning explains (again *Sordello*, a medieval troubadour whom Browning makes a character in his "Ars Poetica" and "Ars Historica"):

> Piece after piece that armor broke away
> Because perceptions whole, like that he sought
> To clothe, reject so pure a work of thought
> As language: thought may take perception's place
> But hardly co-exist in any case,
> Being its mere presentment—of the whole
> By parts, the simultaneous and the sole
> By the successive and the many.

And "Homage to Clio" by W. H. Auden is a very modernist account of the poet asking the muse of history to tell him how to understand it, a lesson more for historians than for poets: Clio whispers, doesn't speak, "Madonna of silence," "Muse of the unique / Historical fact, defending with silence / Some world of your beholding."

In short, modern historiography and poetry seem to have been saying to one another "get out of the way, I'm coming through." As modern ways of knowing, though, I find them connected, at least in thinking cultural history. As crafts, the two fields reject one another. In the interwar years, Paul Valéry—*à la* Wordsworth—found professional history to be of very poor quality ("Regards sur le monde actuel"): "Sous le nom d'histoire de l'Europe, je ne voyais qu'une collection de chroniques parallèles qui s'entremêlaient par endroits" (Under the heading history of Europe, I saw only a collection of parallel chronicles that in places intermingled). For his part, one of the most prominent historians and philosophers of the early twentieth century, Benedetto Croce, declared war on what he called "poetic history" (*La filosofia di Giambattista Vico*), which is what Manzoni demanded not of history but of the historical novel. Manzoni believed that poetic history (the true historical novel) was an unreachable ideal, at least after the success of Walter Scott and of Manzoni's own historical novel, *I promessi sposi* (1827). But historiography, to be sure, could and should attempt to "select, discard, connect, contrast, deduce, and infer. If you do, rest assured that you will arrive at a far more precise, more definitive, more comprehensive, more accurate conception of that historical moment than there was before. But even so, what do you end up with but conceptions only more firmly implanted?" (*Del romanzo storico*, translated by Sandra Bermann as *On the Historical Novel*).

Croce's dislike for poetic history strikes me as odd because he was the one who did the most to revive the thinking of the early eighteenth-century Neapolitan philosopher Giambattista Vico. I believe that Vico's *La scienza nuova* (1725) can be considered, in a way, the founding document of modern cultural history, certainly closer to the understanding that we have had of cultural history since the late twentieth century. Erich Auerbach says that *La scienza nuova* advanced "historical perspectivism," that is, historicism: "The 'Copernican discovery' in the field of historical studies" ("Vico's Contribution to Literary Criticism").

Vico intended his book to be a history of society from its beginnings in the state of nature until the eighteenth century. He believed that humans could not decipher divine creation but could do so with their own creation: history. And his point of departure was "una nuova arte critica" (a new critical art), that is, the historical consideration of language, myths, and poetry. For Vico, and I'm taking liberties with this summary, truth is in the making. Something is true because knowledge is made in two ways, "the true"—a thing for philosophy, ergo universal, the closest thing to the absolute truths that humans cannot entirely know—and "the certain"—a thing of human consciousness, of historical and personal change. The true and the certain correspond to philosophy and to philology (that is, history): "philosophy contemplates reason, whence comes knowledge of the true; philology [history] observes the authority of human choice, whence comes consciousness of the certain" (*The Autobiography of Giambattista Vico*). I suggest that philology/history was the union of knowing empirical reality (reason) and knowing other human realities that are not necessarily empirical. For in Vico, the modern idea of "poetic wisdom" is intrinsic to the historical imagination. That wisdom was, for Vico, the origin of every nation; besides, it was the tool for imagining the past. Of course, Vico also maintained that poetry was not this or that poem but human genius par excellence; the poet as creator in the sense of maker, of demiurge. In Vico, then, poetic wisdom is not only rhetorical but also cognitive.

The origin of nations, according to Vico, resided in fantasies, myths, and invented memories, and thus he also calls the wisdom of mythmakers "poetic wisdom." Myths are important for the history of societies, because Vico believed that all social institutions arise first from the immediacy of the senses, of the emotions, curiosity, fear, doubt, superstition, and from the ability of humans, like children, to give the world human form. Vico said: "in the world's childhood men were by nature sublime poets" (*The New Science*). History ought to be in some way sensitive to the poetic, because every nation was poetic in its beginnings. However, the "poetic wisdom" in *La scienza nuova* is more than praise for the poetry of myths; it is more than the use of poetry's rhetorical resources in the science of history; it can also be read as an early form of historical relativism that contains the historical imagination woven with poetry as knowledge. We are dealing with an eighteenth-century relativism unlike the nineteenth-century relativism used by the Romantics to prove the uniqueness and greatness of one culture or nation over the rest (Johann Gottfried Herder and Germany, for example). Nor does it look like the historical relativism of the late twentieth century, in which it's difficult to believe in a reality beyond the historian, in facts that can exist without being known; it is a relativism obsessed with the poetic, as it were, in the historian's writing but not in the way in which she sees and knows (William Dray, "Narrative and Historical Realism," in *On History and Philosophers of History*).

Without faith in the objectivity of the late nineteenth century, or in the "anything goes" of the late twentieth-century relativists, Vico advanced a tamed historicism. Erich Auerbach explains it: in Vico, historicism is not eclecticism or the cultural relativism of the twentieth century, "[i]t is a difficult and infinite task to understand the particular character of historical forms and their interrelations—a task requiring, apart from learning and intelligence, a passionate devotion, much patience, and something that may well be called magnanimity: a state of mind capable of recreating in itself all varieties of human experience, of rediscovering them in its own 'modifications.'" Therefore, "in performing such a task, the historian does not become incapable of judging; he learns what judging means" ("Vico's Contribution to Literary Criticism").

By the way, for someone like me, educated in Spanish and in Mexico, who still lived in the intellectual life of institutions founded during the Spanish exile (El Fondo de Cultura Económica, El Colegio de México), discovering Vico was from the start mediated by poetry. The first Spanish translation of *Principios de ciencia nueva* that I read was by the Catalan poet Josep Carner—published by El Colegio de México in 1941. I don't know if it's the best translation, but it was the one with which I slaked my thirst long before I had access to Vico in any other language. And as a young man I read it like poetry because that's how it was translated. On rereading Vico, now as a professional historian, I've discovered that his proposition was much more historiographical than poetic.

I believe that Carner was a better poet in Catalan than prose writer in Spanish. In excessively ornamented language, Carner's preface to the translation told Spanish speakers that *La scienza nuova* was an "isla mágica" (magical island), "isla incógnita" (unknown island): "Con la que no sólo la ignoraron esos patronos de cabotaje: los tratantes en tratados y autorcillos sin autoridad, sino hasta los mayores nautas de la especulación en aquellos días" (Which was unknown not only to skippers of the coastal trade, the dealers in treatises and the literary hacks lacking authority, but even to the greatest seamen of speculation in those days: *Principios de una ciencia nueva*). Beyond the high-flown diction, it's true: Vico was an unknown in Europe and America for a long time. A curious note: in Spanish, Vico's work was more or less disseminated by the brilliant Spanish reactionary Juan Donoso Cortés (1809–1853), thanks to the influence of Jules Michelet, who admired Vico. But even earlier Vico had gained a degree of Novo-Hispanic fame through Lorenzo Boturini Benaduci (1698–1749) and Mariano Veytia (1718–1780). As Álvaro Matute and Franco Venturi indicate, as a result of his travels around New Spain, Boturini conceived the idea of writing the history of "Septentrional" America, and his model was *La scienza nuova*. Thus, he collected myths, legends, and pre-Hispanic artifacts (Álvaro Matute, *Lorenzo Boturini y el pensamiento histórico de Vico*; Franco Venturi, "Un vichiano tra Messico e Spagna: Lorenzo Boturini Benaduci"). Veytia, in collaboration with Boturini, also imagined a history of New Spain à la Vico. Boturini's death put an end to those joint plans, although *Historia antigua de México* (1836) included Boturini's research but without being entirely faithful to Vico's inspiration, as his vision of the rights of peoples, and of the philological and political value of myths, did not mesh with orthodox Spanish and Mexican Catholicism.

It was Croce who brought Vico into the historiographic debate in

English, German, and various Romance languages. Thus José Ortega y
Gasset could mock Vico ("Latin chaos," as cited in José Manuel Sevilla, "La
presencia de Giambattista Vico en la cultura española"), and Vico could
be admired by Edmundo O'Gorman, Eugenio Imaz, Erich Auerbach, and
R. G. Collingwood. Croce took up the Vico banner anew at the beginning of the twentieth century, but he mixed it with admiration for G. W. F.
Hegel. The result: a humanized Hegel via one Francesco Sanseverino—an
imaginary Vico that Croce came up with in a fictitious dialogue between
Hegel and Vico. Sanseverino finds humor in Hegel, which strikes me as
an amazing discovery. "Behind the philosopher," says Sanseverino, "it's
a pleasure to find a man who gets impatient from time to time and who
has a sense of humor . . . for example . . . when you said to your esteemed
colleague Schleiermacher, he who reduced religion to the 'sentiment
of dependence,' according to which terms 'the finest Christian would
be a dog'" (*Una pagina sconosciuta degli ultimi mesi della vita di Hegel*).
But Croce also made Vico a little bit Hegelian and rejected Vico and
Manzoni's idea of "poetic history" because, Croce believed, poetry in history is myth, rhetoric, not a tool for understanding what it is to be human
(*Teoria e storia della storiografia*). Poetic history, says Croce, cannot be accused of being poetry, "a form necessary for the spirit." The problem lies
in calling poetry history, "a contradiction in terms." "I am so far from
rejecting poetry woven with historical information that I wish to state
that a great part of pure poetry, especially in modern times, can be found
in books called history." For Croce, examples of such a tendency would
be affectionate biographies of friends, satires knifing enemies, national
histories that sing the glories of the nation of the historian in question, or
world histories "illuminated with the ideals of liberalism or humanism, or
those composed by socialists." As a fervent anti-Communist, Croce was
a fascist for a couple of years, but he was never a nationalist. He believed
that the history sponsored by the Italian Risorgimento was poetry pure
and simple, not history.

However, history and poetry remain intertwined, even in Croce, if by
poetry we mean a way to reach knowledge that can't be captured in any
other way. I don't think that Vico would have objected to Croce's well-
known collection of maxims: "History is a living chronicle, the chronicle
is dead history; history is contemporary history, the chronicle is past history; history is primarily an act of thinking, the chronicle is an act of will.
All history ends in chronicle when it is no longer thought" (*Teoria e storia
della storiografia*). For both Vico and Croce, the imagination is the mentor

of poetry and of history. For Edmundo O'Gorman, the historical imagination contains and drives reason; it is, at one and the same time, a "reproducer" (it reasons and calculates) and a "creator" (it is poetic, ethical).

Thus it would not be extravagant, although it would be a bit outmoded, to follow the poetic road to the historical imagination. Throughout the twentieth century, in the trenches of the modern historical discipline, it was mandatory to assume—without a second thought—that since its professionalization history had left poetry behind, the latter being to science what monkeys are to humans. It would seem that the discipline of history achieved more power and importance than poetry in this way, via its pretension to being science. And so it could be said that my discussion of poetry together with history is like taking Saint Teresa's mysticism seriously in order to understand the Spanish Empire—or like believing that students of history can find clues for their work in modern poets like W. H. Auden or Antonio Machado or Paul Valéry. In effect, I'm pressing my point farther than I should, but I want to entertain this reflection, if only briefly, so as to "fall into" the historical imagination, though it is inappropriate for a professional historian to cook the modern "how" of history and poetry in the same pot. In order to be in tune with academic fads, I would be expected to expound not on poetry but on "discourses" or on "metanarratives" or on "epistemes." But I speak about poetry without aspiring to any truth whatsoever, unless it is the usefulness of poetry for cultural histories.

2

Regardless of what professional history argues, poetry and history never formalized the end of their Aristotelian marriage, neither in Vico nor afterward. The total objectivity of history, through science, was a utopia of late nineteenth-century and early twentieth-century historians, so unattainable that it acquired the status of Ramón López Velarde's "Fuensanta" or of Dante's "Beatrice." Leopold von Ranke's well-known quotation—history "wie es eigentlich gewesen" (as it really was)—was not innocent empiricism; "eigentlich," explains G. Igger, also means something like "essential characteristic" (introduction to Leopold von Ranke, *The Theory and Practice of History*). That mythical Rankean moment was never a total consensus; to be sure, there were many racist, positivist, pseudo-scientific historians whose treatises are totally forgotten today, just as the majority of our metanarratives, postnarratives, and counternarratives will be consigned to oblivion. No historian of note, between 1880 and 1930, believed in the total scientific nature of history, in its separation from narrative as rhetoric and from poetry as a form of knowledge. In the end, many prominent historians who called themselves scientists in the late nineteenth century were philologists, great readers of poetry, and frequently poets: Leopold von Ranke was a philologist and translator of classical poets before he was a historian; Alexandre Herculano wrote the modern positivist history of Portugal and was a recognized poet, as were Justo Sierra and Bartolomé Mitre: historians, poets.

In the eighteenth century, according to Carlo Ginzburg, the learned skeptic François de La Mothe Le Vayer returned to the relationship between poetry and history; he believed that classical poetry was readable as history, though poetry could not do without the "fable." However, history "is worth mentioning only for its truth" (Ginzburg, *Il filo e le tracce*). The issue remained, even in the late nineteenth century, when history was professionalized as science. Ranke believed, of course, that history was a science, but in the next sentence he stated, in Aristotelian fashion: "History is distinguished from all other sciences in that it is also an art . . . as a science, history is related to philosophy, as an art, to poetry. The difference is that, in keeping with their nature, philosophy and poetry move within the real of the ideal while history has to rely on reality" (*The Theory and Practice of History*). Ranke was one of those who wrote little about the how of history and many volumes of history, but it's clear that he never thought that the essential knowledge produced by poetry had completely abandoned history: "History is neither poetry nor philosophy but demands a union of the intellectual forces active in both philosophy and poetry under the condition that the last two be directed away from their concern with the ideal to the real." Indeed, not even Leopold von Ranke was a complete Rankean; that historian, bête noire of our historiographic postmodernism, simply sought to control, via facts, the historian's indispensable poetic impulse—aesthetic, imaginative, shrewd, intuitive. He was, like many, a racist and believed in the racial superiority of Europe—not necessarily of the Teutonic race. It may be that he was deluded and even a bad person, but he was not an innocent empiricist.

But that's not the end of it. Throughout the twentieth century it is almost impossible not to find the idea of poetry in the best professional history. Marc Bloch (*Apologie pour l'histoire ou métier d'historien*) said: "Let us guard against stripping our science of its share of poetry. Let us also beware of the inclination, which I have detected in some, to be ashamed of the poetic quality. It would be sheer folly to suppose that history, because it appeals strongly to the emotions, is less capable of satisfying the intellect." Another outstanding professional historian, Johan Huizinga, without needing to talk about poetry in history, used it like eyes to see and as evidence for analysis; skeptics, read *The Waning of the Middle Ages*: "All this general facility of emotions, of tears and spiritual upheavals, must be borne in mind in order to conceive fully how violent and high-strung was life in that period." And, in Spanish, Edmundo O'Gorman, in his *ars historica*, relocated history's DNA in poetry:

> I want a history as unpredictable as is the course of our mortal lives; a history susceptible to surprises and accidents, to fortunes and misfortunes . . . a history free of the shroud of essentialism and the straitjacket of an allegedly necessary causality; a history that is only intelligible under the light of the imagination; a history-art, close to its literary narrative cousin; a history of daring flights and always as suspenseful as our loves; a history that mirrors the changes in the manner of man's being, which thus reflects the movements of whim so that the degrading metamorphosis of man as a mere plaything of an inexorable destiny does not operate when we focus on understanding the past. (in Jean Meyer, ed., *Egohistorias: El amor a Clío*)

I'm certainly not appealing to that old discussion about history versus fiction, to those familiar debates about history as text, rhetoric, and narrative strategy, or to the tiresome textual relativism that does not conceive historical reality beyond discourses (Jacques Derrida). When I refer to knowing past culture, I'm talking about poetry and history. Both attempt to capture realities of different empirical burdens—for history, a lot; for poetry, a little—but once they are clearly pronounced, those realities materialize as "second natures": proofs of a reality so certainly experienced that it creates consciousness of being, feeling, acting, belonging—a kind of reality similar to what Susan Howe, a poet, finds in the poetry of Wallace Stevens: "As if from some unfathomable source, Knowledge derived from sense perception fails, and the unreality of what seems most real floods over us" (*The Quarry*). We find and feel this conviction in the poet, even if he is not modern (Shakespeare, *A Midsummer Night's Dream*, act 5, scene 1):

> The poet's eye, in a fine frenzy rolling,
> Doth glance from heaven to earth, from earth to heaven,
> And, as imagination bodies forth

The form of things unknown, the poet's pen
Turns them to shapes, and gives to airy nothing
A local habitation and a name.
Such tricks hath strong imagination.

The historian also postulates her treatment of past craft things as "turn[ing] them to shapes, and giv[ing] to airy nothing, a local habitation and a name." In 1821 Wilhelm von Humboldt, the influential historian and philologist in addition to being Alexander's brother, said with metaphors that cannot be reduced to concepts ("On the Historian's Task"): "historical truth is, as it were, rather like the clouds which take shape for the eye only at a distance. For this reason, the facts of history are in their several connecting circumstances little more than the results of tradition and scholarship which one has agreed to accept as true." Because, Humboldt adds, the historian "becomes active, even creative—not by bringing forth what does not have existence, but in giving shape by his own powers to that which by mere intuition he could not have perceived as it really was. Differently from the poet, but in a way similar to him, he must work the collected fragments into a whole." And he can do that "like the poet, only through the imagination." And so it should surprise no one that the *ars historica* is akin to the *ars poetica*.

Marc Bloch believed that "where calculating isn't possible, one is forced to suggest," because for its explorers "le passé est leur tyran" (the past is their tyrant) and historians have to know how to join the indecisive to the precise (*Apologie pour l'histoire ou métier d'historien*).

Wallace Stevens explains the reality that the poet sees and creates ("An Ordinary Evening in New Haven"):

This endlessly elaborating poem
Displays the theory of poetry,
As the life of poetry. A more severe,

More harassing master would extemporize
Subtler, more urgent proof that the theory
Of poetry is the theory of life,

As it is, in the intricate evasions of as,
In things seen and unseen, created from nothingness,
The heavens, the hells, the worlds, the longed-for lands.

Take this as parallel to the sense that Huizinga found in cultural history: "cultural history is distinct from political and economic history in that it is worthy of the name only to the extent that it concentrates on deeper, general themes . . . only when the scholar turns to determining the pattern of life, art, and thought taken all together, can there actually be a question of cultural history. The nature of those patterns is not set. They obtain their form only beneath our hands" ("The Task of Cultural History").

I repeat: I'm not talking about rhetorical modes versus history, I'm talking about ways to capture the cultural dust that has accumulated with the passage of time. I'm talking about what poetry captures:

> Poetry suffers the martyrdom of knowledge, punished by lucidity, by clear-sightedness. It suffers because poetry continues to be mediation and in poetry consciousness is not a sign of power but of the inescapable need for a word to fulfill its purpose. Precise clarity so that what is designed in nothing more than mist becomes firm and precise and acquires "number, weight, and measure." (María Zambrano, *Filosofía y poesía*)

That fulfillment of the purpose of the word led to the reunification of poetry and history in the twentieth century. Poetry does not need history, but it is the essence of the human need for consciousness of the past, the need to have a history.

3

So what is it that makes the affinity between poetry and cultural history survive, and what makes it revealing? Let's reconcile the imaginations of poetry and of the history of culture. Various currents of knowledge end up joining the effort to narrate the cultural past so that the narrative becomes present culture. We're dealing with wisdoms and practices as difficult to deny as it would be arduous to say where they come from; such is the logic that makes it possible to intuit what would otherwise be mere suspicions, fantasies, or irrationalities. "It is known that life's great (happy or terrible) events," José Ángel Valente wrote, "pass . . . almost without our realizing it. It is precisely about that vast field of reality that is experienced but not known a priori that poetry speaks. For that reason, all poetry is, above all, *un gran caer en la cuenta* (i.e., an ultimate realization: *Las palabras de la tribu*). Cultural history is of the same nature.

Poetry is puddles of realizations about a nonphysical (though also physical) reality. A reality that is knowable through poetry, a knowledge that is at the same time a technique, an acquired craft, and something inexplicable about the imagination (questions, flashes, lucidity, intuition, memory, sensibility). The knowledge that poetry can offer, however, is rigorous but cannot be translated into mathematical formulas or exact reflections of reality or total theories of language or of the imagination. It is not merely a rhetorical game, although it is that, nor a romantic accident, nor a mirror of the real, nor a clearly delimited circuit of neurons. Croce, analyzing the marriage of poetry and history in Vico, said: "Poetry is produced not by the mere caprice of pleasure, but by natural necessity. It is so far from being superfluous and capable of elimination that, without it, thought cannot arise: it is the primary activity of the human mind" (*La filosofía di Giambattista Vico*, translated as *The Philosophy of Giambattista Vico* by R. G. Collingwood). That is, poetry is an eternal "linguistic turn" directed toward the extremes of what can be pronounced by human memory and imagination:

Schreib dich nicht
Zwischen die Welten

Komm auf gegen
Der Bedeutungen Vielfalt

Vertrau der Tränenspur
Und lerne leben.

(Don't write yourself
in between worlds,

rise up against
multiple meanings,

trust the trail of tears
and learn to live.)
(translated by John Felstiner in *Selected Poems and Prose of Paul Celan*)

In the 1940s philosopher Susanne Langer said that "the business of poetry is to create the appearance of 'experience,' the semblance of events lived and felt, and to organize them so they constitute a purely and completely experienced reality, a piece of virtual reality" (*Philosophy in a New Key*). Here we see the deep connection between poetry and cultural history, with its capacity to create a second nature, as liberating and enslaving as the first. This capacity (of either poetry or history) to create the "virtual," what Manzoni called the "verisimilar," is not an Internet game but is, rather, the raising of simulacra of past experiences, which are like those things that, as soon as they are named by poetry or as soon as they are well told by history, become as real as, say, "the class struggle," "Western decadence," or "diversity rocks." Thus, for a positivist historian like R. G. Collingwood, the gist of history was "to reenact"—to relive, to feel the past again. Collingwood criticized the historian who so deeply influenced him, Benedetto Croce (especially Croce's essay on Shelley, "Difesa della poesia"), because Croce resorted to philosophy without acknowledging that historical understanding "cannot be acquired by reading their [historians'] books but only by re-enacting their mental drama in one's own person, under the stimulus of actual life" (*The Idea of History*). Collingwood never wrote history that put into practice this "reenactment"; Croce did, and I don't believe that he would have objected to Collingwood's view: historical understanding is a "reenactment" that includes personal memory and life. Of course, "reenactment," reactivating, and reliving are concepts linked to a mental attitude necessarily tied to memory and poetry. It is imagination. Thus, for more contemporary philosophers of history, like Frank Ankersmit (*Sublime Historical Experience*), what history should do is *erleben* (make [the reader] experience, witness, feel), which provides a simulacrum of the past so real and well documented that it changes our consciousness of the present and vision of the future. One more thing: experiencing history or poetry inevitably produces the "suffering" (Croce) of a "common humanity" (*The Defence of Poetry*).

The good knowledge produced by the imagination, while it turns out to be indispensable, is not inevitable, predictable, or repeatable. For instance, if the history of contact between Mayas and Spaniards in *Ambivalent Conquests* by Inga Clendinnen ceased to exist, it would be impossible to write that book again even if we had access to all the documents that Clendinnen reviewed. There would be no way to find the same things she did, which is not to say that there is no reality beyond the historian or the poet. Both endeavor to create a verisimilar (likely or believable) world; in the case of the historian, she never strays from what are assumed to be facts. But in essence we can say about history what poet Fernando Guimarães said about poetry: "A dificultada em se conceber um poema é menor que o escreves novamente no caso de ele um dia ter ficado esquecido. É mais fácil encontrar o que nao sabemos" (The difficulty of conceiving a poem is less than that of writing it anew should it one day be forgotten. It is much easier to find what we don't know: in Nuno Júdice, *Antología de la poesía portuguesa contemporánea*).

To return to Humboldt's simile, if historical truth is the metaphor for giving form to clouds from a distance, they are never the same clouds; never does the eye see them in the same way; the imagination must constantly reimagine them; and the more similes it has to its credit, the more experience it has in imagining the clouds' shapes, the better. Hence history's intricacy; hence, as well, its dangerousness and its usefulness. Because history, like poetry, raises "second natures" that can liberate, changing expectations for the future in the present, which is nothing to sneeze at. It can be a poison or an antidote; poison because history is "dangerous to the extent that it is ambitious, and it is ambitious either when it longs to identify grand general mechanisms or when it longs to become the ideological heritage of an ethnic or social identity" (Giuseppe Sergi, *Antidoti all'abuso della storia*). On the other hand, history is an antidote when it makes it possible to escape from atavisms given as facts (racial, cultural, political). Observing the past, imagining the illusive outlines of something that is no longer, and which we cannot change, confers a certain advantage: imagining a future better than the past and than the present . . .

For as similar as history and poetry are in their realizations, poetry does not have to do something that is indispensable for history: marking the border between past and present. Maybe poetry comes to what it reveals because of the possibility of being a point of view indifferent to time. History, especially cultural history, has to build solid walls between what is past and what is present. It helps that time passes and that before long everything is memory, evidence, or forgetfulness. Ginzburg has suggested that the idea of "historical perspective" owes a lot to the Christian feeling of superiority over Judaism (*Occhiacci di legno*). And, in general, historians love to say "this is the great change, marking a before and an after." But the boundary must be established, and that is done by the imagination trying to rid itself of the straitjacket of the present. That is, imagining the line between past and present is, first, a constant reimagining. The line moves. And, second, it is a political decision, which is to say that it is not just the historian's existential action but a social action. "Freedom and progress depend on the distinction between past and present. The founding principle of history is therefore also a founding principle of politics" (Constantin Fasolt, *The Limits of History*). There are no options: we have to imagine in order to live in the modern world, and that means imagining the border between past and present.

In short, they say that Stéphane Mallarmé wrote to Edgar Degas that poetry was not made with ideas but with words, but whoever touches language, according to one poet ("An Interview with Stanley Kunitz"), touches "the evolution of the tribe's consciousness and history." Because the imagination of the poetic or of the past of culture happens by chance when "a way of life becomes a way of language and when a way of language is transformed into a way of life, both inseparably" (Henri Meschonnic, *Célébration de la poésie*). Venturing to the limits of words, then, is knocking simultaneously on the doors of consciousness, memory, and history.

4

The concepts that the historian creates or reveals are few and cannot be translated into poetry. The *stories* they come up with are completely inhabited by poetry, from Robert Browning to T. S. Eliot, from Jorge Luis Borges (whose perennial narrator is the very image of a historian) to Octavio Paz (who was inspired by pre-Hispanic history, as well as by the histories of New Spain and India). They can be found even in the very latest Mexican poetry: Luis Felipe Fabre (*La sodomía en la Nueva España*) investigates cases of sodomy from 1657 and 1658 to write poetry that brings the human dilemma of seventeenth-century homosexual mulattos and Indians into the present, aesthetically and politically.

But the poet's expertise in metaphor is what the cultural historian uses to understand what cannot be reduced to concepts, facts, or dates. Using metaphors to tell the past is not only a rhetorical resource of the historian but is, as for the poet, the way to capture otherwise incomprehensible human "realities." History is seeing "en bloque" (in bloc, all together), the metaphor, said Valéry, "is thinking *en bloque*, nothing is thought by itself" (*The Art of Poetry*). It's obvious, but it bears repeating: metaphors are indispensable for the historian of culture, so Vico is still up to date. To put together metaphors, Vico believed, is to understand the intricate relations among things or phenomena that appear to be completely different. Of course, Vico turned to the classics (Aristotle, Cicero) to defend the metaphor at the height of the eighteenth century, though not as a rhetorical resource (Cicero) but as knowledge. And it happens that in the late seventeenth century the metaphor as knowledge had been attacked by more or less rationalist thinkers—like the Jesuit Dominique Bouhours (*La manière de bien penser dans les ouvrages d'espirit*) or like John Locke himself. The criticism of the metaphor was unrelenting, and it made sense: metaphors are false arguments that seem true or true arguments dressed as false ones. Because the critics of metaphor believed that the baroque of Baltazar Gracián or Luis de Góngora had abused the decorative, thus endangering truth and logic. To understand the rhetorical arabesques of Gracián or Góngora demanded patience and an immunity to the seduction of metaphorical tricks, while the truth, the critics of metaphor believed, should be clear and direct. Vico defended metaphor from these attacks by maintaining the importance of the half-meaning of metaphors, their ironies, their ability to reach unexpected similitudes, as indispensable sources for the historian's understanding of the past of all that is human. Centuries later, María Zambrano continued to defend the cognitive power of the metaphor in poetry, a power that I believe concerns the historian as well, due to what Zambrano called "continuity": "The metaphor has performed a deeper—and prior—function in culture, which is at the root of metaphor as used in poetry. It is the function of defining a reality that cannot be encompassed by reason but that can be grasped in another way . . . a form of continuity with times and mentalities that are now gone" (*Hacia un saber sobre el alma*).

With its linguistic turn in the twentieth century, philosophy returned to fighting for metaphor. Donald Davidson claimed that metaphor produces only similes, nothing of revelatory meaning, because "metaphor is the dreamwork of language" and, as happens in the interpretation of a dream, interpreting metaphor "reflects as much on the interpreter as on the originator" ("What Metaphors Mean," in Sheldon Sacks, *On Metaphor*). Another philosopher, Max Black, beginning in the 1960s, defended the cognitive power of metaphor and even used Davidson's own metaphor ("metaphor is the dreamwork of language") to demonstrate why metaphor creates knowledge that cannot be reduced to simple literality or to a concept ("How Metaphors Work: A Reply to Donald Davidson," in Max Black, *Perplexities*). One of Black's followers, Evee Feder Kittay, put it even more clearly: "The cognitive significance of metaphor arises from its capacity to restructure or to induce structure on a given content domain . . . We can give an exposition of a metaphor but not a paraphrase—not if the metaphor is still a live metaphor and has not collapsed into literality" (*Metaphor: Its Cognitive Force and Linguistic Structure*). It goes without saying that these contemporary philosophical quarrelers didn't care in the slightest about what historians did or did not do with metaphors. Nevertheless, what happens to the historian is what happened to

Borges, who said "metaphor is a habit of my thought" (quoted in Martha Lilia Tenorio, "Más inquisiciones").

The metaphor in writing about the past, I believe, is what the historical imagination reveals about itself, working, as though by chance, in three ways: when the historian, in his involuntary habit of making metaphors, revives the dying embers of old metaphors that served as ways of seeing the world; when the historical imagination constructs stories of the past that turn into metaphors that take on meaning in the context of the present; and finally, when the historian creates new metaphors with the past that make us see, as a whole, as a structure, what is nothing more than the chaotic occurrences of the past.

I here give some simple examples, not to display, as it were, the nature of time but to show its clockwork. To imagine the cultural past demands that we speak metaphor like a native tongue, not only to translate the metaphors of the past into concepts but to understand what those metaphors revealed in their own time. Marcelino Menéndez Pelayo in his *Historia de los heterodoxos españoles* included an "Oda al Mariscal Suchet" by Leandro Fernández de Moratín, a liberal poet who supported the French in 1808. The unfortunate verses—not because they are treasonous, but because they are bad—went like this:

> Dilatara la fama
> El nombre que veneras reverente
> Del que hoy añade a tu región decoro
> Y de apolínea rama
> Ciñe el bastón y la balanza de oro
> Digno Adalid del sueño de la tierra
> Del de Vivar trasunto
> Que en paz te guarde, amenazando guerra,
> Y el rayo encienda que visó Sagunto.
> (Spread the fame
> The name you reverently venerate
> Which today adds to your region's decorum
> And Apollonian learning
> Grasp the staff and the scale of gold
> Worthy Commander of the dream of the earth
> Of Vivar [El Cid Campeador] replica
> Who in peace awaits you, threatening war,
> And the lightning that Sagunto saw blaze.)

An expert in the history of Spain can decipher the weight of each image and metaphor in these verses and thus explain how the Spanish *afrancesados* (francophiles) thought. Menéndez Pelayo, however, referenced these verses merely to mock them and to kill their metaphors with another image: "si los huesos del Cid no se estremecieron de vergüenza en su olvidada sepultura de Cerdeña, muy pesado debe ser el sueño de los muertos" (if El Cid's bones weren't rolling over with embarrassment in his forgotten grave in Sardinia, it's only because the sleep of the dead is very deep: *Historia de los heterodoxos españoles*). My point here is to emphasize not the correct or mistaken historical view of Fernández de Moratín's verses but rather how the dead embers of metaphors chilled by time can be revived for one purpose or another. Fernández de Moratín's metaphors could be revived in 1880, with the publication of the *Historia de los heterodoxos españoles*. It may be that this century-long dialogue is no longer of interest today.

Nevertheless, I can mention metaphors from the past and join them to those from the present, for example, to write the history of Mexican intellectuals in the twentieth century. I call, then, without further ado, upon Don Benito Jerónimo Feijóo (*Teatro crítico*, 1748):

La superficie se miente profundidad, y el resabio de Ciencia, Sabiduría. [The surface lies about its depth, and the aftertaste of Science about its Wisdom.]

No sé por qué ha de ser más que hombre quien es tanto menos que hombre, quando se acerca a estatua: no porque siendo lo risible propiedad de lo racional, ha de ser más racional quien se aleja más de lo risible. El ingenioso Francés Miguel de Montaña dice con gracia, que entre las especies de brutos, ninguno vio tan serio como el Asno.
[I don't know why he who is so much less than a man has to be more than a man when he is almost a statue: not because laughableness is a property of the rational should he who distances himself most from the laughable be more rational. The ingenious Francés Miguel de Montaña says with charm that among the species of beasts, no one looked as serious as the Ass.]

He visto entre profesores de todas facultades muy vulgarizada la quexa de falta de memoria, y en todos noté un aprecio excesivo de la potencia memorativa sobre la discursiva: de modo, que a mi parecer si hubiese dos tiendas, de las quales en la una se vendiese memoria, y en la otra entendimiento, el dueño de la primera presto se haría riquísimo, y el segundo moriría de hambre.

[I have seen among professors of all schools the very common complaint about lack of memory, and in all I noted an excessive esteem for the strength of memory over the discursive: so that, to my way of thinking, if there were two shops, in one of which memory were sold and in the other understanding, the owner of the first would quickly become very rich, and the second would die of hunger.]

These are just examples, but they help to understand how metaphors become a "lingua franca" between past and present. I could attempt to undo the metaphors explaining Feijóo's modern spirit in Spain and his quarrel with Spain's stagnant intellectual life; or I could put aside the metaphors and offer statistics on the number of times four or five important Mexican voices between 1990 and today have offered opposing views on politics or on cooking, soccer, Germany, the United States, or sex. But the knowledge is already there—it comes from Don Benito Jerónimo: "Porque los hombres son como los cuerpos sonoros, que hacen ruido mayor quando están huecos" (Because men are like sonorous bodies, they make more noise when they are empty: *Teatro crítico*).

On the other hand, a poem creates metaphors—knowledge—but only occasionally does the poem as a whole constitute a metaphor starting from its relationship to its historical context. Verses made into popular songs, such as the lyrics of Chico Buarque de Holanda in Brazil in the 1970s and Lluís Llach in Catalonia during the last years of Franco, spoke of a lot of things, but at the time they were understood and sung as metaphors for protest and resistance to dictatorships. Maybe in another hundred years no one will be able to revive the metaphorical sense of those songs and someone will discover an old recording that talks about a character who asked "Grandfather Siset" about a stake (Llach): "que no veus l'estaca / on estem tots lligats? / Si no podem desfer-nos-en / mai no podrem caminar!" (Can't you see the stake / we're all tied to? / If we don't manage to get loose / we'll never be able to walk": "L'estaca," a popular song by Lluís Llach). On the other hand, what survives of poetry is its autonomy from context: the living metaphors of poetry take on new contexts with the years, though they lose what they meant in their present.

Now history books, like the lyrics of Chico Buarque and Llach, always follow from a concern with the present. Thus, as it were, the historian says "amor, amor" in place of "amen, amen." And so there have been important history books that are in and of themselves complete metaphors for something in the present, without ever mentioning that something. In order not to go to Alexis de Tocqueville or to Edward Gibbon or to Thomas Carlyle, I will say that Richard Hofstadter, for example, in the 1950s wrote what was then the most important history of 1890s United States populism (*The Age of Reform*), a history of poor, antimodern, anticosmopolitan Southern farmers who, fearing their extinction, turned to racism and fanaticism. In its time, the book was a metaphor that everyone understood: populism meant McCarthyism, lynchings in the South, and persecution of New York intellectuals in the 1950s. Another example: the book *Zapata and the Mexican Revolution* by John Womack was published in 1968. The author talks about Emiliano Zapata, about a people who rebelled in order not to change, to maintain their autonomy and their egalitarian way of life. The work was, and still is, the best history of Zapata and his struggle, but at the time it was a metaphor for Vietnam, the radical and anticapitalist struggle for equality, and a generation of sixties boys and girls understood it as such. The same can be said of many history books from the nineteenth and twentieth centuries.

In short, by simple instinct, the cultural historian turns to metaphor. Bloch used the metaphor of an ogre: the historian is like the ogre of legends—he knows he'll find his material where he smells human flesh. Maybe this metaphor merely "adorns" the historian's dedication to all things human, but the metaphor fulfills its task: it is understood that the historian feeds on the human evidence left in the past, that he goes sniffing it out, that he enters into it eagerly. This may be a minor metaphor, but it is one of thousands that any historian turns to when she sits down to recount and explain past culture. Renan left more indispensable metaphors; for example: "But liberty is like truth; scarcely any one loves it on its own account, and yet, owing to the impossibility of extremes, one always comes back to it" (*Souvenirs d'enfance et de jeunesse*, translated by C. B. Pitman as *Recollections of My Youth*). And Huizinga, through the metaphor of a bell, manages to make us feel the daily experience of order and harmony that ought to have existed, to his way of thinking, in medieval cities: "One sound rose ceaselessly above the noises of busy life and lifted all things unto a sphere of order and serenity: the sound of bells. The bells were in daily life like good spirits, which by their familiar voices, now called upon the citizens to mourn and now to rejoice, now warned them of danger, now exhorted them to piety. . . . Every one knew the difference in meaning of the various ways of ringing. However continuous the ringing of the bells, people would seem not to have become blunted to the effect of their sound" (*The Waning of the Middle Ages*). Inga Clendinnen, with a delicate historical imagination shared by few recent historians, learns and teaches via metaphors in *Ambivalent Conquests*: "But colonial situations also spawn multiple realities, and that painful fissuring within the Spanish world is perhaps better caught by a different image: a hall of distorting mirrors in which each individual sees himself, as he thinks, truly reflected, while those about him are disquietingly altered into grotesques, as familiar gestures and expressions are exaggerated, parodies, even inverted."

In effect, for the historian of culture, to resist metaphor is to go against nature and thus the close relationship with poetry: they say that history is the teacher of life, and the teacher of metaphor is none other than poetry. If the cultural historian needs metaphor, poetry turns out to be the necessary point of view. However, poetry constructs and destroys metaphors, grants revealing realities through metaphorical images, and makes of a metaphor a weak cliché either as rhetoric or as knowledge. But "the intimate freedom of the poet to risk new forms," George Santayana wrote in 1922, "does not eliminate the freedom of all men to adopt the old" (*Soliloquies in England*). Poetry always returns to the storeroom of past metaphors, as does history. Cultural history, however, does not search for but "falls into" metaphor. In order to make the past capable of being experienced in the present, the historian makes the literal meaning of an image (the ogre, flesh) the symbol of a figurative, metaphorical meaning (the historian's embrace of evidence of the human); that is, the historian makes that literal meaning explain what she doesn't manage to name directly with a concept or a noun or a statistic or a fact.

But beware: the metaphor is also the vice of the cultural historian . . . and the anthropologist . . . and the cultural critic. Good historiographical metaphors work like provisional and inevitable images that grant sense to things from the past to which we don't have access without metaphor. Those images accumulate in volumes of history, and each new historiographic revision recurs to them to inhabit or finally escape from the metaphor in question. Thus, the metaphor in history is always a message launched to the future historian that says: "Now it's only in this fashion that I can understand this; how does it look to you from there (the future)? You get into my metaphor or exchange mine for another or stop fooling around and bring knowledge of the past down to something more concrete."

The reader can find in George Lakoff, Hans Blumenberg, Susanne Langer, Sheldon Sacks, and Max Black examples of the use and abuse of metaphors in history and in philosophy. In Wolfgang Kayser we find that the same is true for literature. And for anthropology it's enough to read any post-1980 text to bear witness to the metaphorically baroque. An example, from an excellent book, of course, but one whose author constructs metaphor on top of metaphor (Ann Laura Stoler, *Along the Archival Grain*):

> Ethnography in and of the colonial archives attends to processes of production, relations of power in which archives are created, sequestered, and rearranged. If ethnographies could be treated as texts, students of the colonial have turned the tables to reflect on colonial documents as "rituals of possession," as relics and ruins, as sites of contested cultural knowledge. Here I treat archives not as repositories of state power but as unquiet movements in a field of force, as restless realignments and readjustments of people and the beliefs to which they were tethered, as spaces in which the senses and the affective course through the seeming abstractions of political rationalities. I take sentiments expressed and ascribed as social interpretations, as indices of relations of power and tracers of them.

Believe me, dear reader, there is something very interesting within the crossfire of so much metaphor, but it turns out to be difficult to make out what it is, as in the genius of Gracián or Góngora. Metaphor is also abused in the writing of history. Here are just a few examples. The historiography of Spain from 1898 is replete with metaphors. Américo Castro, Claudio Sánchez-Albornoz, José Ortega y Gasset, and Miguel de Unamuno offered the ones about the "Spanish enigma," "invertebrate Spain," "modernity short-circuited," and the land of "an unliving living."[1] What these metaphors represented was a mix of realities and intentions: Spain's imperial and economic decadence, its endemic political instability, the secret nostalgia for a mythical golden age, the very technical regenerationist thought that proposed ways to modernize Spanish industry, education, and agriculture. Also behind those metaphors was the belief in the weight of Catholic tradition and its impact on Spain's "spirit." These were too many things to express in the format "the history of Spain is _____." Then comes this or that metaphor. But so much metaphor made the problem of Spain's backwardness and decadence vis-à-vis Europe seem to be a problem of finding the best metaphor. By the 1950s, in light of the defeat of the Republic and Spain's rapid authoritarian modernization, so much metaphor seemed like an excess of filigree rather than an explanation of tragedies and practical problems. Maybe that's why Catalan historian Jaume Vicens Vives found that the debates among Castro, Unamuno, and Ortega y Gasset were a lot of prattle. Vicens Vives, then, destroyed the metaphorical excess, like Sancho vis-à-vis Quixote, with worldly details: "too much Unamunian anguish for a Mediterranean community with very real, identifiable, and 'epochal' problems: those of how to procure a modest but dignified life for its thirty million inhabitants" (*Aproximaciones a la historia de España*). It's not that metaphors are not useful, it's that they can become a vice.

Another example: *mestizaje* in modern Mexican history. This is, above all, a sexual metaphor, dealing with lineage or caste (originally derived from horse-breeding manuals). In the seventeenth century it took on a juridical and religious sense, that is, it became a legal category and an acceptable way to understand the inevitable (promiscuity) and the necessary (demographic growth in the American realms). With the blessing of God and the king, racial mixing was the perfect corollary to the idea of purgatory: recognition of facts (promiscuity), the possibility of redemption (via the Church and good laws), and equality before God (all together in purgatory). By the end of the eighteenth century, what David Brading called "creole patriotism" (*The Origins of Mexican Nationalism*) began to use the *mestizaje* metaphor as a synonym for an American nation. By the end of the nineteenth century various scientists and Porfirian historians had begun to secularize the metaphor: from a religious and monarchical meaning to a more racial, scientific, and historical one. That is, they made of *mestizaje*/purgatory a metaphor for the origin, present, and future of the nation. The sense of redemption was maintained through education. Regardless of how racist the "Porfirianos" were, they made the *mestizaje* metaphor the founding myth of a new nation-state. And all of that in decades when racial mixing was unacceptable. (Perhaps the only earlier exception in America was the *métis* nation in Canada, a French-speaking group that began to ask for recognition not as a nation but as a mestizo group in accordance with the lands and privileges to which they were entitled precisely due to their native origin, their Christianity, and their service to two monarchies, the French and the English.) After the Mexican Revolution, *mestizaje* acquired the unbeatable power of the nation's supreme metaphor, because *mestizaje* turned into the literal meaning of a greater and more complete figurative meaning: a corporative/collective welfare state. Thus, the metaphor acquired impressive durability and prestige. Beginning in the 1990s, with the dismantling of the welfare state and the corporatist system of the single-party state, *mestizaje* began to function as a metaphor with no referent. A vast historiography began to be written, showing that *mestizaje* was racism, a clear and hard strategy of domination, nothing to do with metaphor. But it was always clear that postrevolutionary *mestizaje* did not mean interbreeding between Spanish and indigenous peoples, but was, rather, a myth of inclusion, possibilities, and a leveling of the playing field, the very synonym for "Mexican." That is, *mestizaje* was a metaphoric reserve. Of course, today *mestizaje* is an orphaned metaphor in search of new meanings. There are none, but there has also been no reinvention of a new, solid, shared "we" for Mexicans.

I won't burden the reader with more examples of this tool, the metaphor, which is indispensable to the historian.

It would not occur to anyone to "prove" the empirical validity of a poem's metaphor. There are indications, but in essence no empirical reality lies behind a poetic metaphor. Nor, fundamentally, in the metaphors of the historian of culture, whose power is measured by what they reveal, not by their empirical exactitude. Past cultures explained through metaphors necessarily carry their dose of intuition, of realizations, of making things clear, of conveying feeling. They are like the metaphors of poetry: "an enigmatic presence that directly attests to itself" (Hans-Georg Gadamer, *Von der Wahrheit des Wortes*). But the metaphor in history and culture has another explanatory strength for the past: it creates the possibility of "as if." In two senses: narrative and political. With metaphors the historian does not ask the reader to assume that the past was like this or that, rather, metaphorically, he implores the reader to consider "as if" the past could have been like this, and hence the similes, the half groping, the intuitions, the ironies, the data, and logical reasoning to maintain the strength of those metaphors directed to the "as if such and so."

On the more political and moral side, the historian of culture uses metaphors as a tool both for inhabiting the present with dignity and for carefully trying to escape from it. Because the "as if" of the good cultural historian is a kind of calling on the possibility, in a given present, accepting a certain simulacrum, a certain falseness if you will, to imagine, in a here and now, peace, justice, and the possibility of a human future. This is what an old German philosopher, Hans Vaihinger, called *Die Philosophie des Als Ob* (1911, *The Philosophy of "As If"*). Because all past, seen correctly, is irrational, if by irrational we mean war, injustice, inequality, humiliation, chance. It's no surprise that the historical imagination of a noble American historian from the 1930s, Carl Becker, would take his inspiration from Vaihinger and his "as if," secularizing it and joining it to the notions of experience and the social and moral usefulness of American pragmatism (John Dewey). Creating the metaphorical possibility of pasts "as if," more or less empirically sustained, logically argued, is, like Renan, to maintain that we have to fight for freedom "as if" it were for the truth, knowing that it is unachievable and false but impossible to renounce as a position, because in history political and philosophical extremes are dangerous.

By way of their metaphors, of course, history and culture settle into pragmatism. The "as if" that is essential for living the present, and for escaping from the present toward possible futures, requires an imagination subjected to experience, to risks, to trial and error, to the responsibility of saying what we don't like, and accepting the consequences of what we like. What's more, the metaphors that are shared between history and culture tend toward pragmatism because of the very mechanics of their existence: the historian constructs metaphors either because she finds it impossible to reduce her intuition to a concept or a fact, because of the limited space available for every story, or because she knows that a given "as if" is perfectly understandable in her time and space. That is, the historiographic metaphor places the responsibility on the reader for providing the "epochal," linguistic, cultural, and moral elements that are necessary for the metaphor to be decipherable. Reading history thus becomes a common ground in which the reader is a participant in the construction of the explanatory power of metaphors, adding to and transforming the historian's original intention, whatever that might be. Therefore, neither the historian's selection of metaphors nor the knowledge that she produces with them is arbitrary; it is experimental, it is pragmatic in terms of here and now and as long as it lasts. Cynthia Ozick said: "I want to argue that metaphor is one of the chief agents of our moral nature, and that the more serious we are in life, the less we can do without it" (*Metaphor & Memory*).

5

The Siamese life of poetry and history has another common artery: the memory that I don't know what to call other than poetic. At one time, this kind of memory belonged as much to history as to poetry—when history was one of the rhetorical arts. In the sixteenth century the retentive faculty used by poetry reached the category of "evidence," as a source for knowing the past. In the nineteenth century that retentive faculty was diluted into the rituals of nationalist historiography. The best example: the lyrics of national anthems, the thousands of patriotic poems memorized in the classrooms of every country. The poetic memory won reputation once more in the waning years of the twentieth century, when it became customary to look for the true history, the history of identities, which, it seems, demands the same memory-retentiveness and self-absorption as poetry. No identity can be maintained without poetry.

I belong to the generation of Mexicans who were badly educated in the "active" schools; we didn't have to memorize the Krebs cycle or the names of New Spain's viceroys because "to memorize" was a verb that only applied to poetry and verse. Poetry was to be memorized or not to be read at all. Knowing and appreciating poetry meant being able to recite it; our access to poetry was through anthologies with titles like *El declamador sin maestro*: a nutritional supplement of bad poetry for our anorexic memories (the book, originally compiled by Homero de Portugal, was published in the 1930s; it has been enlarged, republished, and plagiarized in a thousand and one ways ever since). I still remember the tasteless verses of Enrique González Martínez included in *El declamador*: "Cuando sepas hallar una sonrisa / en la gota sutil que se rezuma / de las porosas piedras, en la bruma" (When you learn how to find a smile / in the subtle drop that oozes / from the porous stones, in the mist). I learned them to save myself from things even more tasteless, such as "El brindis del bohemio" (The Bohemian's Toast). Anyway, that was a bad education and nothing more. But few human questions have been so tightly linked as memory and poetry have always been. The poet works from memory, and his fate is to live in someone else's memory. Poetry seems to fulfill its purpose when the reader remembers not an argument or a plot but some exact verses that take on a distinct meaning in each new evocation. It is only natural: poetry self-constitutes through the indescribable sum and total of memory, trapped in moments of language: alephs to enter into memory's worlds.

The poet remembers—and often poetry, which is an escape from the here and now, manages to create the illusion of a past without present or vice versa. The poet can remember a mountain or a lost love not to objectively reconstitute the mountain or the loved one but to reflect on and to exercise the why, how, and even to what extent we remember—all with the vain ambition of elucidating love, beauty, forgetting. In *Deutschland, ein Wintermärchen* (Germany, a Winter's Tale) by Heinrich Heine, the poem speaks of a nighttime stroll in Cologne in the company of a masked man; the poem inquires who the narrator is and who the masked man is. The masked man ends with: "Ich bin dein Liktor . . . Ich bin / Die Tat von deinem Gedanken" (I am your master . . . I am the fact of your thought—or the thing about which you are thinking). Poetry is consciousness before a mirror, especially modern poetry that makes of memory what recalling was, say, for that hipster Marcel Proust for whom memory was like a rope tossed from the sky to pull us out of the "abyss of not-being" (*Swann's Way*). Thus, César Vallejo and eddying memory: "Hay golpes en la vida, tan fuertes . . . / ¡Yo no sé! / Golpes como del odio de Dios; como si ante ellos, / la resaca de todo lo sufrido / se empozara en el alma . . . ¡Yo no sé!" (There are blows in life, so strong . . . / I don't know! / Blows like the hatred of God; as though before them, / the undertow of all that has been suffered / stagnates in the soul . . . I don't know!": "Los heraldos negros," 1918).

In addition, since its classical origins, poetry has been a sophisticated mnemonics designed to squeeze from language the rhythms and connections that human consciousness demands—for some mysterious neurological reason. Mnemonics seeks to crystallize Memory (an era) in memory (a poem), overcoming given times and spaces, facilitating the retention not of memories but of moments of memory (through rhyme, meter, simile, metaphor, hyperbole . . . consumed in specific personal contexts). The *romanceros* (collections of traditional oral ballads)—it is said that Lope de Vega described them as an *Iliad* without Homer—are a living monument to anonymous human mnemonics. Ramón Menéndez Pidal (*Estudios sobre el Romancero*) and Antonio Alatorre (*Cuatro ensayos sobre arte poética*) explain that *romances* were glossed by the poets of the Golden Age. I present as a witness the memorable and memorizable "Romance del Conde Arnaldos": "¡Quién hubiese tal ventura sobre las aguas del mar / como hubo el Conde Arnaldos la mañana de San Juan!" (Who would have had an adventure like that over the waters of the sea / as did Count Arnaldos on the morning of Saint John!: *Romancero español y morisco*).

Finally, poetry, or at least modern poetry, is an experimental plumbing of the depths and breadth of a human memory. It is a knowledge that reflects not only on the possible combinations of remembrances but on the human vice or instinct of remembering. The poet remembers spaces, landscapes, histories, and lives; he also experiments with memory's limits at the edges of language: he puts memory to the test, thus transcribing the flavor of forgetting. The poet wants his reflections to be memorizable (Antonio Machado, "En estos campos de la tierra mía," *Poesías completas*):

imágenes de grises olivares
bajo un tórrido sol que aturde y ciega,
y azules y dispersas serranías
con arreboles de una tarde inmensa:
mas falta el hilo que el recuerdo anuda

al corazón, el ancla en su ribera,
o estas memorias no son alma. Tienen
en sus abigarradas vestimentas
señal de ser despojos del recuerdo,
la carga, bruta que el recuerdo lleva.
(images of gray olive groves
below a torrid sun that stuns and blinds,
and blue and dispersed mountains
with red tinted clouds of an immense afternoon;
but the thread that ties memory to the heart is missing
the anchor on its shore,
or these memories are not soul. They have
in their unmatched clothing
a sign of being memory's leavings
the raw load that memory carries.)

In sum, that obviousness, that gift for existing in order to be memorized, that managing of an infinite combination of memories, and that evoking of the very ability to evoke—I want to call all of that poetic memory. With that in mind, I turn to history and suggest two ways in which this kind of memory has been present in the writing of history: memory in history as poetry subject to jurisprudence and history as a capturing (poetic to a greater or lesser degree) of the old ways of remembering (mentalité, Zeitgeist, Weltanschauung, context).

Humanism and the Renaissance brought to light three arguments for the consequences of studying the past: the first revolved around the old "art of memory," the trajectory that, as we learn from Frances A. Yates (*The Art of Memory*), points from Greco-Roman rhetoric (memory, tool of rhetoric linked to space) to the Renaissance art of memory: the analytical craft of thinking up hierarchies, characteristics, and relations between things to facilitate memorization and the search for the truth. As a result, a distinction was made between an artificial memory, which is merely rhetorical and retentive, and an analytical memory that reveals truths. This had consequences in two additional arguments, which were contemporary to the one dealing with the art of memory: one about poetry, the value and importance of rhyme, its usefulness as knowledge and historical document; and another about history and the need to detach the historical from the poetic memory, especially from rhetoric.

Historical memory, then, would have to be a memory of facts, recollections, and rumors but subject to critical, or almost judicial, analysis.

Thus, for example, in England, Philip Sidney (*An Apology for Poetry*, 1583) defended poetic memory and its mnemonic techniques as a way to mix history's plots and philosophy's moral point of view—poetry was, in that respect, more useful than philosophy or history. Hence, as Carlo Ginzburg has shown ("Selfhood as Otherness: Constructing English Identity"), the historian turned into a poet became, as Sidney said, a "discourser" like those who speak "not merely about a fact but about its characteristics and circumstances." From here it became a modern *ars historica* that taught how to read facts, documents, and memories critically, judicially, to confirm their validity and trustworthiness. The Catholic then Protestant and later Catholic thinker François Baudouin did this by writing the equivalent, as it were, of an *"ars historica* reader" for the sixteenth century (*De institutione historiae universae*, according to a reference in Donald Kelley, "*Historia Integra*: François Baudouin and His Conception of History"). Baudouin, a jurist, demanded that all memory be subjected to a legal treatment in search of its validity.

With this began the Spanish disdain for one of the worst versions of memory, that is, the fantasy of chivalric novels, whose last critic was well known (Miguel de Cervantes). But the matter started earlier, in the sixteenth century, with the discrediting of the unreal and immoral fantasy of knightly romances. This had consequences for the writing of the past: poetic memory was subject to evidentiary proof; it was also converted into evidence for history (the traditions of oral poetry taken as historical documents). The historian donned the toga of litigator, rendering judgment on the validity of what was remembered, and history thus turned into poetry under the science of law. Finally, history, any history, declared itself universal, because if, as in poetry, it was a matter of remembering the human, everything had to do with everything else; we couldn't be familiar with Rome's past while being ignorant of the history of Greece, Turkey, or New Spain (Anthony Grafton, *What Was History?*).

The "moral and natural" histories of the "Indies" written after the conquest of Mexico and Peru are an emblematic example of this. Of course, from the end of the Middle Ages, the monarchs of Castile put their legacy in the hands of the chronicler. The chronicle of Pedro I, written by Pedro López de Ayala (1511), already assumed and promoted a tradition associated with memory:

> The memory of men is very weak: and none can remember all of the things
> that happened in past time: for that reason the ancient wise men advanced

certain letters and the art of writing so that the sciences and great happenings that occurred in the world would be written down and protected from evil . . . And thus it was later used and ordered by princes and Kings that books be made, that these be called Chronicles . . . Thus from that moment on, I, Pedro López de Ayala, with the help of God intend to continue in this fashion, and in the most truthful way possible: from what I saw: in what I do not understand if I do not tell the truth: also what happened in my age and in my time in certain places where I have not been. (quoted in María Consuelo Villacorta Macho, "Creando memoria")

It goes without saying that poetry, history, and memory always went together in Castile and in New Spain thanks to a powerful cultural, political, and social institution: lineage. One was what could be proven by inheritance and family privileges, even if it was necessary to lie, as was the custom of the Basque nobility who raised their *hidalguía* against the Castilian aristocracy by calling themselves nobles, "que memoria de omnes no es en contrario" (that no man's memory can object) (quoted in María Consuelo Villacort a Macho, "Creando memoria"). In the shadow of this tradition came the histories of Gonzalo Fernández de Oviedo y Valdés (*Historia general y natural de las Indias*, 1526) and José de Acosta (*Historia natural y moral de las Indias*, 1590). And in them, as Arnaldo Momigliano and Carlo Ginzburg have shown, American indigenous memory was turned into a valid document for historical research. Because we must "fall into" the wisdom of poetry, or at least try to, to assemble history where no written records are available to draw on. Acosta said, recalling Seneca: "En lo que la puede con razón haber es en si Séneca adivino o si, acaso, dió en esto su poesía. Yo, para decir lo que siento, siento que adivino con el modo de adivinar que tienen los hombres sabios y astutos" (In that which can be known by reason Seneca was right, or if not, perhaps, he dealt with that with his poetry. I, in order to say what I feel, feel that I imagine in the way that wise, astute men imagine: *Historia natural y moral de las Indias*).

Acosta's conjecture was based on the absence of written documents in the history of the Indies. Oviedo wrote his history completely from memory, and Acosta, who had been in Peru but not in New Spain, based his work on the reports by his fellow Jesuit Juan de Tovar (who lived in New Spain). Tovar told him what he saw, read, and heard from Indians. "There are now among these and other people," Oviedo wrote, "memories very ancient and modern, although those who sing and recite them do not know how to read, they have not been lost from memory. Thus these

Indians do well in following this advice, since they lack letters, which they replaced with their *areytos*, sustaining their memory and fame; because thanks to these songs they know the things that happened many centuries ago."

Oviedo, one of the first to write chronicles of the Indies, abandoned the chivalric novels that he had written at some point, because that was fantasy and not very moral. Historian Edmundo O'Gorman imagined Oviedo's turning point: ("Prólogo a los *Sucesos y diálogo de la Nueva España* de Gonzalo Fernández de Oviedo y Valdés"):

> One fine day or one bad night, who could tell, [Oviedo] must have understood that he had for many years had an extraordinary and novel subject right under his nose that would exceed the literary ambitions of the most exacting [writer]; and, like a man who suddenly realizes that a pretty neighbor has been smiling at him for quite a while, and regretting his past blindness, decides to woo her, our Oviedo, paying for it with his own fortune, hurried to publish the *Sumario* to claim the subject of America as his own.

Oviedo, then, turned to America and its *areytos* (originally, dances and songs from the Antilles). We have to understand that the Indies changed the world; nothing, not even the thinking of the European past, would be immune. That's why the use that Oviedo and Acosta made of *areytos* was an important step that, at the height of the Renaissance, turned poetry into a document: Oviedo and Acosta (their transcriptions of poetry, legends, dances) were read by Baudouin, who took them as evidence that both a poetic memory worthy of history existed and that it merited being history, and also that history can only be universal. Baudouin was read by Sidney and others who, to demonstrate the universal, innate, and significant nature of the poetic impulse, cited Indian *areytos* (that came from Acosta and Oviedo). If savages who did not know writing turned to poetry, there must be something universal and true in it. According to Momigliano, these uses, by Sidney and Baudouin, changed considerations of the history of Rome during the Renaissance, leading to what was called the theory of the ballad.

In other dominions, for example, the south of India, as Velcheru Narayana Rao, David Shulman, and Sanjay Subrahmanyam indicated (*Textures of Time*), history and poetry or varied rhetorical genres coexisted in a very different way. Before the arrival of Europeans, texts already existed in many languages, but history—telling what happened—did not respect a clear distinction among prose, poetry, legend, myth, and history as such. Curiously, in the Europe of the sixteenth and seventeenth centuries American *areytos* turned into poetry-history precisely for being not writing but memory; the equivalent in the south of India, *kāvya* (*Textures of Time*), did not receive the status of history in spite of being text. Beginning with the eighteenth century, Europe absorbed many of India's poetic traditions as perfect examples of wisdom, beauty, and erotica but not of history: they were text in verse, songs, and narratives full of intricacies. Reading them as history would have required, and requires, being attentive to the "textures of time" in each text (which were considered simultaneously as history and as nonhistory). For example, the tradition of narratives about kings in the Telugu language, known as *karanam*, mixed statistics, facts, and fantasy. They were a text, but they were memories of what happened and memories of every new recitation of what happened, all transcribed in different ways through the centuries. By the late eighteenth century one of the versions of this tradition made "history [flow] toward an adorned poetry motivated by new concerns" (*Textures of Time*) (above all, establishing the idea of the universal king as an ideal type), thus losing the discussions about Realpolitik that various texts in the *karanam* tradition had maintained until then. History was discussed, removing and inserting poetry of all colors and flavors, wars, kings, power, and love: "Many are the powerful castles / that I've conquered in fierce battles. / What remains for me to conquer / this night / are the two powerful castles / of your breasts" (quoted in *Textures of Time*).

But in the languages of eighteenth-century Europe, when "ideas began to be considered goods that could be treated as juridical property" (O'Gorman, "Prólogo a los *Sucesos y diálogo de la Nueva España* de Gonzalo Fernández de Oviedo y Valdés"), the historiographic innovations of the sixteenth and seventeenth centuries passed through a twofold examination: doubt was cast on the validity of poetic memory as a historical document and on the very authority, for example, of Acosta. The plot would make a good detective novel, and O'Gorman, a lawyer who put history on trial, nearly wrote it. In the late eighteenth century, English antiquarian Edward King (Lord Kingsborough) filed *requisitorias* (charges) against Acosta for being "guilty of plagiarism" (O'Gorman, "Prólogo a los *Sucesos y diálogo de la Nueva España* de Gonzalo Fernández de Oviedo y Valdés") because, to his way of thinking, the Jesuit had plagiarized not the writings of Juan de Toledo, whom Acosta recognized as the informant in his *Historia*, but an already existing chronicle. In 1856 José Fernando Ramírez found an anonymous chronicle identical in parts to Acosta's *Historia* in a Mexican convent. Ramírez deduced that it was a Spanish translation, made by Tovar, of a chronicle in Nahuatl by an anonymous indigenous person. Alfredo Chavero hung onto that in the late nineteenth century to manufacture an *indigenista* argument, discrediting Acosta and returning the history to pure indigenous memory. But soon another identical manuscript was discovered, in addition to letters exchanged by Acosta and Tovar: it became clear that those anonymous chronicles had been written by Juan de Tovar, which is what Acosta had always said. Nevertheless, neither Chavero nor many other Mexican historians changed their tune. The chronicles were the product of indigenous voice and memory. History under the science of law, then, ended with the enthronement of Acosta's history, but now, rather than as universal history, as a history and memory that was solely Mexican. In essence, however, the question that Acosta put to Tovar is the one that still echoes in so many debates over history and memory (letter from Acosta to Tovar, reproduced by Joaquín García Icazbalceta in *Don fray Juan de Zumárraga*): "How can one believe that the orations or speeches referred to in this history were given by the ancient rhetoricians referred to in them, because without writing it does not seem possible to preserve long orations, and so elegant of their kind?"

At some point modern history returned to the reconstruction not only of the past but also of Memories of the past. History had to enter into the memory of characters from the past—something that is easier to do with those who left a written, painted, or somehow materialized trail. This is what Jacob Burckhardt and Huizinga did, and they were not bashful about their debt to poetic memory. In the second half of the twentieth century various new schools arose that tried this way of inhabiting the Memory of human groups from the past to understand both the meaning and the origin of yesterday's ideas—the contextualism, for example, of Quentin Skinner ("The Idea of Negative Liberty: Philosophical and Historical Perspectives"). To understand, say, Thomas Hobbes, Skinner suggested, one had to acquire Hobbes's memory—his readings, his routines in joining A with B, the meaning of his concepts in their context. This seems akin to poetic memory, but without the poet's freedom to circulate within and among Memories and memories.

For other historians and philosophers, like Michel Foucault, history should be archaeology not of sounds but of silences and forgettings in order to be able to demarcate the ways of remembering and acting in the past from outside in. Foucault sought unexamined, taken-for-granted aspects of past memories and how unarticulated parts of memories served power structures (what Foucault called epistemes or what more recently François Hartog, with that French delight in catchy academic sound bites, referred to as "regimes of historicity" (*régimes d'historicité*: different ways to experience the past). Thus, history resembles an optical fiber that enters into the Memory of a period, whether into jails or mating customs, in order to observe what seemed to be invisible because it was contained by that Memory from within. The objective: to denounce power and its inescapable networks of meaning.

I believe that the obsessive debate between memory and history in the late twentieth century shows remnants of poetic memory in history. And it is through the category of "identity" that historians, as Croce feared, become bad poets unintentionally. Abdelfattah Kilito (*L'Auteur et ses doubles*) tells the story of the illustrious ninth-century poet Abu Nuwas, asking the poet Khalaf al-Ahmar for permission to write poetry. Khalaf orders him to learn a thousand passages of ancient poetry, the only way to become a real poet. Abu Nuwas memorizes classical Arabic poetry, returns, and spends seven days reciting the poems to Khalaf from memory. Khalaf approves the effort but imposes a new requirement in order to become a great poet: now Abu Nuwas must forget all the lines he had learned—and voluntarily forgetting is much more difficult than memorizing. Nevertheless, Abu Nuwas manages to do it and returns to ask Khalaf for approval. Satisfied, Khalaf says: "Now go and compose poetry." The memory that the poet uses requires the retention of profound structures, each verse in order; his memory is the equivalent of a sophisticated pure mathematics from which the rude technology of obsession with identities can extract only two additions and two subtractions. Memories pertaining to assumed identities claim to be better than history, based on witnesses and testimonies that pick at the personal I—which, God knows why, is always advanced as a collective identity—in order to unveil the true history of X, Y, or Z identity.

I'm not one to dot the "i's" of these historiographic currents. I only want to point out that these exercises—which, before becoming a mere question of identity, were once called mentalités, Zeitgeist, Weltanschauung, later nicknamed context, episteme, or regimes of historicity—share a humongous understanding about remembering. That is, it's a matter of coming to an "epochal" remembering that explains not only what happened or what John Locke thought: not only prisons and forms of exercising and sharing power, but an epochal consciousness. In turn, the recent memory fever is not a search for the memory of Tom, Dick, or Harriet, but the way into a humongous identity, something that can sustain the struggle of a people, an ethnic group, or a society. Don't get me wrong: looking for that giant is to explain, to understand historically, but then we are on our way back to the keen desire for poetic memory.

The poet Osip Mandelstam, who was neither Foucault nor an archaeologist, but who better to dig the deepest, said: "Poetry is the plough that turns up time in such a way that the abyssal strata of time, its black earth, appear on the surface" ("The Word and Culture"). In effect, poetic memory has remained recessive in history like a constant search for the historiographic equivalent of what in neuroscience is called an "engram": the physical site of memory, the physiological change in the brain that codifies memory itself (Jonathan Weiner, *Time, Love, Memory*). Thus, the search for epistemes (Foucauldian engrams), the desire to capture whole Memories from the past through the tiny memory of the present, is reminiscent of Petrarch's determination to evoke Laura twenty years after her death, basing his work, naturally, on Augustine's *Confessions*. Being able to surmount Petrarch's here and Petrarch's today, his being there and our being here, still feeling Laura's absence in the twenty-first century, is the miracle of the poetic memory. For the problem with the overlapping memories of history and poetry is none other than Augustine's original dilemma:

> Great is this power of memory, exceedingly great, O my God—a large and boundless inner hall! Who has plumbed the depths of it? Yet it is a power of my mind, and it belongs to my nature. But I do not myself grasp all that I am. Thus the mind is far too narrow to contain itself. But where can that part of it be which it does not contain? Is it outside and not in itself? How can it be, then, that the mind cannot grasp itself? (*Confessions and Enchiridion*)

I can't resolve these questions about the memories of poetry and history. I know that it has all been an overblown idea, perhaps with diminishing returns. Let's leave it there.

6

The contrast in memories between poetry and history offers another key that is difficult for me to describe. I can only comment on it in the first person, but I suspect that this key has also worked for many cultural historians. I refer to the way the poetic imagination sometimes works like the software of the historical imagination—and here I rely on a metaphor and a very chic one at that. Memory is the historian's tool for observing the past, and it's filled with images, logics, and intuitions that sometimes come from poetry's uncanny mechanisms. It is inevitable, but it is also difficult to determine and to explain. The reader may believe I assume that the historian of culture ought to be a reader of poetry. Yes, I do. There is something in the nature of the evidence of cultures that makes the realization that poetry grants useful.

I wanted, for example, to write a cultural history of Mexico City between 1880 and 1940. I relied on, what else, the historiography on the subject—on Mexico and other cities. I exhausted countless archives, but when putting together some bits of the book I noticed that the logic of my arguments, almost without my having arranged it, was nourished on the logic of urban walks and poetry. If cities have left evidence of their cultural lives, it has been in poems, songs, and novels, and from there I took data and anecdotes to prove my ideas and to conceive new ones. My memory drank in something more, not what I had seen or recorded, but poetry's way of seeing, which is historical—it corresponds to its time—but which also goes beyond because it still makes today's reader's realization. Without entirely trying, I read the past with the poetry software in my head. Another way of putting it: without knowing how or when, in order to show the past of the urban experience, I documented poetry's suspicions. I don't know if Octavio Paz's verses ("I speak of the city," "an I cut off from a we," "an I adrift": Octavio Paz, "Hablo de la ciudad") or the dogs, the buildings, the prostitutes, the rain—all that was the point of departure: poetry as a research guide or the point of arrival, remembering poetry a posteriori, confirming that I had only paraphrased a poem with hundreds of facts and footnotes.

On another occasion I wanted to explain my surprise at seeing the periodization of the nineteenth century in various countries: Mexico, Brazil, Argentina, the United States, Spain . . . And I was surprised that it was so similar in many countries, as though—now I'm resorting to metaphor—we were dealing with a railroad line with the same stations in time. But the railroad line simile helped me articulate my surprise, not to explain the why of what I observed. Some lines from an old Galician verse that I read in Álvaro Cunqueiro made me realize and allowed me to write, for better or worse, a book on the nineteenth century understood as a river: "Ay, madre mía, pasadme en el río / *que le levan as aguas os lirios*" (Oh, dear mother, take me to the river / *the water lilies are taking its water away,* in *Papales que Fueron vidas*). And the entire book became a metaphor of a river in which the water lilies aren't carried away by the water, but rather the water by the lilies: the current isn't moved by the simple passage of time; the great themes of nineteenth-century history—the formation of states, nations, peoples, and races—drive the river's current. In short, now that the "historical imagination" of the nineteenth century has been considered what makes us post-this and post-that; now that it's common to "deconstruct" the historical force that ruled in the nineteenth century, another poem granted me the logic of what happens when we "historicize" a force so powerful that it forces us to stop and see it: (Sandro Penna) "io vado verso il fiume su un cavallo che quando lo penso un poco un poco egli si ferma" (approximation: "I'm going toward the river on a horse that when I think of him a little he stops a little": *Tutte le poesie*).

I would like to illustrate the use of poetry as software for cultural history with other examples, but I can't. It's customary for historians to identify "theoretical frameworks" and ideological or political positions, but who admits that it's the poet in the background who is calling the shots? Nevertheless, in Huizinga, between the lines, I read poets I don't manage to identify; in Luis González y González (*Pueblo en vilo*) I feel the verses of Ramón López Velarde.

Finally, between poetry and history we find that parallelism about thinking, as Harold Bloom said about poetry, "through influences of errors and accumulation" (*The Anxiety of Influence*). History is never written—it is always rewritten, and the rewriting of history is, on the one hand, a theft (of the findings and the imagination of predecessors) and, on the other, an unconscious trial and error within the confines of what is thinkable and sayable about the past in a particular present. What's more, H. R. Trevor-Roper said that imagining the past always involves guessing at "what would have happened if" (*History & Imagination*): an exercise that is not aimed at the reality of the past itself—which is always immovable—but at the imagination that legions of historians have captured in many books on many subjects. We might say about the evolution of cultural historiography what Bloom said about poetry: "poetic influence always proceeds by a misreading of the prior poet, an act of creative correction that is actually and necessarily a misinterpretation. The history of fruitful poetic influence . . . is a history of anxiety and self-serving caricature, of distortion, of perverse, artful revisionism, without which modern poetry as such could not exist" (*The Anxiety of Influence*). Likewise the modern historiography of culture.

In sum, no doubt I have exaggerated the intimacy of the couple in question (history and poetry). But take my exaggeration as the result of the risk of expressing a complicated certainty and not as a charge against the certainty that poetry is knowledge and as such akin to cultural history and indispensable to it.

Chapter 3

THE HISTORICAL IMAGINATION

When writing history, the imagination is both input and output; the imagined is revealed to be the testimony of reality and of the imagination itself. Which came first, the political and social conditions that gave rise to the nation or the very idea of nation? I don't know. Historical fancy comes into play constantly. It creates both tiny and enormous things: the nation, the idea of empire, the notion of the Middle Ages, the certainty of progress—and also trifles about, say, the urban experience in eighteenth-century Barcelona or love in the twelfth century. I want to reflect on this imagination, which serves to intuit, describe, live, and relive the past in the present. It's a vast and tangled subject, of course, but here I will simply attempt a little bit of order and clarity using various intuitions as a point of departure. Because the historical imagination's possibilities were revealed to me in the way linguists who study Aymara discovered a new verb tense (the near remote past).[1] The authors of *Aymara: Compendio de estructura fonológica y gramática* write: "There was a delay in obtaining the complete paradigm of the near remote [past tense]. We had to wait for one of the co-authors to 'age' (turn forty) to finish this section." In effect, Juan de Dios Yapita, the Aymara speaker who served as the linguists' informant, had not informed the researchers about that other verb tense because he had not yet reached the age required to use the near remote, a tense, as those who know say, used "for personal knowledge" (*Aymara: compendio de estructura fonológica y gramática*). To use it, the speaker must have reached forty years of age and be "married and established in the community." So that's it: I had to turn forty, having been a good citizen of my tribe of historians in order to realize at last what sort of thing the historical imagination was and how it worked.

First, let me make the following clear: I supinely accept the insignificance of the historian in current cultural life, whether in Mexico or in the

United States. No doubt there will always be a great historian at Harvard or at the Universidad Nacional Autónoma de México who believes that his voice has the power to save the truth, the poor, the people, or the motherland. As for me, I don't even believe that when drunk. To be or appear to be an "opinion maker" you have to be a media star, a Google intellectual who can talk about everything and anything at the drop of a hat. Most historian aren't like that; we bore people. I believe, however, that those who know about the past are an intellectual army reserve; their works can be called up at short notice because nations, memories, identities, and politics explain and justify themselves through the past. What's more, justice is sought using the past as *magister dixit*. "History has ceased to function as a provider of meaning to our lives," historian Christian Meier has said, so "why not just give it up?" Because, Meier believes, "history will become meaningful, even essential, if only because a striving for an overview, for a sense of accountability for our world, must regain ground" (*From Athens to Auschwitz*). Less than two decades ago, scholars like Eric Hobsbawm and Ernest Gellner believed in the end of the nation-state and the complete secularization of the world. Today nations everywhere, large and small, demand recognition of their existence with historical arguments; today the world is once again split by historical religions; today there's again widespread debate about when things (peace, ecology, the distribution of resources) "got all fucked up." Thus, in spite of their evident insignificance, historians of culture must take as much or more care than historians did in the nineteenth century, although without their megalomania. Sooner or later the story of the past counts, and it is dangerous. And liberating. It demands responsibility. I want to examine this imagination that doesn't count, until it does.

The Imagination Is "Cool"

So much perorating about language, discourses, power, "interstices," resistance, memory, identity, the trans- and the post-, all that and more turned what used to be dangerous and traitorous into something optimal and good—namely, the imagination: "the faculty or action of forming new ideas, or images or concepts of external objects not present to the senses" (*Oxford English Dictionary*). The Spanish-language authority, more fearful of the evil consequences of imagining, states that imagination is the "faculty of the soul that represents images of things real or ideal"; "false apprehension or judgment of something that does not exist in reality or that has no basis"; "facility for forming new ideas, new projects or images or concepts" (*Diccionario de la lengua española*). Already in the seventeenth century Sebastián Cobarrubias's dictionary (*Tesoro de la lengua castellana o española*, 1611), while not ignoring the risks of fantasy, accepted that without imagination no thought would be possible: "pasarla por la imaginación una cosa, es no haber tenido pensamiento della ni primer movimiento" (passing a thing through the imagination is not having had thought of it at all). In a much more modern definition, imagination turns out to be a creative force; and in neurological terms it comes to be the part of the brain that conceives things, emotions, images.

But less than two centuries ago the imagination was the enemy of reason and in its worst guise, fantasy, was to be avoided at all costs. Even so, throughout the centuries no one doubted the powers of the imagination. For Blaise Pascal: "The imagination disposes of everything. It creates beauty, justice, and happiness, which are everything in this world" (*Pensées*). Nevertheless, Pascal also insulted the imagination: "lover of error and falsehood, and even more traitorous because it is not always thus . . . reason can protest in vain." In short, though it now sounds flattering, "imagination" has had rather a bad reputation—especially when it comes to writing history.

Imagination and reason were enemies, not unlike the soul and the body; the imagination was thought to be harmful for memory: it was what made memory mislead. Thus it was for centuries, in spite of the revolution represented by the ideas of Giambattista Vico (1668–1744). Leopold von Ranke, Theodor Mommsen, and Ernest Renan preferred to speak directly of the poetic rather than of the imagination in history. Considering their trade poetic turned it into supreme knowledge. Flirting with the imagination was another matter; it meant approaching fantasy or, worse, lies, madness.

I can't say precisely when or why, but at some point in the twentieth century the imagination acquired a flattering pedigree. Here are some examples of its good reputation in common usage: "imagined communities," "social imaginaries," "liberal imagination," "educated imagination," "sociological imagination," "imagining the self," "political imagination"—or the feverish pursuit of the "imaginary" (more common and chic in French: *imaginaire*). And remember the title of the most important historiographic book published in the second half of the twentieth century: Hayden White's *Metahistory: The Historical Imagination in Nineteenth-Century Europe*. In short, the imagination has acquired positive usage and reputation.

It's been a long time since philosophers and historians stopped believing in the separation of the imagination from reason, or consciousness from the body. Not even scientists believe in that now—they talk
about what would have been absolute nonsense three centuries ago, the
"rational imagination." Ruth Byrne (scientist of knowledge) states that
"[r]ational thought has turned out to be more imaginative than cognitive scientists previously supposed" (*The Rational Imagination*). Among
neurologists, the imagination is discussed at the same table with memory
and consciousness. Arnold Modell (*Imagination and the Meaningful Brain*)
believes that the old philosophical debates about the imagination and recent studies of the brain have given way to the modern idea of the "creative
imagination," an imagination that is not equivalent to reason, but acceptable, good—indispensable. What Vico believed almost three centuries ago
neurologists like Giulio Tononi and Gerald M. Edelman have made plain:
"Memory has properties that allow perceptions to alter recall, and recall
to alter perception . . . every active perception is to some degree an act of
creation, and every act of memory is to some degree an act of imagination"
("Consciousness and Complexity").

Based on these developments in the neurosciences, we understand the
lucid confessions of Brazilian thinker Eduardo Giannetti da Fonseca, who
fervently believed in the autonomy of the imagination but wound up con-
verting to "physicalism." That is, he became a distressed convert to the
idea that it is the neurons that are in charge, the fluids, not the soul (*A
ilusão da alma*). And all because one day a brain tumor made it impossible for Giannetti to remember the speech he was going to deliver and he
was not able to improvise. After the tumor was removed, Giannetti spent
his time reading everything available on consciousness and memory and
fell into the opposition between Democritus (who believed that reason
and thought were physical and mechanical processes, complex but having
nothing to do with spirits either human or divine) and Socrates (all spirit,
pure thought). Giannetti's imagination, humanist through and through,
found consolation in a story by Joaquim Maria Machado de Assis ("O
espelho," in *Contos*) in which a character expresses this theory of the soul:
"every human creature has two souls, one that looks from the inside out
and the other that looks from the outside in." And thus Giannetti resigned
himself, not without tragedy, to the unity between brain and imagination:
he wanted to throw in his lot with "the Socrates of the Phaedo, but [he
recognized] that the palm of victory belonged, in the end, to Democritus,
his true adversary, in the contest of the centuries between mentalism and

physicalism" (*A ilusão da alma*). His physical tumor, he says, became metaphysical: "the soul seen from the outside in lacerates and suffocates the soul seen from the inside out."

Despite this collapse of the borders between mind and imagination in the neurosciences, by the second half of the twentieth century, for some unclear reason, every discipline and form of knowledge seemed to need its private imagination: Lionel Trilling and "the liberal imagination" and the various resurrections of Edmund Burke's idea of "the moral imagination," and two or three versions of "the anthropological imagination." Perhaps the best known of these many imaginations was C. Wright Mills's *The Sociological Imagination*, which, astride Marxism, history, and psychoanalysis, stated:

> The sociological imagination enables its possessor to understand the larger historical scene in terms of its meaning for the inner life and the external career of a variety of individuals . . . The first fruit of this imagination—and the first lesson of the social science that embodies it—is the idea that the individual can understand his own experience and gauge his own fate only by locating himself within his period, that he can know his own chances in life only by becoming aware of those of all individuals in his circumstances. (*The Sociological Imagination*)

An imagination, then, to notice that we are not alone and to realize that we have and share imagination; you imagine me, I imagine you. So it's no surprise that a prominent Brazilian political scientist, Wanderley Guilherme dos Santos, has taken this old thesis to its ultimate consequences: "Remembering without being remembered. That is loneliness" (*Acervo de maldizer*). I could add: imagining without being imagined, that is loneliness.

With so much hubbub about the imagination, it is odd that the discipline of history hasn't ventured many definitions of "the historical imagination," maybe because it seems obvious what "imagining the past" should mean: none of that imagining business, just document, describe, and recount the past. Benedetto Croce (1866–1952) criticized the excesses of the imagination in the historiography of the early twentieth century (*Teoria e storia della storiografia*), but he also sketched his version of the historical imagination: "without a doubt, the imagination is indispensable to the historian: empty criticism, empty narrative, they are completely sterile . . . we have demanded a living experience of the events whose history we have decided to relate, which also means their re-working as intuition and imagination. Without that reconstruction or imaginative integration, it is impossible to write history, to read it, or to understand it." However, Croce feared the imagination: he longed to discipline it in the historian. Croce believed that history should be distinguished from the "free poetic imagination, so beloved of those historians who hear the voice of Jesus on the Sea of Galilee." And to those fans of an empirical, objective history— Leopold von Ranke, for example—the imagination was an uncomfortable idea, though they were in their element appealing to poetry as a way of knowing. Croce, on the other hand, felt secure attacking "poetic history" through his faith in a domesticated historical imagination.

A historian closer to our own time and to social history, E. P. Thompson, makes reference not to the imagination but to "historical logic," although he was talking about imagination, pure and simple:

> In investigating history, we are not flicking through a series of "stills," each of
> which shows us a moment of social time transfixed into a single eternal pose:
> for each of these "stills" is not only a moment of being but also a moment of
> becoming . . . Any historical moment is both a result of prior process and an
> index towards the direction of its future flow. (*The Poverty of Theory*)

While Croce longed to discipline the imagination, Thompson wanted to formalize it; that is, the imagination of the historian is the logic, the flow of images of the past. In reality, Thompson called upon the imagination to undermine the rigidity of historical materialism (a domestic feud among Marxist historians).

R. G. Collingwood, inspired by Vico, Croce, and the discipline of archaeology, attempted a modern definition, at the same time rational, logical, and falsifiable, of the historical imagination: "Historical imagination . . . is (if I may borrow a Kantian phrase) *a priori* . . . it is characterized by universalism and necessity. What the historian imagines . . . insofar as he does his work right, is what he must imagine, not simply what he may imagine" (*The Idea of History*). Thus, Collingwood believed that what historian X imagines, if it is well imagined, is what historian Y—exposed to the same data—would also imagine. The definition still surprises me, not because it's penetrating but because it's a trap: it's a way to entertain the problem without entering into it. Croce and Thompson, for good or ill, did not flee from the problem, namely: how to imagine but not altogether imagine when writing history.

Later in the twentieth century the imagination was called upon in order to return to the old idea that history is not science but, rather, rhetoric. Hayden White uses the word "imagination" sixty-three times in *Metahistory*, but he never takes a moment to define it; nor does he include it in the index, though the word appears in the title. In subsequent works White attempted to tackle the notion of imagination, and he did it in relation to—what else?—poetry, but with an interest in the poet's pen rather than in his gaze (*The Content of the Form*). History, says White, orders (disciplines) the imagination, which "in the sense of poets is operative," but which "in the world of the historian" is useful "at the last stage of his labors, when it becomes necessary to compose a discourse or narrative in which to represent his findings." For White, the modern historical imagination is a "social convention" that operates when writing the past. And if we accept that there is no thought without language, then the modern historical imagination that White proposes is all the imagination the historian can afford.

Another theorist who had his years of academic fame, Paul Ricoeur, like Vico and the neurologists, conceives of memory and imagination in constant interaction and reinvents the wheel: "The constant danger of confusing remembering and imagining, resulting from memories becoming images in this way, affects the goal of faithfulness corresponding to the truth claim of memory" (*Memory, History, Forgetting*). In short, I'm interested in the imagination that is deceptive memory, not reduced solely to the rhetoric of history but rather to the very conception of images of the cultural past.

Quixote and Sancho

Cultural history appeals to memory, almost never to personal memory but to that too. The past is potentially either personal or collective memory. The imagination is like a pair of scissors, one of whose sharp blades, on cutting, creates concepts and ideas via the senses, memory, and experiences of the outside world, including the materiality of a document, the adventures in finding it, conversations on the subject, visits to museums, archives, cities. The other blade of the scissors (the imagination) is not an intermediary between the senses and consciousness but consciousness itself; it is the capacity to create images, to abstract, to intuit, to feel, to suspect beyond any tangible reality. Thus, as was believed until the nineteenth century, the imagination can be the enemy of memory. I call as my witness the most emblematic of the excesses of the imagination, the "ingenious" (as in very imaginative) hidalgo Don Quixote de la Mancha, who, carried away by his imagination, lost all memory of reality. In turn, memory and feet on the ground turn out to be enemies of the imagination: hence Sancho Panza, whose memory never fails, rides astride the animal of memory par excellence, the donkey. Cervantes knew well these old, common distinctions of his time between memory and imagination and therefore calls Quixote *el ingenioso hidalgo*: he who falls into fantasy, imagination's most harmful expression. Quixote contracted the disease of fantasy from excessive reading of Amadis de Gaula; Sancho, on the other hand, is earthly, all memory—he is ignorant but recognizes the mundane, imagines nothing.

In a way, early twentieth-century empiricist historians were fond of Sancho Panza; they feared and scorned imagination. Hence it is ironic that their hatred for the imagination took such an anti–Sancho Panza stance— the antiplebeian erudition of antiquarians and philologists. In terms of memory, however, the antiquarian's erudition was like that of Sancho, but in an aristocratic style. The truth is that many great historians, in English, Spanish, French, Portuguese, and German, recognized the poetic in their work without completely accepting that they were victims of the imagination. They sought, of course, to tame the imagination, never to let it fall into involuntary fantasy or, worse, into deception. In fact, recognizing their link to poetry was a way of taming the imagination, because appealing to poetry was to resort not to the literary imagination but to knowledge of a reality that is beyond the material but not divine.

History as a text results from the imagination, but the historical imagination is more than just the rhetoric of that text, especially when it deals with the cultural past. To be able to talk about values or art or music or politics, historians imagine things that are not entirely exchangeable for data or material facts. Few historians faced the problem directly; it was assumed that the historian was, above all, a searcher for sources who did not have much need of imagination and must tame it if he had it. Because of this long-standing embrace of the domesticated imagination I see the historian as a bit like Sancho and a bit like Don Quixote. For historians are readers and then writers more than they are detectives, and with that comes a risk of being Quixotes.

Throughout the nineteenth and twentieth centuries, however, historians believed that the past had to be transformed into an experience in the present, which is something that only the imagination did and does. In the guise of the historical imagination, some notions came into being, like "reenactment" (Collingwood) and "verisimilitude" (Manzoni) and "experience" (from Croce and Huizinga to Frank Ankersmit) and "reality effect" (Roland Barthes). All of these figures call for a variegated balance between Sancho Panza and Don Quixote. In essence, this means that the historian's imagination re-creates what the great historical novel of the nineteenth century did (Gustave Flaubert, Honoré de Balzac, Alessandro Manzoni, Leo Tolstoy, Walter Scott, Benito Pérez Galdós). (Today we would say that the historical imagination works like the staging of the best historical film or television series.) The imagination serves to document each detail, "recreating" the presence of the past in the present without errors or anachronisms and with empirical fidelity. The problem is that, in the case of the cultural past, to re-create, relive, experience, and create the illusion of reality—all of that makes the imagination come into play not only in the act of re-creation (the writing, staging) but in the process of finding and understanding the evidence of past cultures. We need a good imagination just to take note of the massacre of cats on the Rue Saint-Séverin in eighteenth-century Paris and then to connect that event to revolutionary working-class thought and the *Encyclopédie* (Robert Darnton, *The Great Cat Massacre*).

For the historian, a good mix of Sancho and Quixote is in the balance of "finding" evidence, "describing it," "recounting it" (measuring and narrating it), and "explaining it." But cultural evidence is not the same as the evidence of tobacco production in Virginia in 1800 or evidence of weather conditions in England in 1750 or Mesoamerican demography in 1500. The ruins that the cultural historian studies demand an ability to imagine something like cultural evidence before and after we know the facts of the past. The cultural echoes of the past can be mistaken for silence or for the historian's own voice, if she believes herself to be possessed by echoes from the past. Due to the very nature of cultural evidence, the historian is constantly imagining, stumbling, going back and forth between the past and the present, such that she comes to realize how, in her own hands, a poem, a sign, a song, or a coin becomes an important piece of evidence of a past culture.

Of course, we always imagine from the present. There is no other point of entry except the here and now. This is how Carlo Ginzburg explains it: "Historians start from questions using terms that are inevitably anachronistic. The research process modifies the initial questions on the grounds of new evidence, retrieving answers that are articulated in the actors' language, and related to categories peculiar to their society, which is utterly different from ours" ("Our Words, and Theirs"). Thus, a historian from 1900s Mexico might be familiar with the medical literature published at the time on maternity, hysterectomies, care during delivery, and demography. But he couldn't turn these texts into evidence of the cultural construction of the female body (present and future of the nation). A historian today can enter into that evidence with this vision of the female body but will have to learn the medical idiom of the 1900s if he hopes to say something relevant about the past in the present. Shifting constantly between past and present, cultural evidence becomes a moving target. In just a few years new social or cultural contexts in the present, or some odd readings or personal experiences that are difficult to explain, can suddenly turn some object or text from the past into solid cultural evidence. Therefore, historians return to the same archives and libraries not only to see whether there is something new but to see if they become aware of something important in material that they have already seen a number of times. The mathematician, perhaps, hopes that during the next review of the theorem, his imagination will find the key. Frequently, the solution is an accident, a fortunate error that takes the mathematician serendipitously to the revelation. Eurekas are not routine in the work of cultural historians, but they do come about from time to time. Every attempt is a new present, a different social and personal imagination.

In sum, the historical imagination constitutes the possibility to see nothing in a windmill, or to see something more than a mere windmill. Sancho and the historian know that the windmill is tied down to mundane empirical evidence, but the historical imagination allows for connections, recollections, and images that make it possible for the windmill to say something that, to a certain extent and with luck, re-creates a verisimilar and convincing experience of the past in the present.

Sadly, imagination is a scarce resource; it is not widespread or predictable or teachable or repeatable, at least not to the extent that it makes "sublime" experiences of the past possible (Frank Ankersmit, *Sublime Historical Experience*), as great poems and novels do. Therefore, we must expect cultural historians to have only modest imaginations, creative but above all workmanlike: imaginations that serve to recount, to search for, and to create evidence of small scenes from the past, turning them into present culture, into messages to the future. This modest sort of imagination is crafted and perfected through practice and the acquisition of technical skills—from paleography to music to poetics to philology to the mastery of several languages and mathematics. And, to be sure, it demands memory, a great deal of memory, which must also be educated and polished.

The cultural historian, however, has a complicated relationship with his own imaginations. He feels vulnerable before the imagination because he misses it when he doesn't have enough of it and even if does, it has to be disciplined. Perhaps a historian writing a study of cotton production in Texas can do a more or less competent job with little imagination, if he finds good data. There is no way for a cultural historian not to yearn for more imagination, because without it he may not even realize that he has found a gold mine of cultural evidence from the past. He searches among the data and in his erudition for the material to feed his imagination—like a novelist—but also to limit it. The novelist imagines; the historian goes forth imagining and disimagining without pause, while he researches, while he reads, and while he writes.

Disputes between different imaginations must not be confused with the antagonism in history between the partisans of imagination and its opponents. At times the dispute between description and explanation has been considered a quarrel over the imagination, as was the case in eigh-teenth-century England with the clash between Edward Gibbon (explain, recount, imagine) and Henry Edwards Davis (describe with erudition, discover) or in nineteenth-century Argentina between Vicente F. López (philosophize) and Bartolomé Mitre (describe, document). These old histo-riographic quarrels were duels between shadows; to describe is to explain, to explain is to describe: the imagination reigns over both tasks. The same duels between shadows occur today between "narrative" and "theoreti-cal" historians. Which historian does not aspire to narrate (imagine)? And which historian does so without a point of view weighed down with the-ory, with personal experiences, and with so many other things?

The cultural historian needs her imagination so much that she fills it with moral, methodological, political, and aesthetic filters. Don Quixote let his imagination be governed by the criteria of honorability and heroism that he encountered in Amadis de Gaula's novels. Don Quixote's politics, his justice, and his morals were part of his fantasies. The cultural histo-rian's imagination is not only limited by the empirical evidence but also by moral, political, and methodological criteria that may or may not be part of her imagination. Her imagination controls itself through almost imperceptible moral criteria that pertain to the present. Likewise, the his-torian controls her imagination through notions of justice or method that she herself imposes—for example, reading only images, like an art historian, or reading only texts, as the majority of cultural historians did until recently. Thus, not everything is imaginable. A cultural historian can now imagine evidence of "alternative sexualities" in the ruins of the past in a way that was not possible previously. What she could do but would not allow herself to do is to imagine that traces of sex with minors in classical antiquity or in the eighteenth and nineteenth centuries constitute evidence of the "naturalness" and justice of pederastic desire.

Current consensus about justice, liberty, and equality are so hardwired in our ability to imagine that it's impossible to come up with ideas beyond certain parameters. This does not mean that justice is on the side of historical truth or the imagination. Hence, for example, Isaiah Berlin believed that the historian should report the errors, lacunae, and human infamies in history, while his opponent, E. H. Carr (the author of *What Is History?*), believed that personalities were not important and morals even less. What mattered were processes, the progress of class struggle. In reality, justice limits and at the same time surpasses the historical imagination. At times justice requires more imagination than history does, to such an extent that sometimes we must dispense with history to do justice in the present, imagining possible reconciliation scenarios beyond what may have happened in the past. In itself, history is the eternal dominion of injustice.

There is another risk in the imagination of cultural history. Imagination and cultures are wrapped together in a clumsy bundle with the burdensome "us" and "them." We know why Quixote lost his mind, and we also know that other story by heart: nations were "imagined communities" that homogenized and erased local identities. But those presumed local identities, ethnic, prenational, postnational, or paranational, weren't they also imagined? The textbook answer is that every identity is a social construction—that is, imagination. This makes the problem of the historical imagination not whether it is disciplined, but whether it is good or evil. "The dance around the golden calf of identity," says Peter Sloterdijk, would not exist "if it were not basically a question of the fixed form of the ego" (*Critique of Cynical Reason*). There's no need to share Sloterdijk's cynical view in order to remember that identities are a rocky road and a bad habit for the historical imagination.

A distinguished contemporary historian, Pierre Chaunu, explained his dedication to the past thus: "I'm a historian because I'm the son of death and the mystery of time has haunted me since my childhood. As far back as my memories go, I find myself fascinated by memory. It holds the foundation of the spirit, the secret of our identity; memory hands us over to the vertigo of being and of time" (in Maurice Agulhon and Pierre Nora, eds., *Essais d'égo-histoire*). What historical narrative escapes this siren song of identity and memory? It seems obvious, but why are we so obsessed with identity and memory?

Both identity and memory act like recent titles of long intellectual battles. Identity summarizes and assumes language, race, history, and psyche—a kneading together of physical and cultural anthropology, ethnography, and Sigmund Freud, Octavio Paz, Sérgio Buarque de Holanda, Erik Erikson, Louis Hartz, Paul Gilroy, and Gayatri Spivak. Memory, in turn, soaks up and absorbs the authenticity of true history and its undeniable suffering (from John Locke to the Holocaust). It's difficult for historians to escape this seduction, but most have no problem repeating that memory and identity are "social imaginaries." Even so, the historical imagination builds its own jails and finds it difficult to imagine a way out. Nowadays it seems undeniable that identity, the intimacy of the I (personal and collective) is in the past, which we access either through memory or, with increasing frequency, through DNA—the natural consequence of so much obsession with genealogy. Because, as Carolyn Steedman has shown (*Strange Dislocations*), taken together, the nineteenth-century theory of the cell, history's scientific turn in the late nineteenth century, the rise of the idea of childhood beginning in the eighteenth century, and abundant doses of Freud and post-Freudianism gave rise to today's undeniable axiom: the past is the home of identity, the house of intimate subjectivity, individually and collectively, sometimes because it is memory and sometimes because it is DNA. The imagination, then, serves to produce a Public Broadcasting Service show in which a famous Harvard professor makes genetic family trees for regular everyday people like Meryl Streep and Steven Spielberg. Or the imagination serves to make the interior "I" speak: the "I" that is undoubtedly the total sum of history and memory, the only and integral "I" that emerges from within: "In the everyday world of the twenty-first century," writes Steedman (*Strange Dislocation*), "we operate within this mode by means of a politics of the imagination in which the past has become a place of succor and strength, a kind of home for the ideas people possess of who they really want to be."

This is how memory is made to serve as the police of the bad historical imagination (Sancho taking care of Quixote). Thus, I don't imagine, we don't imagine; I remember, we remember. The witness of history doesn't imagine, he remembers. Memory, understood as the mysterious millenary reserve either of the imagination or of reality—who knows?—of a people, of a race, of a "community," doesn't lie. Sometimes it can be memory reborn from its own ashes: data, languages, and the pre-Hispanic past have been lost, but not the imaginary (it exists in living indigenous people). At times it is an argument against the imagination: what X and Y remember of the past as they experienced it is the truth: the rest is historical imagination.

Nevertheless, I believe that the historical imagination of cultures, if it really comes into play, can be neither self-help therapy nor nostalgia for cultural, ethnic, or historical essentials. The historical imagination and memory (personal or collective) do not work very differently from the imagination tout court. Both incessantly lie, distort, invent, evoke, and reimagine. Finding empirical proofs, constructing evidence, and reimagining is a never-ending task . . . for history and for memory.

Clearly, it's a law: "memory is identity"—remembrances rest in memory like the bricks of the edifice of personal or collective identity. This is a common and perhaps inevitable self-deception. Memories do not rest; they are not the perennial presence of an "I am," of a "we are," this or that, there, here, yesterday, today, or tomorrow. Memory makes us believe that it is a pristine spring of identity when in truth it is a messy survival mechanism. It is not a matter of fixed presences but of various versions of the same presences and, above all, of absences. Memory has to have something to do with identity, although not in the sense of the accumulation of the parts of the "I am" or "we are," but as the framework for imagining absences and redefining presences. But who has an identity that he doesn't have, that is foreign to him, that is revealed to be alien to his very own presence? We are what we remember but we are also what we have forgotten, because we have forgotten or because we have preferred not to remember. What sort of identity is that? It cannot be conjugated: I am who I don't remember.

Let's look at this more calmly. It is ironic and tragic that the advocate of the concept of "collective memory," old Maurice Halbwachs, spent his last days conversing and strolling around with the young Jorge Semprún among the barracks of Buchenwald, the concentration camp where Halbwachs later died. There they were, the interpreter of "collective memory" and one of the most important exponents of the contradictory and bitter weight of personal memory molded by the tragedies of the twentieth century (Semprún). For Halbwachs, all remembering happens in a group: it is the result of social interaction, so distinguishing between collective and individual memory is complicated. He believed that what is important is constant and dynamic "remembering" (always more than individual) and not static memories. And Semprún's life was a constant "recalling," always between a very unique and changing "I" (the Spanish aristocrat who winds up being a French leftist writer) and a variable "we" (the losers of the Spanish Civil War, the antifascists, the Communists, the survivors, the honorary Jews, the French, the Spanish). Semprún's memory belonged to so many "collective memories" that in the end it was not any of them. The combination lived only in him. Semprún's life and work proved that, if the constant and variable remembering of which Halbwachs spoke truly functions, the individual or collective memory cannot be thought of simply as a pressure cooker that is always about to explode because of the pressure produced by the steam of tragedy and evil in the past. Because, though the late Semprún advocated for making justice through memory, his formula was actually quite different: "writing or life" (*L'Écriture ou la vie*). That is, to imagine starting from memories so that it will then be possible to narrate, tell, relive, feel so as not to die from the unhindered operation of mutinous, incoherent remembrances that are constantly being transformed in the memories of those who, like Semprún, experienced the horrors of the twentieth century. For Memory kills (Primo Levi, Paul Celan). The imagination, that is, writing, doesn't erase, it only tames memory and forgetting. A character in Elias Canetti's *Die Blendung* (1935) has such a good memory that he makes lists of the foolish things that he wants to forget; that is, he writes to forget. Semprún, as he remembered, made use of what is indispensable to memory and to human life: blessed forgetfulness.

This is how tangled the relationship between memory and imagination is. It is absurd simply to believe in the existence of a set of recollections that come together to form something like an identity, accumulated there as though in an individual or collective storeroom. Each recollection does not live alone in the memory of the "I" or the "we." It is impossible to conceive of, as is common in autobiographies, our first memory. The mere fact of calling it to mind is already the product of the kneading together of remembrance on top of remembrance, of clear or ambiguous images that feed into one another. The "blank mind" is as mythical as the idea of memory arranged like a storeroom of recollections neatly boxed and labeled, with a clear chronology and causality. Each new reminiscence, learned or lived, false or true, changes that which has already been remembered and, at the same time, conditions what will merit remembering. Each new memory, potentially, changes the vision of the past and conditions perspectives on the future. Moreover, what the new recollection will be like is already marked by the chaotic circulation of recollections in every memory.

Today, for example, a Jewish thinker evokes the fourteenth-century pogroms in the kingdoms of Castile and Aragon in a very different way than a Jewish thinker would have one hundred years ago. The Holocaust has conditioned every new remembering of everlasting anti-Semitism. Until only two decades ago the way in which any Spaniard could accumulate new memories about political, personal, family, local, or national life was marked by vivid recollections of a war and a long, repressive dictatorship—whether they were personal memories, the stories of a family or a town, or those of a group in a city. Today there are at least two generations of Spaniards who accumulate memories of political life in a very different way than their parents or grandparents did—though they think of themselves as bearers of those memories. And there is no need to get bogged down in how the same thing happens for each person who goes about accumulating and redefining memories and forgetfulnesses throughout life. The problem is not that I am not the sum of what I remember and forget and that this sum isn't shared with others—whether it gives way to a group's or a nation's identity is a horse of a different color, the horse of history and politics, not memory. The problem is that no sooner do we believe that our own memories are under control than a single old recollection that comes to mind due to X circumstance, or a new present, or the triumph of forgetting at the neural level, disarranges and rearranges the order that we thought we had achieved.

Thus, we shouldn't confuse memory with Memory—what anthropologists, politicians, activists, and historians hold up high in the name of this or that political or social cause. No matter how noble the cause, that Memory is political. It is the struggle to grant political and moral meaning to the past, to make sense of power negotiations in the present. This has little to do with that other uncontrollable and incomprehensible human mechanism: memory. There is no truth in memory that can deactivate whatever is false or true in Memory (history), unless remembrances materialize in a coherent historical imagination, in another history that, in turn, other memories will assume to be false and subject to the whip of their evocations. In a way, the recollections of "subalterns" are theirs and theirs alone only before they become another coherent and well-constructed historical imagination, with forgettings and presences clearly selected. What is presented today not as historical imagination but as memory, ergo identity, if anything, will tomorrow simply be one more story about a "we are" that is no more.

Don Alonso Quijano's imagination appealed to a reality that does not recognize Sancho's worldly retentive memory, and from that comes the tragic and comic, heartbreaking and ironic, nature of the Quixote. By contrast, there seems to be no room for irony in the memory and the historical imagination when they are called to produce truth about the past. Because their truths are akin. Both memory and the historical imagination assume a sense of reality: it was like that because that's how I remember it; it was like that because that's what the data show, or it was like that because the DNA says so. But history, when it lies, lies in a different way than memory. It plays a different trick. History's power to deceive comes from the present: from power, sometimes from poor interpretation, current traumas, intentional falsity, or the scarcity of sources. Memory's ruses may or may not derive from power, poor interpretation, voluntary or involuntary forgetting, traumas, but its verb tense is the chaotic coming and going of human consciousness: between a yesterday deformed by longing and an imaginary tomorrow understood as "what if this or that hadn't happened?" It could be said that history is rewritten in every new present and that it also takes pleasure in the counterfactual. The essential difference is that human memory doesn't recognize the present. The historical imagination is the present.

Memory

For a historian to be forgetful would be as absurd as for a painter to be blind or a dancer lame. Or maybe not? No. The ability to remember dates, facts, names, battles, numbers, or events is not absolutely necessary for the historical imagination. I've known few colleagues who had the memory, say, of sixteenth-century Jesuit missionary Matteo Ricci, who was able to memorize whole lists of Chinese characters in seconds. Very few historians are omniretentive of sacrosanct dates. The sort of memory that is indispensable to the historian is that which creates and retains general images, conceptual maps, whether chronological or spatial; the memory that remembers where to find clues, facts, dates, or the forgotten reading that suddenly comes to mind in light of a new fact or image or as a result of a personal experience. This type of memory, most certainly, is workmanlike—it creates, re-creates, and perfects itself—but it is not just professional: it is inseparable from the memory of anyone who writes, researches, suffers, and lives history.

In a book review, Virginia Woolf said that we can escape the historian's eye but not the novelist's gaze (*The Common Reader*). True, but the cultural historian's eye isn't too different from Woolf's own. "I find that scene making is my natural way of making the past," Woolf wrote in her autobiographical notes ("Sketch of the Past"). She added: "A scene always comes to the top; arranged; representative; this confirms me in my instinctive notions—it is irrational; it will not stand the argument—that we are sealed vessels afloat upon what it is convenient to call reality; at some moments, without a reason, without an effort, the sealing matter cracks." I believe that memory and the historical imagination work in a similar way. First by accumulation: the historical imagination searches, digs to find pieces, to imagine and put together bits of evidence, which go on accumulating for no reason; they are imagined because they are imagined. In procuring pieces, the search is as important as what is found. Going to archives, researching in libraries, observing pictures in museums, walking through old cities and buildings, feeling the weight of history in a street—everything goes into the memory and is as much a part of the historical imagination as the document, the book, or the remembered image. As Michel Foucault, Roger Chartier, and Robert Darnton have taught us, for the historian of cultures, the archive and the library are not only places where documents and evidence from the past are stored. They are, in reality, one more document about what we want to know. The cataloguing, the errors, what is mislaid among papers, the sounds and the silences of the archive are essential documents about the ways in which order, power, and memory were conceived in the past.

The National Archive in Mexico City, for example, is emblematic of power and memory in the late nineteenth century. It is a former jail, a panopticon that stores the nationalized pasts of various indigenous peoples, of the kingdom of New Spain and of independent Mexico, in galleries and cells. Modern Mexico is classified, as official history and nationalism demand, under the headings of colonial past, independence . . . empire, Porfiriato, revolutionary period, and then by presidents (Plutarco Elías Calles, Lázaro Cárdenas, etc.). In the Fomento (Development) division, Porfiriato section, to cite an example, the historian finds an article from the *Revue des Deux Mondes* that has been misplaced, perhaps because it had to do with henequen but makes reference to New Orleans (where henequen string was used to tie bales of cotton) rather than to Mexico. To be sure, the story that the article tells, its location, the Mexican panopticon of the late nineteenth century—all of that is no longer the history imagined by those who catalogued the archive. The historian's memory goes along, retaining findings and accumulating "little tricks" to break the shell of order that the archive imposes on the past and thus make the archive tell different stories.

Besides, on reading, say, boxes and boxes of official documents on agrarian policy in the late nineteenth century, the historian's memory learns almost unconsciously about the structure of documents: the first paragraph says nothing, the second reviews previous communiqués referred to in the document in question, and the meat of the document begins in the final paragraphs, and, above all, in the notes in the margin, in black, blue, and red pencil, colors corresponding to different levels of decision-making. In the margins, the verbose nineteenth-century prose becomes surprisingly direct and clear: "refuse to do it," "say yes but do not follow through," "confidential: remit MP [Mr. President]." A memory for learning and deciphering these codes, that's what the historian needs— that and resistance to the fetid odors that prevail in Mexico's archival surroundings, to the chill of the galleries. Even the signs left by other historians who have reviewed the same papers: it all enters into the memory that has to interpret the past.

Summing up, to the historical imagination, memory is the remembering of a fact, but it is also the retention of having seen, having read, having felt, having intuited, having learned, having lived; it is the simple habit of trying to make sense again and again. Thus, it is a tying up of loose ends, a reading between the lines, a knowing how to follow and how not to follow archive catalogues and knowing where to look and what to look for: evidence, inspiration, details . . .

But in the historian, what breaks the membrane, liberating a mountain of pieces, of personal experiences, of evidence, taking them to a true "scene" of the past? Accumulation, of course: the more pieces, the better. But not only that. It's also trying again and again to restore sense to what one is investigating; it's also straying, managing finally to realize, thanks to a new fact or an image suddenly revealed by a painting or by reading another historian or a novel or a poem or after a chat with a friend or a child. That is, the scenes from the cultural past are the quarrels between Quixote and Sancho; they are not just wild game hunted and caught by rhetoric, with a touch of poetry; they are a poetic hunt, though "poetic" doesn't mean unaccountable in logical, aesthetic, empirical, and political terms.

Marx, for example, after years spent in the newsrooms of radical newspapers, hours of study in the British Library, seeing and suffering, tried to explain Louis Bonaparte's coup d'état in 1851 (*The Eighteenth Brumaire of Louis Napoleon*). He accumulated data and images from Victor Hugo, Pierre-Joseph Proudhon, from the history of the Roman Empire, from his idea of the class struggle, from G. W. F. Hegel's philosophy of history, and thus created a magnificent general image of the historical character of a coup d'état. He explained the event, of course, but also how history works in general. He realized its essence and, with hard, ironic metaphors, said: "It is not enough to say, as the French do, that their nation was taken unawares. Nations and women are not forgiven the unguarded hour in which the first adventurer who came along could violate them" (Karl Marx, *The Eighteenth Brumaire of Louis Bonaparte*). If there were concepts to explain this, I would say: "It was their fault, now let them face the consequences." Based on ironic metaphors, Marx comes out with a true question to put to the past. (Knowing what to ask the past earns one the thirty-third degree in the historians' lodge.) Here's the question: "How can a nation of thirty-six million be surprised and delivered without resistance into captivity by three knights of industry?" Then Marx even comes to realize the pertinence of poetry and the need for an all-embracing scene of historical change that challenges the past to arm the future: "The social revolution of the nineteenth century cannot take its poetry from the past but only from the future. It cannot begin with itself before it has stripped away all superstition about the past . . . The revolution of the nineteenth century must let the dead bury their dead in order to arrive at its own content. There the phrase went beyond the content—here the content goes beyond the phrase." Behold the contents of the phrase, the historical imagination at work, with metaphors, ideas, images, facts:

> Men make their own history, but they do not make it as they please; they do not make it under self-selected circumstances, but under circumstances existing already, given and transmitted from the past. The tradition of all dead generations weighs like a nightmare on the brains of the living. And just as they seem to be occupied with revolutionizing themselves and things, creating something that did not exist before, precisely in such epochs of revolutionary crisis they anxiously conjure up the spirits of the past to their service, borrowing from them names, battle slogans, and costumes in order to present

this new scene in world history in time-honored disguise and borrowed language. Thus Luther put on the mask of the Apostle Paul, the Revolution of 1789–1814 draped itself alternately in the guise of the Roman Republic and the Roman Empire, and the Revolution of 1848 knew nothing better to do than to parody, now 1789, now the revolutionary tradition of 1793–95. In like manner, the beginner who has learned a new language always translates it back into his mother tongue, but he assimilates the spirit of the new language and expresses himself freely in it only when he moves in it without recalling the old and when he forgets his native tongue (*The Eighteenth Brumaire of Louis Bonaparte*).

Marx remembers, his imagination works, and each accumulated piece finds a place in a general landscape. Because the historian does what the poet does when faced with an emotion or a landscape: he tries to capture the emotion or the landscape one way or another, he accumulates attempts, he adopts this or that point of view, until, with luck, he traps a complete scene from a slice of the past. The scene aspires to be neither the only nor the absolute truth, but in the best of cases it will succeed and make the emotion or the landscape from the past felt in the present. That is how the historical imagination works, and that's all there is to it.

Cultural historians are tied like Quixote to Sancho; we can't fly—due to either lack of imagination or respect for our trade—beyond the evidence that we find and construct from the past. We are like nineteenth-century landscape painters: before the landscape of past cultures, we see a bit here, we see a bit there, we take a mental snapshot, but it doesn't work, it doesn't have what we need to tell or understand, so we do another mental take, and somehow, with the baggage of all the takes, with the help of everything we have seen, lived, read, we put together a landscape, a simulacrum of what and how it might have been. "When our gaze," said Maurice Merleau-Ponty, "travels over what lies before us, at every moment we are forced to adopt a certain point of view and these successive snapshots of any given area of the landscape cannot be superimposed one upon the other. It is only by interrupting the normal process of seeing that the painter succeeds in mastering this series of visual impressions and extracting a single unchanging landscape from them" (*The World of Perception*). Thus, the painter manages to capture the landscape as something natural and objective, although, Merleau-Ponty believes, with the inevitable consequence of killing "the trembling life" of nature. Past cultures force the historian to do the same as the painter. And the true historical imagination also always feels that it has killed something of what it suspects existed in the past but knows itself unable to express in its entirety—it can only try.

A User's Manual

I want to bring all these high-flown ideas down to earth: how to get the practicality of a Sancho and the best of a Quixote. I say, then, that the modest historical imagination of past cultures aspires to create a simulacrum of experiences from the past in the present that fills the past with value for the present and the present with a minimum of suspicion about the future. The scene should be verisimilar by being informative, by describing with logic and empirical rigor, and thus should use concepts, facts, metaphors, impressions, and intuitions. I believe that the boundaries of this modest sort of imagination are erudition, melancholic irony, the classroom, pragmatism, and the nature of the evidence.

I understand erudition to be what I've been describing as the historian's own memory: the ability to accumulate snapshots of the past, which is not what the antiquarian does but is a matter of returning to books, archives, and images again and again—to everything about the period we hope to become familiar with. That's all there is to it. It often happens that, lacking the erudition I've been talking about, cultural historians take refuge in a fashionable point of view, be it a theory or just common jargon. Neither the anti-intellectual love for more or less colorful anecdotes nor a passion for the latest theories will help the historical imagination do what it can do: imagine. Only erudition can do this.

In short, it sounds pedantic and elitist, but I believe that without this kind of erudition the historical imagination does not work well or cannot exist at all, especially when the matter at hand is the cultural past—and especially the history of "popular" culture. Strangely, in recent decades two opposing beliefs have arisen among historians. On one hand, there is the belief that erudition hampers the study of popular culture. Complete nonsense. To understand theater in seventeenth-century New Spain, we naturally have to read whole libraries of "elite" culture. To study popular representations in the same place and time, we would have to read those and more. Proponents of the new anti-erudite trends, generally linked to the defense of ethnic identities, that is, to things that are non-Western in some way, have not realized that their anti-erudition is the most Western and "civilizing" of gestures. Here I call upon Edmundo O'Gorman and his ironic criticism of 1940s Mexico ("El caso México"): "Civilized man has the right not to engage in culture, the right not to give a damn about culture. This right is one of culture's established conquests and one of civilization's greatest benefits. Not giving a damn about culture offers the maximum comfort, and if the civilized man has a right to anything, it is to be comfortable."

On the other hand, maybe as a reaction to the proliferation of second-rate histories of popular culture, the neo-erudites have arisen: learned persons who wave the weight of their vast erudition in our faces, academics who without much imagination go from one old quotation in Latin to another in sixteenth-century German to end up with something in classical Greek. Nothing is farther from the kind of erudition that inspires the historical imagination, but it goes without saying that we must study the tracks of the neo-erudites.

Quixote's imagination, tempered by Sancho, always ends in irony and finally in melancholy. As does the historical imagination, which knows that it cannot know everything; it knows, besides, that it imagines, that it creates simulacra of truths based solely on hours and hours of searching for pieces, reading between lines, and organizing and disorganizing archives. An imagination that tries to escape from its present but never succeeds cannot ignore the fact that neither happiness nor unhappiness, neither truth nor doubt, exists as an absolute. That is, if the historical imagination is not put on hold, it cannot stop auto-imagining itself, destroying itself and yet again putting itself back together. Therefore, it tends to end in irony, which in good time filters into melancholy. The melancholy of knowing that we are certainly not going anywhere, that God has died, that we escape and don't escape from the present at each attempt, that science is not everything, that we are as incapable of invalidating all certainties as we are of defending all doubts. Therefore, the historical imagination can only frequent great utopias through political decisions that stop the imagination and leave what is imagined as a goal. Carlo Magris said: "[M]elancholy is born when one cannot want, that is, tend toward a goal, because one doesn't know and doesn't care to know what one wants. But our fate is to settle accounts with this indolent sadness, if we don't want to yield to megalomaniacal illusions about happiness and authenticity" (*Itaca e oltre*).

This, then, is what the historical imagination, if good, should be: melancholy because it knows that its designs are provisional, incomplete, obscure, or dangerous. Irony and skepticism are its natural habitat.

In order to fall into the temptation of laws—universal (progress, for example) or divine—or to be caught on the hook of some utopia, to take itself very seriously, the historical imagination would have to stop imagining. Therefore, about this imagination we could say what German philosopher Odo Marquard said about the "skeptical I": it is, "without a doubt, evil, but it is the least possible evil; it isn't an I in truth but an I in quarantine; it is not a fetish but an antifetish" (*Schwierigkeiten mit der Geschichtsphilosophie*). Perhaps doubt, skepticism, and irony are not the ultimate solution for imagining cultural history, but I don't know of a better guide.

Nowadays the classroom is—maybe it was not two hundred years ago—another limit to and criterion of truth for the historical imagination. So much debate about the discursive, about objectivity in history, historical neutrality, and truth, about power in and the power of history, has missed the fact that for at least two hundred years all of that (objectivity, truth, neutrality, and power) has been happening not at the level of history as text but of history as lesson, as reading in the classroom and in textbooks. Culture, low or high, to a large extent is socialized in classrooms. Since its professionalization, history has become a form of education, whether good or bad, that liberates (Croce would say), that "introjects" power (Foucault would say). History does not fully come into being until it reaches the classroom. The historical imagination finds in the classroom a laboratory in which it can attempt to put information on trial, to venture explanations, and to provoke reactions. It is in the classroom that we attempt something like "let's see how it sounds if I explain it like this."

Besides, the classroom is to the historical imagination what the *molcajete* (stone mortar) is to a good Mexican salsa: you can do without it, you can use the food processor, but it's just not the same, it tastes different. It isn't good salsa, that much is clear. The lack of classroom hours is just as noticeable in histories that are written as though the author were standing before a mirror: "Just me and my lucidity," which ends in platitudes that the author takes for grand discoveries. Without the classroom, historians' books are vulnerable to exaggeration or nonsense—and they're certain that the reader's ignorance is to blame. In teaching we learn the meaning of objectivity in history, because the real meaning of judiciousness is negotiated in the classroom. The classroom creates and challenges the historian's erudition—especially today when it is no longer possible to get a name or a date or a fact wrong without some know-it-all instantly discovering the error on the Internet. Of course, a cultural history cannot be declared good, objective, false, or revealing according to the number of hours its author logged in the classroom. But if for two centuries history has served primarily to educate, it is already inevitable: the classroom, at its best, marks the limits of what is imaginable for the historian, decrees the need for synthesis and logic; at its worst, it is a stage and a captive audience for the ego displays of those megalomaniacs so given to fantasy: professors.

In turn, the politics of the historical imagination of past cultures is pragmatic, because it functions as experience and experimentation—the experience of imagining time and again, collecting data and events, putting together images, trying to escape from the present, falling into it again, searching for the meanings of justice. It is also pragmatic because it comes up with not only true pasts but useful pasts, sometimes weak, sometimes dangerous, but which can always be overcome, reimagined. In fact, it would be almost impossible to disassociate the historical imagination from politics. When the imagination and politics work well, they control one another. The responsibility of the political imagination nourishes and tempers the creativity of the historical imagination and vice versa. To imagine a politics that is responsible and possible is to put "checks and balances" on the historical imagination. It obliges the historian to be skeptical, to doubt her interpretations, to talk about what doesn't fit in or what contradicts her ideas, thus forcing her to think through the consequences of this or that utopia built out of the past.

It is often said that politicized, ideologized history is bad history. We also frequently hear that it is not possible for the historian to escape politics, that all history is political. In terms of imagining the past, neither statement is terribly consequential. What vital cultural past can be imagined without politics and a heavy load of the political present? But being conscious of this doesn't free the historian to turn herself into an ideologue or to imagine new heavens and hells in the past or the present. On the contrary, it makes her responsible for presenting ambiguities, risks, and possible scenarios as well as their gains and losses.

Of course, there is always the temptation to become a prophet, in these times no longer in the fashion of the patriotic or racist historians of the nineteenth century but of the posteverything academic. Odo Marquard calls this the "law of the historical avant-garde." Modern times, he says, have meant the acceleration of time, and speeded-up changes make it increasingly difficult to understand the past and present and their ties. Thus, the temptation arises to "surpass [history] in acceleration": "Human beings escape indictment for the evils of the present by becoming its avant-garde, because the avant-garde, which is always swifter than the indictment, escapes the tribunal by becoming it: by flight into issuing indictments (flight from *having* a conscience into *being* the conscience)" (*In Defense of the Accidental*). In making history and politics the most chic of avant-gardes, the most innovative and insolent, the historical imagination leaves its natural habitat of skepticism and irony, assuming itself to be the final judgment on the unfolding of history and political action. Academic fashions attract crowds of these prophets, and this is dangerous and mistaken. But, as though by the mandate of some mysterious ecosystem of the historical imagination, these tales don't usually make it beyond the little world of academia.

Finally, the nature of the evidence is the greatest curb on the historical imagination. The poet finds his limit in language (Óscar Hahn, "Invocación al lenguaje," in *Archivo expiatorio*):

Con vos [language] quería hablar, hijo de la grandísima
Ya me tienes cansado
De tanta esquividad y apartamiento,
Y tu látigo húmedo
Para tiranizar mi pensamiento.
(With you [language]I wanted to speak,
son of the greatest bitch.
You have me tired by now
of so much evasion and distancing,
And your wet whip
tyrannizing my thought.)

Language is the historian's limit as well, but filtered by the type of evidence or the lack thereof. For example, it is possible to imagine ways in which a "mestizo identity" was imposed or negotiated politically in Mexico or in Guatemala in the nineteenth century. To do this, we would have to dig and dig through legal documents, letters, paintings from the period, and scientific treatises. But the evidence places limits on the imagination: we have to know nineteenth-century law, nineteenth-century artistic debates, biology, philology . . . The imagination's success in breaking through these limits will tell us how revealing, how effective the historian in question is at creating culture in the present. In fact, a particular historical imagination may not be made for a certain type of evidence. It may sound silly, but it has to be said: a historian who does not know music or mathematics will not be able to do a history of eighteenth-century Spanish music or of statistics in nineteenth-century Argentina. A historian who does not know Quechua and Aymara can't talk about "agency" among nineteenth-century Peruvian or Bolivian indigenous people. If we don't have some almost philological knowledge of the humor and blasphemy of nineteenth-century New Orleans, we can't imagine the popular culture of that city. There have been so many linguistic turns and so much relativism, but excursions into the cultural past cannot be undertaken without long and tedious intellectual preparation to command the nuances of language.

Coda: What Will Happen to the Sources?

For some time now the historical imagination has faced a new challenge: the digital revolution, the Internet. Online archives and data banks are changing radically old conceptions of the nature of evidence, of the ruins, of the past. Never before in the history of the discipline have we had such immediate access to sources. An increasing number of archives are digitalizing their collections, and two enormous digital library projects—Google Books and the HathiTrust—have changed the historian's relationship to her sources. We can now access an archive in Paris or New York without ever setting foot in the city or the archive itself. We can look for phrases, concepts, in thousands of books and documents simultaneously, without paying attention to the classification of books and documents. If documents could talk, they would be able to say that "Funes el memorioso" (Jorge Luis Borges) now really exists on the web. But we know that they can't talk, and that isn't history. We still need imagination, memory, to tie up loose ends, to know what has to do with what and where to look.

This revolution in immediacy and accessibility should not be mistaken for a democratization of access to historical knowledge or a democratization of the writing of history. All the material needed to write history is not on the web and maybe will never be. In addition, the majority of the large digital collections are not open access—colleagues in Morelia or Mexico City have much less access to the digital paradise than those at Harvard and Chicago because neither they nor their institutions can cover the high entry fee. The World Wide Web is transforming but not replacing the historical imagination. What's more, it is making it more necessary to give meaning to so very much information. In some sense, the great historian used to be one who found clues here and there and managed to put them together. The ability to find clues is losing pedigree, but that does not mean that on seeing thousands of dots any observer whatsoever can connect them to form the figure of a historical argument.

Indeed, two aspects of the old ritual of the meeting between historian and archive are being lost. On the one hand, it is becoming easier to dispense with the authority of the cataloguer. A powerful search in electronic data banks obliterates centuries of order imposed on the past by history books, archives, and national libraries. On the other hand, it may no longer be necessary to travel to an archive in Paris to find the element that we are looking for or take the metro to the center of the city or stroll among library stacks. For the historical imagination, it is uncertain what sort of revolution all this may bring.

The digitalization of sources is already changing the nature of the evidence, whether texts, musical scores, images, diagrams, formulas, or songs, because the conventional rituals of the meeting between the historical imagination and its sources have changed. This could produce more of the same: the geometric multiplication of novelists who, without reading a single book of history, get the three facts that they need to put together a bad but successful historical novel in just two "Googles." However, the good historical novelist still needs that boring, academic historical imagination. Take, for example, a single paragraph from Marguerite Yourcenar's *L'oeuvre au noir* (translated by Grace Frick as *The Abyss*):

> From a high point on the mountain, Zeno spied at last the hamlet of Heyst
> . . . That hamlet on the edge of the vastly deep had, on a very small scale, all
> the essential commodities of a city: a covered market, which probably served
> for auctioning off fish, a church and a mill, an esplanade with, of course, a
> gallows; its low-roofed houses were tucked in between lofty barns. The
> Pretty Dove, the inn that Josse had indicated to him as a rallying point for
> the fugitives, was a mere hovel near the dune, with a broom stuck in its dove-
> cote to stand for a sign, thus announcing that this poor hostelry was also a
> rustic brothel.

What a wealth of cultural historiography on social, political, and economic matters—as well as on the sexuality and customs of the town in question—inspires this paragraph! The Internet will facilitate the historical novelist's task; but if the novelist has no historical imagination and erudition the Internet will not grant what nature denied.

It might also be that the Gibbon epidemic is upon us: great popular history writers with narrative imagination and salesmanship who absorb the modest imaginations of the professional historians who publish boring monographs on this or that subject. Edward Gibbon freely admitted that he copied sources from all sorts of antiquarians; he believed that he truly gave life to those burdensome histories, filtering them through his vast imagination. This sort of fast and popular historical imagination will now have direct access to thousands of sources. They will no longer need us, I mean the boring historians. It remains to be seen whether this type of imagination works for knowing where to look, how to read those digital sources, how to tie up loose ends, or if in fact they will continue to need the old boring historical imagination of professional historians.

For nineteenth-century philologists, it was indispensable to memorize thousands of words to find relationships among different languages. They had to memorize whole grammars in different languages in order to be able to understand the functioning of words and the historical evolution of meanings. Before Google it was impossible to search for words without memorizing a certain amount of grammar, which led to common sense about how words, meanings, and worlds work. Google is now the extraordinary memory that philologists never had, but it does not know and isn't interested in grammar. We are stripping ourselves of memory, leaving everything in the hands of an electronic search engine in the largest archive humanity has ever known, and thus we can know everything without understanding almost anything. Google can analyze the frequency of a word or phrase (if you put it between quotation marks), according to algorithms designed to maximize users' possible consumption habits, prioritizing occurrences on the sites that are most lucrative for Google. Google is the memory that no human being will ever have, but it is like that patient of Oliver Sacks who after a stroke could read every letter in a text but was unable to understand a sentence (*The Mind's Eye*). I'm not nostalgic for old paper archives; I am attesting to the enormous usefulness of something like Google for whoever still retains something of the old memory of the historian or the philologist, of those who had several grammars of words and worlds at their fingertips. But what will happen in two generations' time, when all of us have ceded to Google the ability to memorize?

For the craft of the cultural historian, the digital revolution in sources is changing the possibilities of imagining. As I hope I have explained, going to an archive, reading a rare book in an old library, or seeing an old painting in person are part of the historical imagination. These experiences often lead to unexpected sentiments, unsuspected findings, and unpredictable clues. Because sometimes the key to interrupting the mere accumulation of facts is to see not only the images in oil paintings but the painterly events, studying the brushstrokes of a painting up close, experiencing the craftsmanship of the oil painting, which in addition to representing, say, the father and son of Jean-Léon Gérôme before a provincial house, is also a series of dabs of color, with texture, relief, and different intentions. Going in search of an old book in an obscure library takes us, serendipitously, to the discovery of the unexpected book next to, above, or below it, an unknown text that sometimes gives us the key to imagine the past. And what will become of the contact of the imagination with the past without the sensation of paper, the experience of feeling that someone, six or four centuries ago, put ink on that paper? What will become of the imagination if the source does not include the walk through the old city, the experience of the buildings? I can't explain how, but these experiences have been part of the historical imagination.

But digitalization promises to benefit the good historical imagination, and here's an example that has captivated me. In the 1940s a German art historian, Wilhelm Fraenger, had spent years trying to interpret the paintings of Hieronymus Bosch. He didn't lack erudition in considering the pictures by Bosch as chiliastic expressions of a heretical movement, the followers of Gioacchino da Fiore in Bosch's town, 's-Hertogenbosch, in the early sixteenth century. Fraenger's interpretation has been the gossip of experts, but what is interesting is what he did with the evidence, which now seems inconceivable. How did a historian have access to paintings by Bosch in the 1940s if he could not see them in the Museo del Prado? (A good part of the Dutch painter's work ended up there thanks to Philip II's great love for his paintings.) Most certainly, he had access to *The Garden of Earthly Delights* in black-and-white reproductions and perhaps some in color, but without much detail. Therefore, this German historian—a Communist and anti-Nazi who was nevertheless a friend of the Nazi jurist Carl Schmitt—took advantage of Schmitt's visit to Madrid in 1943, asking him to look at some of the painting's details carefully. Schmitt, of course, was admired by Francoist intellectual circles. He was a German spy in Madrid during the war and after the war gave a number of lectures in Spain, where he had a daughter and was considered less repulsive than in postwar Germany. Eugenio d'Ors, a former star of the Catalan cultural movement who wound up as a luminary of the Franco regime, wrote a story about his visit to the Prado as Schmitt's guide, describing the care with which the jurist paid attention to details for Fraenger. He tried to determine, for example, if what he saw hanging from some female figures was a whip, because that would have proved Fraenger's interpretation, being a symbol of the chiliastic rites of members of the millenary kingdom to which, according to Fraenger, Bosch had belonged. Of course, the whip turned out to be a branch, which had something like eggplants hanging from it instead of knots. But what I want to point out is that the historical imagination depended on this kind of improvising in order to come face-to-face with the evidence. The digital revolution would have been delightful to Fraenger; today he could have had access to every inch of *The Garden of Earthly Delights* in high resolution: he could observe every bit of it better than in the Museo del Prado without moving from his table (http://www.hetnoordbrabantsmuseum.nl/english/press-jheronimus bosch/persbeelden-eng/). For someone without his imagination, without his erudition, this possibility would not make any difference. The combination of imagination and technology promises to revolutionize history. With access to digital sources, I don't know if the imagination will be better or more profound, but it will be different. Massive access to sources promises to remove the limitation of finding sources from the historical imagination. The secret labyrinth of the imagination will continue to be its own limit.

Like a poet or a painter, the historian's imagination has the machinery for realizing, experimenting with possibilities, pushing the limits of the perceivable and sayable . . . also fantasizing and leading; also convincing. In his work, then, the perception of the real world enters into chaotic play, not as a mental fact that says ice = cold, sun = warmth but in the form of mental images that interact with the historian's memory. I leave this as a summary of the historian's imagination: (Ida Vitale, "Lección de historia," in *Poesía reunida*):

Que una moneda antigua
hallada—¿por azar?—en el jardín,
te enseñara una fecha: 1804
y un dato no ficticio:
Napoleón rey de Italia,
importó menos que,

luego de la lección de cosas,
el bronce atesorado
se disipara sin palabras.

Quedó en el aire
algo de Historia y Algo
todavía sin nombre:
un comienzo, la insana
costumbre de observar,
atar cabos, alcanzar
la no errada visión
de algún prójimo horrible

Saber que nada es tuyo
para siempre.

(That an ancient coin
found—by chance?—in the garden,
would teach you a date: 1804
and a nonfictitious fact:
Napoleon, king of Italy,
mattered less than,
after the lesson of things,
treasured bronze
would dissipate without words.
It stayed in the air
something of History and Something
still without a name:
a beginning, the mad
custom of observing,
tying loose ends, reaching
the unerring vision
horrible of some fellow man
Knowing that nothing is yours
forever.)

Chapter 4

READING HISTORY TODAY

Nowadays there are more books—print and electronic—than ever before, which is not to say that variety and readership have increased. Adrian Johns (*The Nature of the Book*), Robert Darnton (*The Case for Books*), Fernando Escalante Gonzalbo (*A la sombra de los libros*), and Gabriel Zaid (*Los demasiados libros*) have already explained, and well, how we came to conceive of the book habit and why today it is more a matter of business than of wisdom and aesthetics. I speak of history books and of unpretentious readers, because some read for work (reading is part of their jobs) and some read for passion (reading as vice). And I hold this to be true: persons addicted to reading history books, who are passionate about it, do exist. I speak to those readers, to those devotees, nonexperts, who read history for the same reason they eat, sleep, and think. But with so many books available, what to read?

1

The relationship between the "ordinary reader" and "history" involves two entwined paradoxes:

(1a) Professional historians cause readers to nod off. ←→ (1b) History sells.

(2a) Never before has so much history been easily accessible (books, articles, and digital archives, Internet, films). ←→ (2b) In terms of historical knowledge, there is no great demand for or available supply of much more than variations on the same stories that have been told time and time again for more than half a century.

There's no need to prove or disprove 1a (historians are soporific). The proposition is irrefutable. Whether what we professional historians do is good or bad is debatable, but the boredom that we produce in the ordinary reader is not.

To prove 1b (history sells) in rigorous fashion, we could point out the many history books and historical novels on the best-seller lists of the last decade, say, in Argentina, Spain, France, Mexico, and the United States. I won't do that, but I repeat: history sells. Agreeing with me doesn't require faith: anyone who goes to bookstores, watches television series or movies, or frequents magazine stands will conclude that history must sell: because if it didn't, why would there be so much of it?

As for 2a (never before has so much history been easily accessible), I say that it's an absolute but deceptive truth. A simple search in the most complete catalogue of the world's libraries (Worldcat) reveals the following: the subject "Mexico—History," with publication dates between 1950 and 1970, has 14,500 entries, the subject "United States—History" has 93,500; between 1971 and 1990 the numbers increase to 30,000 and 200,000, respectively. And from 1991 to 2014 there are 91,000 entries classified as history of Mexico and half a million as United States history. Impressionistic data, clearly, but they only serve to describe the obvious. Historiographic production has increased: there is not necessarily better history but more university output and more demand for history.

We would also have to add the digital revolution: the (virtual) "archive" contains millions of pages of all kinds on historical themes and periods, reigned over by her majesty Wikipedia, the oracle of wisdom for our students, opinion makers, and newspaper commentators. In addition, some archives have begun to digitize their collections, and thousands of documents are now available on the web: on the Middle Ages, the nineteenth century, declassified United States State Department files. And that's in addition to Google Books and HathiTrust (almost 12 million volumes digitized), two immense virtual libraries that make it seem that, in theory, historians, historical novelists, and smart op-ed writers should not have to get up from their chairs to write about almost all of known history.

However, access to all that history is deceptive. Not everything is on the web, and in terms of historical research nobody has invented a better method than getting lost in archives and libraries for a good while. Besides, any traditional archive offers more freedom for discovery than the Internet does. To what extent are we the searchers or the searched on the Internet? Google's algorithms, the order in which results appear, either lose us or prescribe an interpretation of what is to be considered important. As we access Google for research, Google turns us into accessible material as consumers and merchandise. Then we get to where we are: lots of Internet, but what to read?

In Mexico or Brazil it's a dream to believe that everybody has access to the web; on top of that, the large digital collections of books, magazines, and documents are private and have very expensive subscription rates that only universities and institutions with resources can afford. But to be sure, we live in times of access to "lots of history" and it's hard to see with so much sun—the abundance makes it difficult for the ordinary reader to consume history.

What to read? How to begin? What information is trustworthy? What interpretation is good or revealing? Whom to believe? This, I'm afraid, continues to be a matter for experts, for obsessive readers, for those victims of the vice of books and of history. And so the history debate remains ugly and elitist.

As for 2b (that, in terms of historical knowledge, for the ordinary reader what is available is more of the same), I can't speak with data, just from experience based on years of teaching and giving talks to students, high school teachers, physicians, lawyers, and scientists. To give an example: in Mexico, during the centennial and bicentennial fever of 2010, lots of "Google historical novels" repeated the same old patriotic stories. There wasn't even a new historiographical summary that revolutionized public thinking about national history, as Justo Sierra's *México: Su evolución social* did in the 1900s. In the United States, in effect, "mass-market" books and documentaries have fostered variations on the national historical consciousness. Subjects like the American Revolution or the Civil War are in demand and consumed with new and interesting takes and appendices through new syntheses, documentaries, exhibitions, and more or less public debates. For instance, after two or three decades this criticism has spread, inspiring many social movements in the South to demand the removal of monuments erected to General Robert E. Lee and other heroes of the old history of the South as honorable "enemies."

But in Mexico this is what's happening: not long ago I shared a lunch table with two well-known lawyers, an educator, an economist, and an editorialist and nationally famous cartoonist, all cultured and well-traveled, of course, excellent prototypes of the ordinary reader of history. One of the lawyers is so cultured that he's concocting a historical novel and asked his historian friend (me): "Why is there such a difference in development between Mexico and the United States?" I had my own ideas to air but no opportunity to do so. The editorialist launched into a tremendous explanation that the rest of the table seconded in unison and supported with variations on eternal themes: Protestantism versus Catholicism, they killed the Indians versus we didn't, individualism versus collectivism, England versus Spain, the Protestant ethic and capitalism versus the ethic of the *gachupín* (Spaniard) and crony capitalism. And yes, here and there the old arguments were sweetened with genetics, economics, biology, and game theory, all taken from the latest bestsellers by Niall Ferguson or Steven Pinker. Because I was with well-read people, consumers of "mass-market history," they're up to date on the latest half-academic hit published in English. But in terms of history proper, it seems that they haven't taken in anything different from what was read in the late nineteenth century. It also seems that they would rather not know more. It's not that I, the historian, could not have inserted a doubt into their clichés in straightforward language; it's that they have no use for doubts in their historical convictions. In any event, proving 2b is a lengthy and complicated process. Here, yes, I ask the reader to trust me: I know what I'm talking about. And even if you don't believe me, grant me that the vast professional historiography produced every day doesn't get to the ordinary reader and that with all those books and the Internet it's hard to decide what to read.

Faced with these paradoxes, we need a road map in order to know what and how to read in our time of too many books, publishing monopolies, famous book prizes, and ephemeral bestsellers. Conventional guides include book reviews and historiographic discussions in newspaper supplements and magazines. History programs on radio, television, and the Internet also serve as guides, as do magazines on what is called "public history" in English. There are a few guides in the English language; not nearly as many in Spanish. Every anniversary of this or that historical event will have an issue of magazine *X* dedicated to it but not many reviews of history books. And talk-show guests who discuss public history in the media talk about facts and provide anecdotes or promote their own books, but they talk very little about history books and about any history that doesn't pertain to Mexico. Discussion about history in Spanish exists, for good or ill, in specialized magazines. In Mexico *Istor* systematically reviews history beyond Mexico with a nonspecialist public in mind. *Nexos* and *Letras Libres* include a work of history in their book review section every now and then. Why that particular book and not the other twenty recently published? The answer, almost always, has to do with networks, with friends and enemies, but not with guiding the reader of history.

Like most members of my guild, I'm not very good at translating and summarizing what we historians go around discussing and discovering. *Culpa nuestra* (Our fault). I want at least to offer a basic map for the ordinary reader of history. But first let's recall the anatomy of a history book.

2

In brief, a history book has the following characteristics: a point of view, a synthesis, a narrative, and a dress. Naturally, these characteristics are all present simultaneously, but for the sake of clarity let's explain each separately.

Any account of the past is, above all, a point of view, a set of ideas that explain and organize the account and, at the same time, produce specific ideas about how the past might have been. It may be an explicit point of view or it may not. If I say "the class struggle" or "from the traditional to the modern" or "what's important is: follow the money," these are points of view that need no explanation. Through them the past is organized and ideas about what happened and how it happened arise—for example, the Mexican Revolution was a bourgeois revolution or Latin America's problem is its colonial heritage (tradition).

The common ailments that afflict the point of view are its absence, its omnipresence, its simplicity, and its unconsciousness. In fact, the construction of the point of view is the most complicated and indecipherable part of a historian's job: it's where all possible erudition and imagination is processed and is always constructed through calibration against facts, making adjustments as research and writing proceed.

Synthesis is transforming an almost infinite universe of information and connections through the point of view into a finite representative universe that serves to say "this is what this particular history was like" and at the same time fits in a book. The historian digs up, searches for, discovers, accumulates, intuits, and deduces as much information as possible. If synthesis is not required, it's because there is no well-researched story to tell. Synthesis is how history thinks. Making good history is a thankless job: the historian has to accumulate and digest not just information but many points of view about the same information, until patterns and trends appear, until he can say with confidence "I know the forest" and "it is like these few trees." Examples, evidence, and demonstrations follow from the synthesis.

At times the synthesis can be almost mathematical, such as in certain kinds of economic or demographic history. One recent study written by an indispensable and boring professional historian (Moramay López Alonso: *Measuring Up*) analyzes inequality in Mexico—not a trivial subject—by examining nutrition through Mexicans' height between 1850 and 1950. After collecting and processing annual data from soldiers' records and from passports, a graph provides the most eloquent history on the subject: a line that doesn't move much beyond 1.5 meters (4 feet 11 inches). The synthesis is clear, visible, and graphically expressible. To get to it, it was essential to have a point of view, educated by many readings and intuitions, and hours and hours in the archives, collecting thousands of data points that together shouted "synthesis!" Other historians cannot rely on such an expeditious and graphic method of synthesis. Often it seems that the simple passage of time provides the synthesis: X happened and then Y and then Z. But it's never like that, not even with histories that seem clear, as in "this happened and then the next thing happened." History is synthesis because when X happened, A, B, and C also happened; therefore, X, in the best of cases, is a synthetic representative decision arrived at by a disciplined point of view.

In the worst of cases, the common ailments of synthesis are lack of synthesis, mentioning how little is known without any idea of connections or echoes, and examples that aren't illustrative—either because they are the entire universe of the sample or because they are an irrelevant anecdote. At times evidence and demonstrations flutter like moths around a tiny flame, because all the rest is darkness. It is also common that the historian is unable to tame her erudition and prescribes for us an enormous tome filled with facts and figures more or less connected by means of a chronology. I know, it's a disease, but we historians are hopelessly addicted to these hodgepodges and tend to welcome them. But that's our problem: there's no reason to share it with the ordinary reader of history.

Because history bestows meaning on human actions, it is necessarily political and moral. It is sometimes a moral, an accusation, a tragedy, or vainglory, but it is always a more or less explicit ethical or political position. Often history is nothing more than politics and morality, like many nationalist histories, the partisan histories of a war, or the social histories that make it very clear who the perfect villains and the spotless good guys are. But history is political, and nothing can be done about it: that's why it's important, that's why politicians, ideologues, and opinion makers bring it to the table. In order to engage in public debates, we have lots of other ways of knowing; but without the raw material, history, how can we discuss subjects as political and as vital as the people, the nation, citizenship, inequality, justice, and violence?

Thus, the common disease of morality in history is precisely that sort of politics that turns the past into what we ourselves choose as a moral and political decision; rather than learning history, we pledge allegiance to flags, ideologies, and feelings. But history is political: a pact, a truce, an agreement, a brief meanwhile, an acceptance of villainies, and a forgetting of history itself to bring about justice and peace.

In addition, history is words and narrative, and as such, involves elements of rhetoric and literature, from the metaphor to the anecdote, color, flavor, texture, and many echoes and scenes derived from the old storyteller's craft. For the ordinary reader, and for the professional historian, this is vital. The perfect anecdote at the right moment, the color of the scenes, and the texture of the narrative are what makes history what it is, an account that all signs indicate we need in order to provide the past with significance, to feel it, to decipher the present, and to sketch the future. There's not much more to say on this subject, except that the ordinary reader should be aware that point of view, synthesis, and narrative are not a protocol for action but an inseparable combo. The imperatives of narrative are determined by and determine the point of view, dictate and are dictated by the synthesis. There is no transcription, evidence, or demonstration that is not also a narrative decision—that is, a stylistic choice. The emotion that the economic historian feels before his graphs is also aesthetic. For example, which came first in Sérgio Buarque de Holanda: his great narrative style or his extraordinarily complicated point of view, which was based on philosophical, legal, political, and literary readings, his difficult life, or his erudition regarding the history of Europe and Brazil?

Many of history's ills are ills of narrative that cause history to attract and repel at the same time; its eloquence fools us with so much filigree, and its lack of eloquence bores us because it is badly written.

Finally, what I call the dress of the history book includes things like the press that publishes it; the publicity it gets; the blurbs on the front and back covers; the use or lack of bibliographies, quotations, and illustrations, and how they are included; the kind of paper or the electronic format that is used, sales distribution, and so forth. In short, all that is related to the production and sale of the "book" as merchandise. Just like the mamey (a tropical fruit), books have to be eaten from the outside in. Publishing companies and author identification are a guide, but in our current monopolistic publishing world, in the star system in which we live, those clues aren't altogether trustworthy. Clearly, in Mexico, the Fondo de Cultura Económica, the Colegio de México, and the Colegio de Michoacán are more or less reliable academic imprints, but, like every publishing company, also publish a lot of dreck, as do Harvard and Princeton. Academics often complain about the lack of distribution of books published by Universidad Nacional Autónoma de México and similar presses. Readers often assume that if a book can't be found in the bookstores or on Amazon it must not be very important. But in fact distribution says little about the quality of a history book.

There's a prejudice that damages the reputations of human beings and books alike: fatness. Fat books aren't necessarily ugly; in fact, it's only recently that books have gotten rail thin, the result of the marketing of self-help books or the imaginative anorexia of the "fragmentary" postmodern novel. History books are something different, fat or skinny. What's more, the "minimal histories" that prestigious publishing houses like the Colegio de México and Cambridge University Press have launched are excellent guides, especially if we read more than just the volume corresponding to the history of our own country. The ordinary reader who is a fan of Mexican history, rather than the skinny version of Mexican history, almost certainly needs the one for Guatemala, the United States, or Spain. And as for the fat books, I recommend that the reader take a look, read a few paragraphs, and check the table of contents. For certain, it's a good idea to mistrust any history book, skinny or fat, that doesn't offer a clear guide to its sections and the evidence that it uses. To believe that mass-market history doesn't need to reveal the sources from which the information was taken, or to include a bibliography, is like assuming that government cheese does not have to be made of milk, because it's for popular consumption.

Ironically, although we hear more about interactive systems, social networks, and Internet activism, the book publishing industry is readying itself for ever more passive readers. It's increasingly difficult to publish well-documented history, full of provocations and complications: stay away from strange names and exotic theories—the publishers tell us—keep it simple, like an airport novel. I still believe that the ordinary reader of history is much more active; though he may be disoriented in the face of so many books, he looks here and there, reads reviews, and searches on Google for the names, authors, and facts that come up in books, in movies, and on the History Channel.

Each of the following is untrustworthy: best-seller lists, reviews in general-interest magazines, documentaries, movies, the Internet. But all of them together help the active reader. The diligent reader should search in more specialized magazines; depending on the subject and the period, she will have to read in other languages. Despite a lot of globalization and a lot of information on the Internet, history is one field that is still written in the vernacular and to some extent—not completely—in English. That is, to get a real understanding of Mexican history, we have to read Spanish and English; to understand Japanese history, English and Japanese. History is still so rooted in the vernacular that readers interested in the modern history of Spain have to read Spanish, Galician, Catalan, and English, at least.

3

Four frequent misunderstandings about history can mislead the ordinary reader:

(a) *Academic history is unreadable: it has no purpose other than aiding the careers of professors, those bloodsuckers who muddle the history that we all want to know.* A cliché. Intellectuals, commentators, and professors emancipated from university "slavery" compete to repeat it as though it were news. And, in fact, a lot of professional garbage is produced, but we have to forget both our grudge against and our fear about this kind of history. It's not important. Professional history, with all of its deficiencies and abuses, produces new points of view, new syntheses, new forms of narrative. This kind of history is, first, generally readable although not always enjoyable and, second, indispensable. The reader has to leaf through it, review academic history on a subject of interest, and follow the clues that those books provide.

A hint: academic history, including the good works, is often a quarrel among historians, perhaps thought-provoking but filled with arguments that are of interest only to professionals. Many of these academic histories are readable for those who are interested and have no academic ambitions because the works meet the scholastic requirements: the central thesis appears at the beginning of the book, ideas derived from the thesis are at the beginning of each chapter, and the essential points are repeated in the conclusion. The rest is data and more data—that may or may not be of interest to the reader—and a lot of showing off among historians that the reader—who has no horse in that race—can avoid like the dog that's come face to face with the family's vicious and spoiled cat.

(b) *Good history for the general public comes from the pens of "contemporary Gibbons" who know how to write, don't follow academic fashions, are very cultured, and don't beat around the bush.* Another fallacy. A work like Edward Gibbon's would not have been possible without the existence of boring historians and antiquarians who combed the archives and wrote the archaeological catalogues on the Roman Empire. And then, yes, a best seller: *History of the Decline and Fall of the Roman Empire* (1776–1789). But what does a mass-market history book disseminate if it isn't nourished by professional history? The fact is that just as much garbage is produced in mass-market history as in the academic variety, and it's just as hard for the ordinary reader to distinguish the gold from the dross in mass-market books as it is in hyperspecialized books.

Go to the bookstores, review catalogues of new publications and best sellers, see what the large publishing monopolies have to offer, review the anatomy of those books. Mistrust books that don't include a good bibliography, that lean too far toward one or another ideological or moral position. Read a few pages: if the color is eye-catching but the book has little more than color, mistrust it; if the book is replete with anecdotes but provides few hard facts, mistrust it even more. But, above all, don't believe what academic historians say (that beyond academia everything is journalism) or what nonuniversity writers and historians say (that academics know a lot but understand nothing). Those are stupidities. What's good is scarce, and a Ph.D. neither precludes nor guarantees good history.

(c) *There is history and there is theory; for some, what's best is a mixture; for others, they must be kept separate.* False. A history without theory (without point of view) isn't history; and what is a theory without history? They are not two domains, they are one; it happens that sometimes historians seem to hold back on theory, while sometimes they have nothing else to give. And there are no quality or labeling rules here: how much or how little theory and history is advisable depends on how convincing, how revealing, how well researched and realized the account is. Whether there is too little or too much can only be dealt with in specific terms: which theory, in order to understand what phenomenon; what historical data and how many, on what subject, seen from what angle, illuminate or refute a theory. This brings us to the conclusion that a reader interested in history consumes theory even if he doesn't want to. Thus, the best approach is to be aware of that as you read, and stop reading if the book turns out to be an unholy mess, but the presence or absence of theory can't be a criterion for opening the book in the first place.

Here's some advice: ordinary reader, don't worry about the debates among historians; read history and know that in it you will find theory and point of view. Now, if you know that you are drawn to theoretical questions, read more about them, follow the clues that books provide. Here, yes, there are experts in the "theory of history"; but if those experts haven't written a single history, don't take them too seriously. Doing so would be like trusting a Catholic priest as your sexologist. And when you get into very conceptual books, follow the rule of three: read a paragraph once; if you don't understand, read it a second time; if you now begin to glimpse something interesting but come up against a term or an author or two that you aren't familiar with, it's time for a dictionary or Google, something that will help you decipher the terms—nobody ever got a hernia doing this. If on the third reading the paragraph doesn't make any sense whatsoever, forget about it: you won't be the first to consign that tome to the scrap heap.

(d) *Reading history builds citizens, makes the nation, and helps us avoid repeating the mistakes of the past.* This is a half-truth. It's not that we don't get something like that out of reading history, but these good intentions shouldn't guide our historical curiosity. While an ordinary reader may be interested in becoming more familiar with the history of Mexico, for example, that history is unintelligible without knowing something about other histories, depending on the subject and the period. Of course, the nation has been the vital analytical unit, but it has also led to the dilemma that history is now so accessible but has so few new views to offer. Patriotic history is a bad guide for the reader; every problem, phenomenon, or historical period is irreducible, conceptually and empirically, to a patriotic history. Even if history is "life's master" and teaches how to be citizens and better Mexicans, it has to be something more than the consideration of a solely Mexican history. To encourage civic culture or love for national accords, we would have to consider a great deal of European history, a whole lot of Caribbean, Central American, and United States history, and the history of things like liberalism, inequality, and nationalism in general terms. Besides, we already have sufficient empirical proof to say without hesitation: humanity has killed and will continue killing, whether it knows its history or not.

Make your own archive of concerns and responses. One subject will lead to another and another—don't be scared. When you realize that there's a book about, let's say, Spanish liberalism or about the war against indigenous people in the United States that will help you understand Mexico, then go for it. And then, after you have made the rounds, it doesn't really matter whether you return to patriotic history. *Nadie le quitará lo bailado* (they can't take that away from you).

4

Finally, I offer my own classification to help you choose from among the excessive number of history books available. The subspecies of academic books includes:

(a) *The specialized brick-like book.* Nowadays, what used to be a hefty tome is usually a skinny book—increasingly gaunt, poor thing, because academic presses refuse to publish fat specialized books—but on occasion it can be fat. This is a book with a lot of bibliography, an infinity of footnotes or endnotes, and numerous references to archives. Its prose tends to be dry and even abstruse, but it's not unusual to find volumes that are well written. In principle, for a nonexpert, reading this type of book produces the sensation of turning on the ball game when the first half is almost over. So if you buy it, it's because you already know something about the subject and want to know more. Generally, this type of book is published by university presses or by the few nonuniversity presses that still publish academic books (in Spanish: Crítica, Fondo de Cultura Económica, Era, Siglo XXI, Anagrama, Prometeo, Archipiélago, Katz, etc.; in English Penguin, Knopf, Hill and Wang, W. W. Norton, to mention only a few).

It may be a beautiful book, full of pictures and with an attractive cover; or it can be a horrible book, carelessly put together. Check to see if it's a doctoral dissertation; if so, look for the main idea at the beginning and figure out if it's interesting. Determine whether the author has published a lot on the topic or on other topics. If its physiognomy, dress, or point of view doesn't capture your interest after reading a few paragraphs, forget it. If it's sort of interesting but not overwhelmingly so, don't buy it right away (these books tend to be expensive). A Google search will tell you whether the author and the book have been written about. It's likely that the author has published an article in which she summarizes the book, which will make your work easier. Don't pay much attention to the blurbs on the back cover that publishers use to promote books. Academic presses do the same as commercial publishers and are not to be trusted in this respect. Don't be worried if in the end you aren't interested in the majority of these books. That's normal: what's good is scarce. For the same reason, you should worry if your library seems to be filling up with history best sellers: what's good is scarce.

(b) *The synthesis brick-like book.* This book shares the physiognomy of the previous type but tends to be fatter. It doesn't usually derive from a dissertation but is a professional historian's second or fourth book. These books are worthy of your attention. Sometimes they are sweeping new syntheses of a century or a subject (the Spanish Civil War, the Mexican Revolution, World War I, the Age of Empires). They are generally the product of a historian's maturity, which doesn't save them: they might be blessed baloney, but don't be put off by their thickness and the quantity of data. Weigh the book's possibilities with the tricks I've been explaining. Also keep in mind that many of the truly new syntheses are collections of essays, which are the best on the market for understanding a particular history. So don't be scared off: jump at the opportunity to get the Cambridge or the Oxford history of this or that or the Colegio de México's *Historia general de México.* These are uneven summae, but they are the most trustworthy accounts, although the cycle of historical production is so slow—because it requires tiresome research—that by the time you read the latest version of any of these compendia it will already need updating. And, to be sure, be suspicious of textbooks: they can be helpful, but in general they are bare-bones syntheses for consumption by a very specific readership (French or American or Mexican preuniversity or university students).

(c) *The historical essay.* This is a book or collection of essays whose physiognomy is fairly similar to the two types described above but which is radically different. Contrary to popular belief, historians are not as boring or asinine as they seem, and their discussions among themselves take place not through heavy monographs based on new archival research but through essays offering a general reinterpretation of a phenomenon or historical period. These books can be highly conceptual or not, but that is not the criterion for deciding whether to read them. They tend to be better written than monographs, offer many more echoes and angles, and are more grandiose and daring. They are always a very serious consideration of all that has been said about a subject as well as a proposal for how to look at it. Sometimes they come like a revolution after many monographs on the topic; in other cases they are proposals that in turn produce great numbers of monographs, the boring kind that scare off the nonacademic reader. On occasion they are just that: essays, brief articles, like Frederick Jackson Turner's very famous piece on the importance of the frontier in American history. At times they are suites of essays like those by Alan Knight on the Mexican Revolution. Then again, they might seem to be on a general topic, moving freely in space and time, such as Michel Foucault's histories of sexuality and prisons, the histories of nationalisms by Ernest Gellner and Eric Hobsbawm, or Edmundo O'Gorman's *México: El trauma de historia* and *The Invention of America*. Generally, these types of books are the delight of readers who are more or less initiated into historical topics; the books are easy to read and brainy. Go out and hunt for them—for the historian and the ordinary reader of history alike, they are our daily bread.

(d) *The biography.* This is a book with a physiognomy similar to that of other academic types. It can be a truly unreadable brick, but there's something about recounting a life that makes the narrative pleasing. Indeed, the biographic genre can be an easy bridge between the heavy academic tome and the mass-market book. Great biographies require as much research as a social or economic history or more, but synthesis through a life makes the account more reader-friendly. Reading well-documented academic biographies of history's protagonists about whom we already know something is valuable and pleasant. It's more useful to read the lives of interesting characters who played a part in histories that we don't know as well. Reading a good biography of Saint Augustine, Queen Elizabeth I, Napoleon Bonaparte, Benjamin Disraeli, Manuel Azaña, Gilberto Freyre, or José Ortega y Gasset requires an active reader, as if you had clicked on a name, an event, or a period in French, English, Brazilian, or Spanish history. While biography is also a genre preferred by writers of mass-market history, I'm afraid that here, dear reader, there is little difference: read biographies, whether academic or not—it's pretty much the same.

Of course, you have to be somewhat, though not entirely, aware that the historian's and the biographer's crafts are like an old married couple who have lived together since way back but are constantly squabbling. In English, from *The Life of Samuel Johnson* (1791) by James Boswell to Virginia Woolf's famous and vituperative reviews about, and against, the genre of biography and the so-called New Biography (of the 1920s), historians, biographers, and novelists have squabbled over who truly captures the past and have accused the other of invention. Sometimes it is the historian who is accused of banality, at other times it's the biographer. The confusion is less extensive in Spanish but no less difficult to resolve, since the time of an Argentine historian whose most memorable work, read throughout the continent, was a biography—Domingo Faustino Sarmiento's *Facundo: Civilización i barbarie* (1845), which narrates the life of caudillo Facundo Quiroga.

During the second half of the twentieth century, in many languages, writing good scientific professional history meant overcoming the "life of the great man" paradigm. Biographers became second-class citizens among the historians. But that was just an illusion. History and biography are always quarreling but always stay together. And the ordinary reader knows this and profits from it. But rather than being in favor of or against biography, what's new is who is considered a fit subject for a biography. Virginia Woolf wrote in *Orlando: A Biography* (a fictionalized biography of Vita Sackville-West): "If the subject of one's biography will neither love nor kill, but will only think and imagine, we may conclude that he or she is no better than a corpse and so leave her."

Historians have been of the same opinion for a long time, producing biography after biography of great men, the kind who killed. But the ordinary reader can now understand the history of difficult philosophical and scientific matters through excellent biographies of philosophers and scientists who neither killed nor loved too much. For example, to understand the Vienna of the early twentieth century and Ludwig Wittgenstein's complex philosophy, there's nothing better than Ray Monk's biography (*Ludwig Wittgenstein: The Duty of Genius*). To understand English and European history of the second half of the nineteenth century, nothing beats the biography of Oscar Wilde (who didn't kill anyone, but, oh my, did he ever love) by Richard Ellmann (*Oscar Wilde at Oxford*). More innovative was the appearance of biographies of apparent nobodies that the reader can enjoy as excellent history and biography—for example, *Il formaggio e i vermi* by Carlo Ginzburg, the biography of a half-mad, half-visionary sixteenth-century miller. In 1980s Mexico Enrique Krauze rescued the genre of biography from the ashes (*Biografía del poder*); criticism from professional historians rained down on him. Krauze took advantage of the situation to continue the shadow boxing between history and biography in his private campaign against professional history, which he calls boring and useless. But biography is an old form of knowledge in Mexican history, and the ordinary reader can find comfort, for example, in *Nezahualcóyotl, vida y obra* by José Luis Martínez; *Santa Anna: El dictador resplandeciente* by Rafael F. Muñoz; the half-novel, half-history *Memorias de Pancho Villa* by Martín Luis Guzmán; *Zapata and the Mexican Revolution* by John Womack; and *Maximilian und Charlotte von Mexiko* by Egon Caesar Conte Corti. You, ordinary reader, pay no attention to the hair pulling between historians and biographers: there's no better history than a good biography.

Among the nonacademic books, we have:

(a) *The new mass-market syntheses, general and specific.* The physiognomy of this book is well known to the ordinary reader of history: generally, it's a book with a colorful cover that says on the front or back that it will change our perspective on a topic or an era; it can be sort of fat, never too skinny or too voluminous. Sometimes it's presented as a work that will demolish something well-known or that will surprise us, with publicity in this vein: "the book that changed the course of the twentieth century," "the book that every Mexican should be familiar with to understand why the bad guys won," "Columbus was Catalan," "the secret role of bankers in the First World War," "the new synthesis of the First World War that shows that Germany wasn't to blame." Or it can be presented as the best and most up-to-date synthesis of the history of modern Mexico or France, illustrated and with maps and sidebars that include original documents. When these books are in English, they tend to be published by commercial presses; their authors may be academic historians (but with literary agents) or cultural or scientific journalists, freelance writers, or independent scholars. When they are in Spanish, they tend to be published by one of the imprints of the two or three large publishing monopolies but on occasion may also be published by the Fondo de Cultura Económica or may be translations of English or French works published by presses like the FCE.

And the same applies here: first comes the diagnosis. If the book is without footnotes, does it have a long and solid bibliographic essay? Does it have an ample annotated bibliography? If you know something about the subject and the book does have a real index (as books in English tend to have), review it to see if it includes the protagonists and themes that you consider important—how many of them, where, and in what context. If it doesn't, that is not a sign that the book is useless, but it is a criterion for continuing the diagnosis. Generally, these books are narratives comme il faut; read a bit here and there, see if the book grabs you, if it has subtlety but also force in the prose and the argument. If it is a simple chronology—in 1910 this happened and then that—or if it has anecdote after anecdote, begin to distrust it. If it starts with something like "nobody has said, nobody has seen this before," distrust it. That's not likely to be true. If it's in English and claims that "there's no other book like this in English," distrust it. You, ordinary reader, are looking for these books, the grand syntheses, from the grand synthesizers (Simon Schama, Hugh Thomas, Eric Hobsbawm, Edmundo O'Gorman, Enrique Florescano), and so am I. But understand that whenever a book of this kind is convincing, we must also undertake to read and continue reading syntheses that are critical of it. We read history not just to accumulate facts but also to contrast points of view and to learn how to see.

(b) *The business school history book model.* This has been the successful type of history book for some time now, the kind that cultured lawyers, physicians, and high school teachers read, that is discussed in cafes and at social gatherings and regurgitated by opinion makers. This type of book is never fat and is always well dressed and elegantly published in English or in Spanish translation by large publishing houses—attempts at this kind of book written originally in Spanish have not had much success yet. We're dealing with a Power Point book: it offers just one or two very powerful ideas as though they were truths that are simultaneously obvious, daring, and conclusive. And then the ideas are developed with bits of history here and there. They generally include phrases like "recent research demonstrates" or "we now know that . . ." They are above all about pushing a catchy scientific "app" or "sound bite." Here we find books that tell us that Western history can be reduced to the existence of four or eight "apps" (the Protestant ethic, patents . . .) or talk about "windows of opportunity," "disruptive evolution," histories being "path dependent" or things being "wired." A historian, a psychologist, or a business professor discovers one day that patents explain the development of capitalism—or no, that the grand truth is that all of history is written in our genes, or that the real truth is war, or growing violence, or diminishing violence, or water, or the air, or whatever becomes chic in business schools and history, economics, and psychology departments.

This type of book appears to follow the model of biology or economics or political science, but in reality its model is business school marketing. The idea is packaged like a product, well manufactured like a *prêt-à-porter* history and offers definitive and absolutely clear conclusions with the logic of a Power Point graph, so that no intelligent person will be able to resist the knock-out punch. There are thousands of books of or about history produced in this style every year. Some catch on—they become common currency among educated people—while others go unnoticed. But if they catch on, beware, ordinary reader, you will see them everywhere. You should read them. I'm one of those people who believe that we can never have too many ideas when it comes to understanding history. These books can be very interesting because, unlike the works of boring historians, they proceed with clear and important questions and solutions: Why do empires fall? Why does inequality persist? Why was England first? But beware: as you know, diligent reader of history, that damned Clio is no friend of monocausality or simplicity. There is no historical phenomenon that can be reduced to one or two causes, and what is interesting and important about history follows from that. This is not to say that you shouldn't consider these explanations, no: take a look at them, don't even criticize them for their selective use of history—they always find what they're looking for and make it seem like what they're not looking for is irrelevant. They should be thought of as historiographic essays, without the erudition of the great historiographic essays with their thousands of echoes; they are merely interesting hypotheses to consider in light of more history.

With this kind of book, reading the front and back covers or the information on the author will be of no help: they are always the greatest geniuses, prizewinners, the sine qua non. Alas, history, dear reader, can be used for anything, even for simulating genius and wisdom when what we really have are some bullet points loaded with a modicum of historical information. In short, read those that seem the most serious and best; but no matter how tempted you are, don't prescribe the bullet points to your colleagues at the academy of medicine or the bar association, don't burden relatives during family dinners. Simplicity is habit forming, and sometimes addicts run around giving Power Point lessons to anybody who will lend them an ear. Digest these books, think about them together with all of your readings.

(c) *The historical novel.* This is the ordinary reader's book of history par excellence. When it's good, it's indispensable for the historian and for life; when it's bad, it's totally unnecessary either as history or as literature. It used to be that the authors of good historical novels were as erudite as historians and in some cases even more so—read Alessandro Manzoni and his quarrel with Walter Scott, read Brian Hamnett's book on the nineteenth-century historical novel, or Peter Gay's on Flaubert and Thomas Mann as historians. Every country, every language, has great practitioners of this genre. Tradition itself, local and universal, can be a guide. In

Spanish, for a time, the *Episodios nacionales* of Benito Pérez Galdós was an excellent paradigm of the marriage between history and fiction. There were imitators of this tradition in Mexico and Argentina. But the reader of history can find good history in the Spanish-language literature. To mention a few titles: consider the majestic verbal baroque that emphasizes rather than erasing the great history of failed emperor Fernando Maximiliano in Mexico in *Noticias del imperio* by Fernando del Paso. Or, to understand the way Spanish bureaucracy worked in the late viceroyalty of the Río de la Plata, nothing beats *Zama* by Antonio di Benedetto. In short, there is a lot that's good and far more that's very bad. The complication comes when discerning what to read, given the boom in historical novels that are published because history sells and Google exists. I won't mince words: most of what is published today as a more or less historical novel is pure Googly, with very little research, the run-of-the-mill history that is a pure product of Wikipedia. Any subject can be sweetened with a plot, some sex, and some obvious reference to the contemporary, all with an eye to selling the movie rights. For this kind of literature, we have no choice but to get a taste for the great historical novels—from Leo Tolstoy to Marguerite Yourcenar, from the *Episodios nacionales* of Galdós to *La voz dormida* by Dulce Chacón, the novel of the Spanish civil war and postwar, seen from the very local level. Then flip through the pages of what is published today and let them fall under their own weight.

(d) *Gossip history.* In the guise of history a lot of mass-market books are sold that deal with the private life of this person or the love affairs of that one or the drunken sprees or homosexuality of another. History is gossip, and there's not a thing that we can do about it. Don't believe serious historians who deny the gossipy nature of history. Enjoy measured, well-informed, and heated gossip that is relevant to historical arguments. But follow the criteria indicated above. Check the source of the gossip, be skeptical of anachronisms: "Sor Juana wrote love sonnets to the wife of a viceroy, ergo . . ." she did the same for God and the world; "Zapata served as head groom in the household of a known homosexual, thus . . ." What? He slept with the boss because he had to, or with the boss's wife because he felt sorry for her? On the other hand, even the most outrageous and baseless gossip is fun to read; enjoy it, but don't believe it. Laugh with or at the book, but don't be gluttonous. These books are a vice.

By way of signing off, I remind the ordinary reader of history to read in order to do research, to understand, to contrast, but not just to feel good about what you already know. If reading history has done nothing more than make you happy that you are right, alcohol does a better job. When history annoys, questions, and creates doubts about identities, beliefs, and affiliations is when it's at its best. Let history do that for you. Of course, you will have to take an interpretation at face value, at least until your next reading. Clio is not only the historian's muse but also the patron of readers of history: she forgives innocence but not stubbornness or dogmatism.

Chapter 5

CELEBRATING HISTORY

BETWEEN *SER* AND *ESTAR*

A preliminary version of this essay was intended to honor my mentor and friend Enrique Florescano in 2008 and as a proposal for the 2010 Centennial and Bicentennial Celebration of Mexico's Revolution and Independence in 2010. Of course, the celebration was something else altogether: Felipe Calderón's government prepared a silly and insignificant nationalist fiesta. For the most part, the historians' guild went along with the affair without protest and won concessions to oversee the insipid celebrations and to publish innumerable books that had been forgotten by 2012 or at the latest 2013. Nothing to write home about. I leave this new version of the essay as a marker on the road to future discussions about history vis-à-vis celebration.

"Knowing by heart" (*saber de memoria*). The expression intrigues me. I want to examine it as a partial answer to the doggedly asked question: "Why history?" I do that to reach the *desmemoria* (memorylessness) needed to see anew an obsession that is close to the heart of history and historiography: celebrations.

Knowing by Heart

"Why history?" We know by heart the question. Let's start there, not with the question, but with knowing by heart. The literal translation of the Spanish phrase *saber de memoria* would be "knowing by memory," but the equivalent in English and other languages is "knowing by heart." In other words, we are dealing with a kind of knowledge that is at the center of our being. It is knowing something that we can repeat or reactivate without looking at our notes, sometimes even without thinking about it.

This, then, is what used to be called knowledge par excellence: the human memory. In addition, knowing by heart implies that we ourselves are the utterance of a language both memorized and pregnant with memory. I can invoke a certain memory, but I can also be called into active service, almost unconsciously, by various forms of knowing by heart.

These knowings by heart, in turn, create intellectual communities that repeat a private language that no one believes it is necessary to define. I refer to the blah-blah-blah of professional historians, philosophers, anthropologists, and literary critics. Nevertheless, at times such private memories become common sense. Think about how little Freud and Marx are read and how present both are in the materialist and therapeutic culture of the Western middle classes. In fact, sometimes private languages turn into common sense and become the memories of great numbers of people. Allow me a personal detour by way of example. When my daughter was eight years old, I, who know hundreds of old Mexican songs by heart, sang her a tune that went like this: "Como a las diez o las once Juana se puso a pensar / voy a matar mi marido para salirme a 'pasear'" (Around ten or eleven, / Juana began to think, / I'm going to kill my husband / to go hang out). My daughter interrupted me in a flash because she knows it by heart: that was, she told me, *violencia de género*, her literal translation of "gender violence." The point is not whether the song is or is not gender violence; the point is that this poor daughter of American-style professors had no choice but to know the private language of hypersensitive, self-serious academics by heart.

At times a knowing by heart transformed into a sort of "academic etiquette book" forces us to act in certain ways, though it does not own us the way, say, the knowings by heart derived from our mother tongue do. For example, when I read in English the word "Hispanic" or that other odd word "Latin@," I don't feel summoned as though my name is being called. The two words put me, like it or not, in a semantic universe in which I know where each thing goes by heart: the Anglo-Saxon here, the others there, the obsession with race at the center, romanticism about authenticity all over the place—and don't forget to behave as a (brown person) is expected to.

Knowing by heart is also accepting that all the rest, what we don't really know by heart, is mayhem, conscious or involuntary. So we have no other way to mark the boundaries of our forgetting and ignorance than from the inside (from what we know by heart) out (what we don't know by heart). Because forgetting is the mechanism that we use to shape and reproduce our knowings by heart—at least that's what the impressive development in the neurosciences over the last three decades has taught us. Memory cannot be relinquished, but it only works if forgetfulness functions properly, especially in dreams but also when we are awake. Thus, when we say that a child or a person now has a memory, what we are saying is not just that she now has sufficient recollections, but above all that she now needs to forget in an orderly manner and knows how to do that.

Finally, knowing by heart is being familiar with, holding forth about, and studying the past in the present. Neurologists, psychiatrists, magicians, mnemonics specialists, poets, novelists, and of course historians know something about knowing by heart.

Mexican Knowing by Heart and Why History?

Some ruins and routines of memory and forgetfulness have somehow acquired the adjective "Mexican." They are what is learned in school or by living in, seeing, and hearing the cities and towns of the territory that we now call Mexico—and also in many towns and cities in the United States. I don't want (nor am I able) to talk about all of them. I merely focus on the historian's complicity in inhabiting and constructing these Mexican knowings by heart. Enrique Florescano long ago demonstrated that since pre-Hispanic times "collective memories," foundational myths, and senses of belonging have been ideations, in part ideologies of power, in part utopias and selections from popular traditions (*Memoria mexicana*). In such a way many knowings by heart have been formed that were gradually shared by more and more people, who, in turn, have mixed them with their own personal and collective memories. Because the writing of history inevitably leads to sociability that is beyond the historian's control.

Therefore, an approach to the question "why history?" should begin from this fact: memory precedes the question. We are almost never a part of complete memorylessness: sets of misleading and fleeting memories are always shared. J. G. Droysen said about history that "knowing about her is her" (*Outline of the Principles of History*). It isn't possible to contemplate memory's raison d'être, or history's, outside of history and memory; our concern for memory and forgetting is perennial and *ohne warum* (without reason). Any historian who thinks from Mexico about the why of history and memory finds herself a guest at a banquet that is always underway, whose diners don't get up from the table, and the conversation is ongoing—from Father Francisco Xavier Claviejero to Lucas Alamán, from Francisco Pimentel to Ricardo García Granados, from Justo Sierra to Edmundo O'Gorman, from Charles A. Hale to Josefina Vázquez, from Luis González to Enrique Florescano . . .

In view of the intricacies of knowing by heart and the very fact of ruminating on memory in Mexico—assuming ourselves to be part of a lasting flow of various moments, of different ways of wondering "why history?"— the asking and the question ("why history?") turn out to be pleonasms. Memory and history have no "why," and the "why?" is history itself: history is the past, the story of a chaotic and memory-filled flow of "why?" Thus, "why history?" is not a question about what history is for but a confirmation in response to a question about history's usefulness.

History's usefulness, however, has commonly been taken to be synonymous with "what or who we are." I hold that the utility of history should not appeal, either in its method or in its ethical reasons, to who we are (*somos*) but to where we are (*estamos*). To be sure, the distinction I'm advancing is subtle and difficult to feel in English. The English verb "to be" encompasses in one single verb what in Spanish is expressed in two verbs: *ser*, which has more ontological connotations, and *estar*, which is a more transitory way of being in specific circumstances, locations, or states of mind. Thus, when the "why" of history addresses the "where are we?" (*¿dónde estamos?*) rather than the "what are we?" (*¿qué somos?*), we turn away from ontological territory (giving up many questions: What are we? How can we be ourselves? Why haven't we arrived at being what we are? Would we be able to forget what we are?—all a matter of *ser* more than *estar*). It's no big thing, but I believe that something can be gained in the renunciation. Accepting that memory has no "why" and that history is a constant "why" creates the possibility of referring to memory and oblivion without embarrassment and without admitting absolute truths. To ask ourselves where we are (*dónde estamos*) is to accept a degree of lostness, to air our unconscious certainties, maybe forget them, in order to experience others, to rescue old plans and start from scratch to the extent that it's possible—it is never very viable. And to ask ourselves *dónde estamos* is to spell out the name of the present, which limits and explains our histories, makes them say exactly what they are able to say and nothing more. Such an exercise doesn't mean renouncing historiographic objectivity but giving it meaning: the past from here and now. Tomorrow we'll see.

From History for Being (*Ser*) to
History for Being Here (*Estar*)

At various moments in the nineteenth and twentieth centuries "why history" became synonymous with justice: history for whom. This use of history as the ultimate and true judge, as the source of real and permanent identity, is nothing new. The German Romantics repeated Friedrich Schiller's poem "Resignation" (1784): "die Weltgeschichte ist das Weltgericht" (world history is the world's tribunal); Ulysses Grant, who was a United States military officer in the war against Mexico and commander of the Union armies in the Civil War, considered the latter bloody war as the penalty that the United States paid for its unjust war against Mexico. John Maynard Keynes allowed the tribunal of history to judge France and England for believing, at the end of World War I, that history was about winning and humiliating the loser, making Germany pay for everything. Fidel Castro believed that history would absolve him. And, to be sure, the current obsession with recovering memories in order to do justice is just the same, though couched in therapeutic jargon.

Before the Braudelization of *Les Annales*, Marc Bloch and Lucien Febvre debated "why history?" Bloch knew geography, sociology, and economics—a good disciple of Paul Vidal de la Blache, Émile Durkheim, and Henri Pirenne—and thus preferred that the response to the question come from structures rather than from individual psychologies, so difficult to discern in space and time. But Bloch had also grown up as a true French patriot, if there ever was one, but Jewish in the France of the Alfred Dreyfus affair. Thus, he believed that no testimony or document was 100 percent credible and that it was better not to get involved in asking what we are racially, spiritually, or ethnically. "By birth I am a Jew," he wrote in *L'Étrange défaite*, "though not by religion, for I have never professed any creed, whether Hebrew or Christian. I feel neither pride nor shame in my origins. I am, I hope, a sufficiently good historian to know that racial qualities are a myth and that the whole notion of Race is a . . . particularly flagrant [absurdity]." His way of being French, of defending and dying for France, was universal citizenship, a category superior to identity atavism. *Les Annales*, and the Marxism of the 1950s and 1960s, maintained something of that republicanism, but in exchange for implanting a historical mechanics that left little room for the pragmatic imagination that founders of *Les Annales* like Bloch had embodied.

In Mexico, until the beginning of the 1980s, we historians knew the true causes of history, the real actors, and the mechanisms by heart. We knew that the rise of capitalism, the class struggle, and the working class were the only true histories to tell. It cost us an arm and a leg to detach ourselves from that knowledge, not because those things were false, but because they were very seductive; they explained almost everything. To the extent that today the only sure thing that can be affirmed about where we are (*dónde estamos*) is that we are adrift in the post-1989, post–Cold War era, after the passing of the socioeconomic and moral paradigm of the welfare state. The economic and social historiography of *Les Annales*, of E. P. Thompson, of the New Left in the United States, and of working-class history in Mexico gradually gave way to an avant-garde of historical subjects.

As in other historiographies, in Mexican history this shift has led again to the question "why history?" in the old sense of "what are we?" (*¿qué somos?*). Thus, it has become a matter of writing history from the bottom up but also an idealization of ordinary people; it's no longer about great men, elites, structures, or the class struggle. Like nineteenth-century Romantic philologists, we turn to the popular vernacular in search of the authentic verbs that were lost during years of affectation. Now we're dealing with the identity of the small and the humble as the secret bearer of the true morality in history, because the "authentic" holds the key to what we are, to the "why" of history. However, before race, gender, ethnicity, nation, sexuality, or class identity became fashionable, in a way we already knew that ontological obsession by heart. We already knew the plot about good and bad guys, the suffering of the authentic versus the glory of the artificial. This sort of memory involves serious methodological, empirical, and ethical risk, although in Mexico it looks like peaceful and healthy ontological reparations and justice.

To avoid getting involved in domestic problems, allow me to take an example from elsewhere. Look at the view of a post-1968 German historian who is disposed to make peace with his past but not ready to throw the baby out with the bathwater. Jürgen Kocka says:

> Let's imagine a historian interested in analyzing the wave of rural anti-Semitism that grew during the 1880s in some parts of Germany, where, for example, in Upper Hesse, a number of candidates to the Reichstag for the new anti-Semitic party won overwhelmingly . . . and subsided again in the 1890s. Let's imagine that this historian limited himself to reconstructing the subjective experiences of those peasants and small landholders of Upper Hesse

drowning in debt, harassed and pressured by moneylenders and livestock raisers (often Jewish), the experience of those people, who, for the most part, professed anti-Semitism in good faith. That would be fatal: it would result in an absolutely insufficient interpretation that would reproduce . . . the prejudices of those ordinary people. (*Sozialgeschichte*)

Kocka invites the reader to consider other things (in addition to the authentic feelings of peasants), including agricultural crises, transportation problems, immigration, the crisis of liberalism, and the failure of the state.

The crisis of social history, then, mixed with the excesses of the new identity-addicted approaches, demonstrates that, in truth, the question "why history?" and its corollary "history for whom?" are inseparable from morals, dogmas, rhetorical styles, and political ethics that we know by heart, inseparable above all from the axiom "we are what we remember and should evoke what we are," which turns out to be a more or less unconscious translation of "what we should be."

No one is conscious of the full extent of her ignorance or of all she has learned, especially the prejudices. Using any identity as a starting point for a true memory or history is to swap the questions "why history?" and "history for whom?" for this sophism: "the true history is ours, where 'we' are the optimal and real result of history." It's better to begin with the question "where are we?" (*¿dónde estamos?*) before asking "what are we?" (*¿qué somos?*); thus, the answer to "why the past?" or "memory for whom?" depends, first, on the time when the question is being asked; and second, on the risk that we are prepared to run in balancing memory and forgetfulness in the imagining of the past and the present in light of where we want to be (*estar*).

Therefore, every time the question "why history" creaks, it's time to make an act of contrition, to look at where we've been. That is what, in their time, Mexican historians Edmundo O'Gorman, Enrique Florescano, and Luis González did; in United States historiography it's what Carl Becker, Richard Hofstadter, John Higham, and Peter Novick did, at different times and in different ways. And it is in essence the question that Raymond Aron put to himself. At the beginning of the 1960s Aron wrote that, after learning philosophy and biology, he got interested in history and "then I bumped into what would be the subject of reflection for my entire life: How is it possible to know oneself and the society in which one lives at the same time? . . . How does one perform the dialectic between society, which makes me what I am, and I, who want to define myself in relation to that society?" (*Mémoires*). This is the historian's task: how to put together a verisimilar, useful, and ethical explanation of the past as a conscious "being here" (*estar*), now and in the near future, hoping for our explanations to be empirically robust and morally responsible though we know they are ephemeral like the present.

Celebration: the Example of 1910

There's no reason to go into a great deal of detail: it's clear that 1910 made a lasting mark on time, in Mexico and in the world. And soon after 1910, nothing would ever be the same. Thus, some sort of commemoration had to be held in 2010. But where were we? And where did we want to be in 2010? What should guide the celebration? To handle these questions, allow me to take refuge in a pre-2010 comparison: the image of Ulrich, the "man without qualities" who in Robert Musil's novel *Der Mann ohne Eigenschaften* works for Leinsdorf, the chief of "Parallel Action": the celebration of the "transcendental seventieth jubilee" of what remained of the Austro-Hungarian Empire.

After the fall of the empire, Leinsdorf suggests that Austrian patriotism should be promoted through the image of an even-tempered, ecumenical emperor. "[W]e keep to our four points," Leinsdorf says to Ulrich, "Emperor of Peace, European milestone, True Austria, property and culture." Ulrich's avatars in the novel's first volume ramble on about preparations for the celebration. This is a novel-essay about the destruction of some memories, the rise of others, and how a generation searched for the solidity that had been lost forever. "Suddenly, out of the becalmed mentality of the nineteenth century's last two decades," says the narrator:

> Nobody knew exactly what was on the way. . . . But people were standing up on all sides to fight against the old way of life. Suddenly the right man was on the spot everywhere . . . people were enthusiastic hero-worshippers and enthusiastic adherents of the social creed of the Man in the Street; one had faith and was skeptical, one was naturalistic and precious, robust and morbid; one dreamed of ancient castles and shady avenues, autumnal gardens . . . Admittedly these were contradictions and very different battle-cries, but they all breathed the same breath of life. If that epoch had been analysed, some such nonsense would have come out as a square circle supposed to be made of wooden iron; but in reality all this had blended into shimmering

significance. (*The Man without Qualities*, translated by Eithne Wilkins and Ernst Kaiser)

That "illusion" was a mix of worldwide contradictions, a balance between memory and forgetfulness that worked well at least for the political and intellectual class that came up with, for example, the fiestas for the Mexican Centennial in 1910. Back then, what Ulrich calls the script, the plot that could organize a narrative, a celebration, was operative in Mexico and the world. But in 1910, or in 1914, the long peace that had lasted three or four decades suddenly came to an end, the peace that had been "la resaca de todo lo sufrido" (the undertow of all that suffering: César Vallejo, "Los heraldos negros") throughout the nineteenth century. The era of "deductive living" was left behind, Ulrich would say, when character was deduced from "certain definitive and absolute universal presuppositions." But after 1914 life went on "without a guiding idea, but also without a conscious method of deduction. We go on muddling through, trying things as stochastically as a monkey would."

Alfonso Reyes wrote in Madrid in 1915: "No matter what historical doctrine one professes (and I am not among those who dream about absurd perpetuations of indigenous tradition, nor do I even much trust perpetuations of Spanish tradition), what joins us to the race of yesterday, without mentioning blood, is the commonality of the effort to tame our angry, rough nature; an effort that is the brute base of history" (*Visión de Anáhuac*). In Mexico there were, then, positions and quarrels, but the consensuses were "wooden iron" (*The Man without Qualities*); "the angry, rough nature" had to be tamed. In 1910 Justo Sierra, during the reinauguration of the Universidad Nacional, one of the most important elements of the centennial celebration, suggested a theory of history, political morals, and the balance between forgetting and memory—which the creators of the centennial were amenable to:

> The founders of the university of yore said: "Truth is defined, teach it"; we say to the universities of today: "The truth is being defined, look for it." They said: "You are a select group charged with imposing a religious and political ideal summed up in these words: God and King." We say: "You are a group that is perpetually being selected from the substance of the people, and to you has been entrusted the realization of a political and social ideal that can be summed up in these words: democracy and liberty." (in Genaro García, *Crónica oficial de las fiestas*)

The historians, artists, politicians, and scientists who prepared the great centennial celebration, beginning in 1907, were governed by a perhaps mistaken but nonetheless crystalline mixture of pragmatism and utopianism: progress, therefore modernization; peace and justice, therefore the state; the nation, therefore the most polished cosmopolitism and universalism that had existed until then in América del Septentrión (America of the North). And Mexico as a modern nation was finally a reconstruction of the local, an echo of the universal, through elitist mechanisms that were conceived as "perpetually selected from the substance of the people." Every detail of the celebration synthetized realities and utopias, contradictions and cravings. Those Porfirians of every stripe created what the intellectuals and politicians of 2010 would eventually know by heart, because the Porfiriato synthesized lasting notions of nation, progress, and state. Twenty-first-century Mexican memory may hate the dreams of the Porfiriato, but it cannot forget them.

Reyistas (supporters of General Bernardo Reyes) and *científicos* (the collective name of a powerful faction during the Porfiriato), liberal *revoltosos* (troublemakers) and military officers plotted everything, from pacts to coup d'états, but very few doubted the need for the state that had been imagined, for the first time in the country's history, by the regime during the Porfiriato. No one cast doubt on the natural and optimal result of history: the modern nation as it should be. Because without idealizing them, we have to give the Porfirians who imagined the centennial credit: rather than knowing who they were (*qué eran*), they knew where they were (*dónde estaban*), and thus the abuse of the term "pax." They had peace, or the best and most widespread peace the country had known since its independence. They knew that peace was the optimal result, a result to be celebrated, but they also knew that peace was fragile, dangerous. It's not that they suspected that one of the twentieth century's greatest popular revolutions would begin in a few months; it's that they were aware that peace was the delicate equilibrium where they were. Thus, they designed monuments to peace not only because they were idiots and tricksters but also because they appreciated peace—because peace was the consensus that made it possible to imagine that any conflict could be contained before it turned into a great revolution. Some wanted a more modern, cosmopolitan Mexico, others a more introverted nation, but no one doubted the very idea of a modern nation. It wasn't true that Mexico was modern, but it was truer than it had ever been. And no one wanted anything other than modernization. Utopia and realpolitik were neighbors. Some wanted the former emperor, the authentic father of independence, Agustín de Iturbide, to come back as a hero, others didn't, but no one doubted that the nation needed heroes. Some believed that national history began with the Aztecs, others that it began in 1521, and others in 1810, but everyone believed in the value of history as the maker of fatherlands and thought that the truth of the Mexican past could be accessible through science. Others believed, with Diotima, the aristocratic and liberal lady in Musil's novel, that all social classes should be consulted about how to celebrate. In fact, thousands of opinions were sent to the office of those in charge of the 1910 centennial. In short, what those Porfirians were celebrating was being in a time when the optimal and the possible were not in complete contradiction. This was the memory that they remembered and that they invented.

What those Porfirians did, whether Mexicans like it or not, is what many Mexicans now know by heart, the memory that they recount and the memory that recounts them. From a distance, it looks like the Revolution wrecked the staging of the Porfiriato's centennial. An optical illusion. The Revolution meant violence and changes but not the end of the script of certainties that the celebration of 1910 prescribed. So solid was the script conceived in 1910 that the revolutionaries who were in power in 1921 followed it to the letter when they celebrated the centennial of the end of Mexico's war of independence from Spain (1821).

Celebrating: Between Ulrich and Arnheim

In Musil's novel Ulrich is doubt and helplessness in the face of history; Arnheim is the wealthy professional who thought he could find the right formula to organize the celebration of Austria's history. Equally, in 2010 Mexico it was impossible to approach the centennial of the Mexican Revolution and the bicentennial of independence with the same certainties and conflicts that reigned in and around 1910 or with a scheme in the style of the Porfirians or Arnheim. Nowadays we historians flirt with Ulrich but secretly long for Arnheim's precision; the sort of history-essay that Ulrich sought, which "considers things from various sides without understanding them completely" (*The Man without Qualities*), was not yet thinkable. If we historians had truly learned from the historiographic debates of recent decades, the apparent consensus would be reduced to little more than a few ethereal ethical categories (diversity, tolerance, multi-this, post-that relativism, environmental consciousness). We exist, alas, in nations, in states, in empires; we believe in peoples, in revolutions, and in the very possibility of recounting innovative and convincing histories that nevertheless, we hope, will not become dogmas. We are also skeptics.

If we are to be faithful to the skepticism of our times, historians should cast doubt on the very fact of commemoration. To speak from the academic world in favor of the campaigns against the old Porfirian and post-revolutionary ideology of *mestizaje* and the campaigns against Robert E. Lee monuments is not doubting but, rather, affirming the need to celebrate history, as if believing in the possibility of an empirically true and morally correct celebratory instinct. Celebrating not by erecting but by removing monuments is still celebrating. Where does that leave the epistemological, moral, political doubts so slowly learned in such a piecemeal and painful fashion? In refusing to celebrate the past, if only hypothetically, the inevitable question would not be "what are we?" or "where are we?" but would history be possible in the unthinkable universe without nations or memory-burdened peoples? Can we do without history?

Truth be told, we historians have never been as innovative or cynical as we think we are. We know a great deal by heart, much more than we would like to know. By definition, we are the children of that "second nature" created by history—which is as natural as the forests and rivers. And today it is our irrevocable duty to write histories in terms of states, peoples, nations, empires, countries, and revolutions. This is what we inhabit—this is what we are: *estamos y somos*.

The historian's dilemma, essential but practical, is to narrate. This is the dilemma that Ulrich, the "Man without Qualities," faced vis-à-vis Arnheim, the character who believed that he knew the formula for history. Ulrich realized what we "post-post" historians know: the past is "an endless system of relationships . . . in which there was no longer any such thing as independent meanings, such as in ordinary life" (*The Man without Qualities*). Ulrich, then, fell into another sort of knowledge, into essayism: the genre of the critical voice that sees the many angles and the duplicities of the definitive formulas and pays attention to the infinite disorder that it is to write the past. Essays (attempts) are the undisciplined shape that storytelling acquires when disciplined skepticism is at work; for the essay, says Musil, "is not the provisional or incidental expression of a conviction that might on a more favourable occasion be elevated to the status of truth . . . an essay is the unique and unalterable form that a man's inner life assumes." Thus, like today's historian, Ulrich faced this dilemma: if he attempted to deduce historical truth and justice from the ambiguity and density of essayism, the essay disappeared. The complexity that frees us from ignorance and dogmatism vanishes. Because, Musil says, what is left of the essay when we attempt to make it functional, when we turn it into a textbook, a celebration, a doctrine, a monument, "is about as much as remains of a jelly-fish's delicately opalescent body after it has been lifted out of the water and laid on the sand" (*The Man without Qualities*).

In light of this paradox, we're left with simply attempting to narrate the past as a "we are here." We can't ride historical monocausality, call it nation, state, class struggle, or the true ethnic or global Mexico; we can't even state, with philosophical and empirical certainty, that we have the sum of the national past under control. We can't serve as posthumous judges of the past or the present. It's not even possible for us to doubt everything. We are left with settling, modestly, for essaying history, if only to ponder what we know by heart almost without meaning to; if only to put into action a number of doubts, knowing that we take too many things for granted.

Let's take the jellyfish out of the sea of musings, though on the sand what remains of the essay is a tiny inert body. And let's say the least: that as historians it's impossible for us to give up the epochal mandate of history, that we must assume that we are among the long list of history's doers, those who were executioners and victims in and of history, and that it is only possible to say of the question "why history?" that this is where we are: in the moment when writing history is imagining how we will fill at least three logics of memory and history in different ways. We cannot turn our backs on these. The first is moral, because who denies the belief that history is civic-minded, although we don't know how to fill this ethical logic of history with content? The second is empirical, although we doubt all notions of neutrality and objectivity, and precisely because we question these we're part of a long tradition and aspire to something more, in spite of still longing—and here is the third logic—to tell stories, maybe only for the purely aesthetic and existential reason that my daughter demanded of me when she was five years old: "Don't explain it to me, tell me the story."

I don't think that any historian can fill these logics with the contents that would render complete and verisimilar views of the past, coherence with concerns of the present, and acceptable visions of the future. No. Since we don't have certainties with which to fill these logics, let's fill them with what we have: a handful of doubts, without believing ourselves better than the old historians, as though we held the monopoly on doubt. We don't.

To sum up, it is not a viable option for historians to be the Ulrichs of any celebration, but we also can't resign ourselves to becoming the Arnheims of the next great patriotic fiesta. After all, we are "people without qualities," we are merely a popular tango called *piantaos, piantaos, piantaos* (crazy, crazy, crazy) ("Balada para un loco").

Chapter 6

SELF-HISTORY AND AUTOBIOGRAPHY

Autobiography is a solitary sin, though as solitary sins go some are better and easier to indulge in. And autobiography is an adventure astride memory, evidence, truth, imagination, forgetting, and self-censorship; as a result, we cannot demand of it either truth or precision, pity or humility. It is a genre so firmly wedged between history and literature that it can be either history or literature when in fact it's merely autobiography. Until the mid-nineteenth century some practitioners of the genre didn't seem to be autobiographers at all. Don Bernal Díaz del Castillo wanted his history of the Conquest to be "the true history" by being autobiographical, and memoirs by Francois-René Chateaubriand, Jean-Jacques Rousseau, and the Marquis de Sade were literature by virtue of being autobiographies. And it's well known that the novel used to be fiction with traces of autobiography but for some time now has been nothing more than autobiography with traces of fiction. The mania for autobiography took off in the second half of the nineteenth century, at least in European languages, and became a flood during the twentieth and twenty-first centuries.

But don't worry, dear reader, I won't attempt to write my autobiography here. Instead I will allow a suspicion to write its autobiography, a suspicion that I held for a while, which I want to declare dead once it has finished telling its story. I essay, then, the ephemeral life of an intuition that some time ago struck me as a result, on the one hand, of my reading of the autobiographies of several historians and, on the other, of my conversations with historian friends—Friedrich Katz, Charles A. Hale, and Jean Meyer. My suspicion became a sort of reading the constructive side of the historical imagination in their books and conversations.

My very dubious suspicion was born with the face of a great *Tractatus* and died, young and in me, of obviousness. It also died of nostalgia and resignation: my biography imagines itself through and contains the good autobiographies that I've read and heard. My life is what I've experienced, including the intellectual and existential experience of the lives of others.

In short, at its birth, the suspicion sounded like this: if the person who recounts her life is a historian, the account should constitute a veritable unique and original subgenre of autobiography. I believed, then, that the autobiography of a historian had to be a genre in and of itself, with its own peculiarities, because any practitioner of the trade of reconstructing the past who decides to tell her own past becomes the agent of a greater auto-biography, that of history itself—Clio inspiring Clio. I suspected that this would be an exercise like a neuroscientist's self-examination, inserting a scalpel between the cerebrum and the cerebellum. A microscope built to observe a creature trained to build microscopes. And that's how my suspicion began to take on a life of its own.

Happy Childhood

The newborn suspicion was exciting. I imagined it to be a kind of trust-worthy thermometer for measuring and understanding the historical imagination. At the beginning, years ago, the suspicion was nothing more than an echo from having read *The Education of Henry Adams*. Then, one fine day, my long dialogue with Hale began. Clio, I realized, is also the muse of intellectual companionship. Hale was a font of wisdom and eru-dition, his gestures and voice communicating generosity, *caballerosidad*, and kindness. Later, in Chicago, the suspicion grew through conversations with Katz in which he spoke in a purely autobiographical manner. Katz was not my teacher, but every historian of Mexico knew and knows the work of this exiled Austrian, who was the historian of Mexico's imperial intrigues during World War I and Pancho Villa's biographer. In Chicago I became addicted to having lunch with him, to long conversations about the history of Mexico, Germany, Russia . . . and about his life.

The suspicion lasted for some years and learned to walk on its own two feet. It led me to identify more than three hundred autobiographies of his-torians and to read many of them, but the problems began there. If reading one of those autobiographies led me to believe that the suspicion was now quite grown up, reading five or six more made me doubt its very existence again. I discovered that many historians whom I admired had written and more importantly published autobiographical notes. Yes, I know, obses-sively reading the autobiographies of historians was a bit egocentric, but I truly believed that I was on the trail of something interesting.

Recounting the details of these readings would bore the reader with an excessive number of scenes from my wanderings in libraries, carrying the suspicion in my head: here three hundred scenes of the historian discovering his calling, there the multiple and tiresome anecdotes of academic politicking, the affected photos of the historian surrounded by bookshelves, and enemies lined up before the unforgiving firing squad of the historian's memory. In short, nonsense.

But no sooner do these words leave my mouth than my mind turns to the delicious megalomania of Edward Gibbon (1737–1794), narcissism translated into exaggerated optimism about the possibilities of knowing the past. That is, for my suspicion, Gibbon didn't reveal much about what autobiography meant to someone who had written a history that was a best seller for two centuries, *The History of the Decline and Fall of the Roman Empire* (1776–1789). I found in his autobiography only ego and conceit, nothing more: "every man who rises above the common level has received two educations: the first from his teachers; the second, more personal and important, from himself" (*The Autobiography of Edward Gibbon*). And there are several like him. In short, what I was reading seemed to be the ravings of an egocentric that might just as easily have come from the mouth of a novelist or a banker or a politician with a good memory.

Though I promised not to, how can I fail to pause for a moment on one of the best autobiographies of a historian, the biography of an era: *The Education of Henry Adams*? My nubile suspicion fed on this book for a long time. *The Education* was the godfather of my suspicion and its sustenance, an autobiography of a historian as an "un-Gibbon–like act": none of the conceit of transcendence, but the pride of insignificance. Giambattista Vico, in the early eighteenth century, inaugurated the genre of the historian's (or philosopher's) autobiography and wrote it in the third person, just like *The Education of Henry Adams*. Adams narrates the life of Henry the way Giambattista speaks for Vico: "with the candor proper to a historian, we shall narrate plainly and step by step the entire series of Vico's studies, in order that the proper and natural causes of Vico's development as a man of letters may be known" (*The Autobiography of Giambattista Vico*). Giambattista's Vico doesn't forgive the indifference of Naples to his unquestionable genius. The Adams of *The Education* is something else: the brilliance of melancholy, the forensic anatomy of an era, the Gilded Age, its patina of grandeur removed through the life of a failure, Henry Adams.

Imagine, dear reader, my intellectual suspicion, so avid for sustenance, reading that patrician who used autobiography to identify a twofold fraud: his own and that of his era. His salvation was in honestly recognizing that fact; his era, however, was unredeemed. Adams, grandson and great-grandson of presidents, painted his life as an insignificant occurrence within the betrayal of the grand republic, stripped now of its glories and the hopes of his forbears, a nation that "stood alone in history for its ignorance of the past." In Adams, my suspicion heard the following confession as though before an altar—the past and life escape knowing: "The sequence of mind led to nothing and the sequence of their society could lead no further, while the mere sequence of time was artificial, and the sequence of thought was chaos." In truth, now that I am writing the life of this suspicion, I realize that it was little more than a prolonged reading of *The Education of Henry Adams.*

My suspicion persevered: I read more autobiographies of historians, and just saying so produces incontinence in my memory. Allow me some more anecdotes. Brilliant historians recounted their lives as tragic and methodic examples of Clio's art, like Benedetto Croce, whose autobiography has a sadly memorable beginning: the earthquake of 1883 on the island of Ischia. There Croce loses his father, his mother, and his sister ("L'autobiografia come storia e la storia come autobiografia" and *Memorie della mia vita*). His autobiography ends up being that of the historical imagination—how and why the historian imagines when faced with the black hole of Italian history (1914–1945). But Croce's autobiographical notes don't entirely accomplish this last task, because they were written before the arrival of fascism and the terrible decades for someone born in 1866—during the "Third War of Independence," shortly before the end of the unification of Italy—who would die in 1952, after the defeat of fascism and of Italy.

What Croce couldn't do, Marc Bloch did—I mean something like making sense of a tragic era, as it were, by interviewing Clio about her whims—in his *Apologie pour l'histoire ou métier d'historien.* This memoir was indeed an account of human existence playing against both history and the historian's life. From the trenches of the French resistance in World War II, he wrote: "If history would only renounce its false archangelic airs, it would help us to cure this weakness. It includes a vast experience of human diversities, a continuous contact with men. Life, like science, has everything to gain from it, if only these contacts be friendly."

With these readings, my suspicion seemed healthy, fat, certain; I was on the trail of something serious. What? I did not know, but something that had to do with the neural architecture of the past. Time and again I ran into the poetic wisdom of Vico or of some historian-autobiographers who created portraits of their subject—say, slavery—through the personal and the inhumanity of humanity, like the autobiographical fragments by W. E. B. Du Bois, *The Souls of Black Folk*. I know, I should have ended this string of souvenirs from my travels with my suspicion paragraphs ago, but how can I not quote Du Bois on history and his dead son? This has to be read:

> Within the Veil was he born, said I; and there within shall he live—a Negro and a Negro's son. Holding in that little head—ah, bitterly!—the unbowed pride of a hunted race, clinging with that tiny dimpled hand—ah, wearily!— to a hope not hopeless but unhopeful, and seeing with those bright wondering eyes that peer into my soul a land whose freedom is to us a mockery and whose liberty is a lie, I saw the shadow of the Veil as it passed over my baby, I saw the cold city towering above the blood-red land.

Also, for a few years, I had lunch with Friedrich Katz two or three times a month, and it didn't cost much to see the simultaneous working of autobiography and the conception of history, just like that, at any excuse (something about Israel, about the Spanish Civil War, about Cardenismo, or about German literature). Katz always joined autobiography and history— I don't know which gave the orders to which. What I do know is that I always wound up saying: "You have to tell that story, *maestro*, write your autobiography."

By now I should have stopped with the anecdotes, but what is the life of a suspicion, or of a person, if not a collection of anecdotes? Here's another: my suspicion was nourished, naturally, on the *Essais d'égohistoire* where, with variegated brilliance, Maurice Agulhon, Pierre Chaunu, Georges Duby, Raoul Girardet, Jacques Le Goff, Michelle Perrot, and René Rémonds dealt with memory and the craft, the past and life. My suspicion was also delighted with Henry Abelove's *Visions of History*, although, without realizing it, my suspicion was dying because of reading the autobiographical exercises of E. P. Thompson, N. Zemon Davis, and John Womack in that book. The interviews and essays revealed much about an important moment in United States historiography but included nothing unique about the historian's life impact on history itself—they might have been autobiographies of people in Silicon Valley or of literary critics of the 1930s, as they said nothing especially revealing about history and autobiography. And, clearly, my suspicion fattened up on the Mexican version of *Essais d'égo-histoire*, Jean Meyer's *Egohistorias: el amor a Clío*, in which the editor collected the few autobiographical writings available by historians as important to me as Edmundo O'Gorman, Luis González, and Alfredo López Austin. They are also of varying quality: some of the chapters in *Egohistorias* are no more than résumés in prose. In addition, sadly, the volume includes nothing autobiographical by the editor, Jean Meyer, the other interlocutor with whom my suspicion traveled to cherished encounters with my people of Michoacán and with the Paris of the 1960s, and to memories about a history teacher, André Meyer, Jean's father, in Alsace and in Provence, during World War II and in the postwar era (Jean Meyer, *Le livre de mon père ou une suite européenne*). Conversing with Jean has been like witnessing those conversations about life and the craft between Jean and Luis González, Fernand Braudel, and François Chevalier—conversations that I in fact never witnessed.

Indulge me a bit more before I proceed to the suspicion's obituary. Allow me to briefly reveal some of my suspicion's more recent favorite autobiographies: Inga Clendinnen's memoirs of the life of history, a method for living, and one of the finest historical imaginations (*Tiger's Eye*); the memoir of my colleague Sheila Fitzpatrick (*A Spy in the Archives*), recollections of the historian's time in the Soviet Union in the 1960s—an autobiography of archives, spies, stories, and intrigue; and *Fireweed* by Gerda Lerner—like Katz, a Viennese Jew who escaped the Holocaust by fleeing to the United States, where she became a pioneer of feminist history. This is an autobiography of the trade's strategies but also of someone who, after writing the history of the feminist consciousness in the Western world, realizes that autobiography is "a questionable enterprise." "One keeps reordering the past," she states, "in light of one's current insights and so what one sets down are not the facts but a story. An explanatory myth at worst, an entertaining tale at best." And that's what Lerner made of her life: a memorable tale of salvation and adventure, a confession from the dreadful twentieth century.

I also remember two "epochal," as it were, autobiographies that cover the life of two different ages of hope: Eric Hobsbawm's *Interesting Times* and Tony Judt's *The Memory Chalet*. They read like self-anatomies of twentieth-century hopes, proving William Hazlitt's dictum: "The season of hope has an end; but the remembrance of it is left. The past still lives in the memory of those who have the leisure to look back upon the way that they have trod, and can from it catch glimpses that make them less forlorn" (*Table Talk*). So the autobiography of Hobsbawm, the English Jew born in Alexandria, incarnates the hopes and disillusionments of the twentieth century. And Judt turns into the historian who, on assembling his life, becomes aware of the assembly of history: "I realized that I was reconstructing—Lego-like—interwoven segments of my own past which I had never previously thought of as related" (*The Memory Chalet*).

Anyway, my suspicion also got fat and began to get sick on the autobiography of the profession in the United States, which Peter Novick wrote (*That Noble Dream*). And then it was nourished by various autobiographies: Tulio Halperín Donghi's *Son memorias*, where my suspicion found delicious notes by a wise man who was going to be a chemist but ended up writing history in Juan Perón's Argentina; the memoirs of Nicolás Sánchez Albornoz (*Cárceles y exilios*), who undertook a film-worthy escape from El Valle de los Caídos and journey to Argentina and New York to devote himself to the rare craft of the economic historian; the recollections of Boris Fausto (*Memorias de un historiador de domingo*); and those of Luis Valcárcel (*Memorias*), which display the historian as *costumbrista* autobiographer and the memorable flavors and colors of Cuzco.

My suspicion, however, felt increasingly betrayed upon reading many tasteless autobiographies by historians. They are memoirs, indeed, but they could have been written by anybody, uninteresting and flavorless, such as the autobiography of R. G. Collingwood (*An Autobiography*) and the many autobiographies by United States historians who have been infected by the post-1990s memory fever. I have the impression that academic autobiographies are now an entire genre, very close to the campus novel: gossip from university halls, a lot or a little sex, overdoses of careerism and ego. They are memoirs already conceived within the post-Holocaust, postlinguistic mnemonic turn, and post–everything else. They have enlarged the size of the "I" out of proportion in the larger scheme of things. They might as well be the memoirs of car dealers or chefs. In the face of so much evidence of nothing, my suspicion lost heart and found no real evidence of how those whose craft and vice is Clio think life and history in unison.

Mexico, of course, went through my suspicion's filter, and it took delight in some notes by Guillermo Prieto (*Memorias de mis tiempos*), parts of *El Ulises criollo* by José Vasconcelos, *Memorias* by Daniel Cosío Villegas (a very interesting testimony but lacking both philosophical and personal depth), and some autobiographical notes included by Jean Meyer in *Egohistorias*. There, in González and O'Gorman, I found something that inspired bastard products of my suspicion, things about life, the historical imagination, and the formation of a style for recounting history. I wrote about that, but my suspicion—alas!—kept on dying.

I was also concerned with taking international Latin Americanism into account, especially in the United States, but found little, apart from Womack's notes. My real and virtual masters—Richard Morse, Irving Leonard, Carlo Ginzburg, Charles Gibson, David Brading, Charles A. Hale, Alan Knight, and Friedrich Katz—did not write or have not yet written autobiographies. Of course, my persistent suspicion got busy deciphering how much of the autobiographical was to be found in their work: Womack, the populist from Oklahoma, and his Zapata; Carlo, the son of Natalia Ginzburg, and his medieval witches: "only many years later did I become aware that my experience as a Jewish child during the war had led me to identify with the men and women accused of witchcraft" ("Our Words and Theirs"). And also the exiled Austrian Friedrich Katz, son of Leo—a populist and Communist who wrote novels in German about peasant rebellions in Eastern Europe—and his own populist hero Villa. The very cultured Morse wrote several pieces that advanced an alternative West, the Iberian Enlightenment, a finding that matched his hopeless eroticizing of the Iberian, fascinated as he was by Hispanic and Lusitanian erudition and promiscuity. The profound liberal Hale embodied the concerns of the best of the mid-twentieth-century American liberal tradition and wrote the most respectful and enduring history of Mexican liberalism. And the lives of Brading and Jean Meyer, whose writings on Guadalupes and Cristeros were marked by their respective Catholic existences.

And thus I finally realized: there is no lucid subgenre of historians' autobiographies. It's just that there are lives that merit being told because they are a magnetic resonance of two things: a stage in the collective historical imagination and a period in humanity's history. And of course that was the lesson of Henry Adams.

Only Turkeys—and Suspicions—Die on the Eve

My suspicion died before its time, just as it had barely managed to exist as a true idea. In effect, I no longer believe there's anything special about historians' autobiographies; as with politicians and scientists, there are good and bad historian autobiographers. What is vital is a life worth telling and the ability to tell it. This is the banal fact that killed my suspicion. In addition, in its zeal, my suspicion discovered that it was already quite a topic. Jeremy D. Popkin wrote *History, Historians, and Autobiography*, in which he makes no mention (as is the rule) of the Spanish- and

Portuguese-speaking world but is at least aware of French and German historiography (Friedrich Meinecke, above all). He offers a conventional consideration of English and United States historiography—nothing about the autobiography of historians from India who wrote in English, such as the excellent autobiography of someone who wanted to be a historian, Nirad C. Chaudri (*The Autobiography of an Unknown Indian*).

Popkin demonstrates that my suspicion merely proved the obvious point that historian autobiographers talk about how they became historians, about their readings, their friends and enemies, rarely about their conception of history as life and craft in concert. I also discovered that Jaume Aurell had dealt with the subject of history and autobiography in memoirs by English and United States Hispanists (*Theoretical Perspectives on Historians' Autobiographies*). But my suspicion did not die the violent death of "the subject has already been dealt with." No, as I've said, my suspicion died of obviousness. I came to conclude that my suspicion--that of the neuroscientist looking in the mirror at the image of his own brain--was not a knowable subject. What in the life of historians explains their historical imaginations? Everything and nothing. How does the disciplined historical imagination grant meaning to our lives? There's no way to know.

Having gotten to this point, to be sure, I could have given my suspicion artificial respiration, with injections from Vico, Henri Bergson, Paul Ricoeur, and Hayden White as well as vitamins from Jacques Derrida and Giorgio Agamben, thus turning the toad into a prince—as if to earn tenure. But it was no use: my suspicion was at death's door, and when suspicions get sick, we must grant them the compassion of a quick and painless end.

Lessons of a Failure

My conceit-filled suspicion died, but something remained: the ability to distinguish the scents of autobiography, history, and relevant lives ready to be told in the air. If Chaudri, like Vasconcelos, was the wannabe historian who ended up being an inspired autobiographer, what about those who have been great historians but above all have lived memorable lives, potential autobiographies slipping into every chat, parenthetical remark, comment, and source? We have all met people who have told us in conversation about a life, a perspective, that instantly reveals a great unwritten autobiography. But I'm a historian, and having wandered about in the historians' small world for quite a while, I've run into colleagues who have left me thirsting for their autobiographies, as though the books I really wanted them to write were the histories of their own lives.

I no longer believe that there is something essential to be found between the historian and the autobiographer, in philosophical or historiographical terms; now I only believe that life offers us few opportunities to know people whose autobiographies would be a necessary complement to our own humdrum lives. Thus, at the beginning of the twenty-first century, Katz was one of those few still alive whose lives embodied the tragic meanings and tremendous weight of the twentieth century in Western history. He told me he would write his autobiography but not in his mother tongue, German; he would do it in English, for his grandchildren. I don't know if he finally did.

I want to return to the original metaphor under which my suspicion was born—that of the neuroscientist—but in harmony with my recollections of conversations with Katz. Because it turns out that there are two parallel lives, the one I read and the one I heard. They are like time capsules that, if they could, would give future readers a good notion of how bittersweet and gritty the twentieth century tasted to us. Katz's nonexistent or unpublished autobiography, then, came together for me with the reading of a great autobiography, not of a historian but of a neuroscientist: Eric Kandel. He was two years younger than Katz, also an Austrian Jew, also wise in the engineering of memory. The work is titled *In Search of Memory*. In effect, the book encapsulates the metaphor that gave birth to my old suspicion, but it's not a metaphor, it's reality.

Kandel is an expert on the brain and on memory, and he pays attention to his own. Katz was a historian who, by way of telling history, made me feel his life; Kandel is a scientist who, by making me see how my memory works, reminds me of the entire weight of the twentieth century, through the autobiography of a science, of a life, of an era. *In Search of Memory* doesn't begin with recollections of the extreme life of a Jew born in 1929 who grew up in Austria. No. It begins with another autobiography, of Santiago Ramón y Cajal, and not with what memory is but what it does. By the way, perhaps my now dead suspicion should come back to life with another proposition—autobiography and neuroscientists—because Ramón y Cajal's autobiographical tales are remarkable (*Recuerdos de mi vida*), as are those of Kandel, Oliver Sacks (*On the Move*), Carlos Castilla del Pino (*Pretérito imperfecto*), and Rita Levi-Montalcini (*Elogio dell'imperfezione*).

Katz and Kandel might have met in the streets of Vienna, where Kandel's father had a toy store. Katz—I asked him—remembered the toy store. But Kandel and Katz fled by different paths: Kandel became a scientist in New York, won the Nobel Prize in 2000, and, like Katz, abhorred the failure of de-Nazification in Austria and missed the old Austro-Hungarian Empire, the tolerant land that had been a family tradition. Stefan Zweig, another Katz or Kandel, described the era before World War II as a golden age, though he wasn't unaware of the fact that it had been a *Traumschloss* (dream castle, *Die Welt von Gestern*). Nevertheless, they all contained something of that golden age.

Katz was *el enamorado de México, el agradecido de México* (loved Mexico and was grateful to Mexico), which granted him and his parents exile from Nazi barbarity. He was the Austrian, the American professor, and, above all, as he once said in his unwritten or unpublished memoir, "one of those without a real country, one of those that fled" (personal communication, 2008). One day I gave him Kandel's book. He was unfamiliar with Kandel, but I told him that it was an invitation to write his own autobiography. We agreed to talk about it once he had read it. But life was no more for him.

Kandel and his family fled to the United States in 1938. The Katzes migrated to Berlin, capital of the German-speaking world, before Adolf Hitler came to power. As for millions of Jews and Communists, the rise of national-socialism meant constant flight for the Katz family: France, the United States, and Mexico, where Friedrich continued his studies at the French Lycée—he couldn't attend the city's German school, the Colegio Alemán, he said, because it was full of Nazis. It was hard for him to socialize at the Lycée with the aristocracy of the *barcelonnettes*,[1] though he spoke French. At least that's what he said—he who felt like a totally assimilated Austrian from a poor Communist family. The flight was a torment and a danger. I asked him to tell me the story a number of times; I didn't mind hearing it again. A young German soldier arrives, looking for his father, Leo Katz, at the family's apartment in occupied Paris. Then tragedy and humanity: the soldier interrogates them, the family lies, stating that Leo Katz hasn't written anything against the Führer, but the soldier leaves saying something like "I don't believe you, but I'm leaving; the next one who comes won't leave without you."

The family looks for a way out in Marseilles and encounters Gilberto Bosques, the Mexican diplomat who helped a number of Jews and Communists flee. Then to Mexico, just as Anna Seghers told the story about similar characters in the excellent novel *Transit*. Seghers was also exiled in Mexico via Marseilles. We had a number of conversations about Seghers and her husband, László Radványi. Katz remembered them in his home in Mexico City. Afterward I was able to confirm in Seghers's correspondence that, on their return to Berlin in 1947, she asked her husband (who remained in Mexico) and Clara Porset, a Cuban pioneer of design in Mexico and the wife of Mexican painter Xavier Guerrero, about Katz and his son Friedrich.

On another occasion I asked Katz about his position on the new German historiography, which finally referred to the German victims, the Russian horrors in Berlin, and the indiscriminate bombing of Dresden and Hamburg. Katz didn't want to read Hans Erich Nossack's account (*Der Untergang*, translated as *The End: Hamburg 1943* by Joel Agee, another one who as a child was in that Mexico of Katz and Seghers), but he did read that book, which relates Nossack's life during the bombing of Hamburg, and we discussed it. Nothing could be sad there except the mind, Nossack wrote (as though he were a neuroscientist), "it's just how it is," because "[the mind] thinks it has wings, but it keeps falling back to earth." "We no longer have a past," Nossack said. "Perhaps we would not feel this so profoundly if there were not people who still have a past from which they derive their standard for tomorrow."

The feeling didn't surprise Katz; for him, Germany had sown terror in all of Europe; what was done in Hamburg and Dresden was not morally justifiable, but it was historically understandable. So Katz believed. Later I read Seghers's letters and understood more. Seghers wrote to Clara Porset from Berlin (June 1947) with the modesty but also perhaps the boldness of those who, like Katz and Seghers, fled and returned and felt but didn't publish: "I'm ashamed to say that I'm delighted (only aesthetically as an artist) by the city's ruins . . . I myself don't say to anyone that each night I'm delighted by those ghostly streets: first, because the Russians were so successful, and second, they give the absolutely perverse or unreal or surreal impression, these staircases that rise to the sky like Jacob's staircase in the Bible and these facades completely empty, that is, burned, where the only inhabitants remaining are the ghosts" (*Anna Seghers: Briefe, 1924–1952*).

The biographies blend: Katz and his elders, exiled German Jews, Communists, the Holocaust, and salvation (Mexico). Kandel makes this joint biography the leitmotiv of his science and autobiography: "One theme of post-Holocaust Jewry has been 'Never forget' . . . My scientific work investigates the biological basis of that motto: the processes in the brain that enable us to remember" (*In Search of Memory*).

Katz told me that Vienna was a city that hadn't been de-Nazified. He told me about his decision to work at the Humboldt Universität in what was then East Berlin and not to return to his alma mater, the University of Vienna. Katz always brought up Austria's sin, with the excuse of some news about Austria or when we spoke of a new Latin Americanist position at the University of Vienna or to explain to me why he had refused to review his file with the Stasi (East German state security service). Equally important is the sense of betrayal in Kandel's parallel life. An example: as a renowned scientist, Kandel was invited to Vienna, to the Ehrenzeichen für Wissenschaft und Kunst, where Elizabeth Lichtenberg, an Austrian scientist in her eighties, approached him. According to Kandel's memoirs, she said: "Let me explain what happened in 1938 and 1939. There was massive unemployment in Vienna until 1938. I felt that in my family, people were poor and oppressed. The Jews controlled everything—the banks, the newspapers. Most physicians were Jewish, and they were simply squeezing every penny out of these impoverished people. It was terrible. That's why it all happened" (*In Search of Memory*). Kandel thought she was joking, but she wasn't. He jumped and shouted, as the calm Katz would have nevertheless done: "Ich glaube nicht was Sie mir sagen!" (I can't believe what you're saying to me!).

The autobiographies of Katz and Kandel, then, although they did not coincide on paper, coincide in their feeling of absolute betrayal. What's more, Kandel explored, as I would have liked Katz to have done, what my dead suspicion wanted to know: memory exploring memory. "How did the Viennese past leave its lasting traces in the nerve cells of my brain?" Kandel asks, as though asking in the name of all those like him and in the name of professionals of memory (historians and neuroscientists). "How was the complex three-dimensional space of the apartment where I steered my toy car woven into my brain's internal representation of the spatial world around me? How did terror sear the banging on the door of our apartment into the molecular and cellular fabric of my brain with such permanence that I can relive the experience in vivid visual and emotional detail more than a half century later? These questions, unanswerable a generation ago, are yielding to the new biology of mind" (*In Search of Memory*).

Of course, Kandel never lived through the second letdown that Katz recounted to me: that of Communist authoritarianism. The Soviet invasion of Czechoslovakia occurred while Katz was on a sabbatical in Mexico. He didn't return to East Germany but instead went to Texas and finally to the University of Chicago, whose authorities had to find a way to wash away the Federal Bureau of Investigation's "Friedrich Katz" file, which identified him as an East German professor. The sparks of autobiography that I heard from Katz mentioned the disappointment of Czechoslovakia and the East German Communist regime without beating around the bush. But Katz took refuge in stories of the kindness of all those who, like his father, like Anna Seghers, and so many others, believed, fought, and saved themselves. The twentieth century passed through his recollections with its full weight, and Katz was given to self-criticism but not to renouncing his elders.

One fine day, I told Professor Katz about reading the biography of another scientist, Juan Negrín, the last president of Spain's Second Republic (Enrique Moradiellos, *Don Juan Negrín*). I was surprised that Negrín used agents in New York to buy arms with Soviet funds in the world's largest black market. "Oh, yes, of course, my father was that agent," Katz replied, just like that, as though it were one more incredible scene from the autobiography that he never wrote. The scene continued: he told me that in *Arms for Spain*, author Gerald Howson asks what had happened to that Leo Katz who foolishly returned leftover funds in the midst of the chaotic final defeat of the Republic. Katz told me that he written to Howson and narrated paragraphs from the autobiography that we don't have: what happened to Leo afterward in France, in Mexico, in Israel.

For the professionals of memory, historians and neuroscientists, as Kandel wrote, "without the binding force of Memory, experience would be splintered into as many fragments as there are moments in life. Without the mental time travel provided by memory, we would have no awareness of our personal history, no way of remembering the joys that serve as the luminous milestones of our life. We are who we are because of what we learn and what we remember" (*In Search of Memory*).

In effect, we are memory, even if only borrowed memory.

If my suspicion didn't get anywhere, it was because History's grand dimensions and the small world of memories only sometimes share an architecture in the writing of an autobiography. Yes, I do believe that when the autobiographer is a professional of memory and has had an epochal black hole for a life, then the coexistence of history and memories becomes an entry point into the engine room of memory. And as is clear, an autobiography is then no longer the biography of its writer or teller but part of the "we" who read it or hear it. But no one, not even I, will miss the suspicion whose fleeting life was told in these pages.

Chapter 7

SIX LIFE STORIES BY HEART

The science of history leaves us uncertain about individuals. It reveals only those points at which individuals were tied to general actions . . . If a book were to describe one single man in all of his anomalies, it would be a work of art akin to a Japanese engraving in which one sees eternally the image of a tiny caterpillar perceived at a precise moment of the day.

MARCEL SCHWOB, preface, *Vies imaginaires* (1896)

[Harold Nicolson's aim was] to put real people in imaginary situations, and imaginary people in real situations.

NIGEL NICOLSON, introduction to *Some People* by his father, Harold Nicolson

1

Doña Guadalupe Aceves Gómez was born in La Piedad de Cabadas, Michoacán de Ocampo, in 1898, according to her birth certificate issued by the parish of El Señor de la Piedad. She died in Chicago, Illinois, at 102 years of age, the victim, she said, of those *aires colados* (unhealthy winds) that were worse, even windier in Chicago.[1] Doña Guadalupe lived in La Piedad until she was twenty-one, when she went to Chicago, promising that she would return. In 1925, when some University of Chicago anthropologists interviewed her in a Mexican barrio on the south side, she explained (all quotations here respect the Aceves's nonstandard colloquial Spanish from the Bajío region]: "Aquí vinemos pa' sacar pa' una casita y pa' poner una tiendita en La Piedad" (we came here to get enough to buy a little house and open a little store in La Piedad). In 1998 Jacky McKean-Aceves, Guadalupe's great-granddaughter, wrote her undergraduate thesis on Mexican Chicago for the Ethnic Studies department of the University of Illinois. Jacky interviewed her great grandmother, asking: "Mama Lupe, you always wanted to go back to Mexico?" Doña Guadalupe responded in the Spanish of the Bajío (she never learned English): "pus claro que quería regresar a La Piedrita, pero ni ansina cuando echaron pa' trás a tantos mexicanos mi marido perdió la clientela de panadero, y pus luego las criaturas nacieron aquí y aquí se criaron, y bueno pa' cuando teníamos dinero pa' irnos ya no teníamos salud pa' l viaje y pus aquí se nos arrejuntaron los recuerdos y aquí nos amuinamos."[2]

Doña Guadalupe's people were campesinos at *rancherías* around La Piedad. Feuds between two families—with deaths on both sides—led the Aceves to move to La Piedad, where Guadalupe's father worked in a mill that ground corn for tortillas and her mother worked as a cook in the homes of some of the small city's wealthier families. Guadalupe left school after the third grade, learned to read and sort of write, and at seventeen became engaged to Agapito: son of the *churrero* (the churro man) who had a stand at the corner of the parish church on Calle Dieciséis de Septiembre. He was an unusually *aguzado* (sharp) young man, a great musician, and a very devout Christian, the favorite altar boy of La Piedad's Señor Párroco (the parish priest). He used to play the organ and guitar at Sunday masses, though Agapito, trickster that he was, made money on the side playing the guitar in cantinas. They came from a family of self-taught musicians who played gigs (*jalaban*) for lower-class weddings in La Piedad, Santa Ana, Churincio, Numarán, and Pénjamo. They also performed at religious fiestas and participated in the Catholic organizations that were involved in the first Cristiada rebellion (1926–1929). Agapito carried a rifle for a few months, and before long he had to hide out in *rancherías* and towns nearby: "árboles de las barrancas" (trees of the ravines), sang those who waved the banner of "Cristo redentor" (Christ the redeemer), "¿Por qué no han enverdecido? Por eso calandrias canten o les apachurro el nido" (Why haven't you turned green? Sing, larks, or I'll smash your nests). But their courage didn't last, and they had to flee.

Doña Guadalupe told her great-granddaughter: "¡Uy!, me quedé rete enamorada de tu Tatapito, no es que fuera guapo, pero pus cantaba rete bonito, con harto sentimiento . . . ¡ay diantre de Agapito!, ¡cómo me chiviaba toda con su 'Perjura' y su 'Viejo Amor' que 'ni se olvida ni se deja!' . . . ya ni mi hablis criatura que nomás se me agüita el alma."[3] Of course, Guadalupe's father was opposed to the relationship, but there was no need to ask for permission. The federal army prowled through the area in search of Catholic rebels who participated in the Cristiada. The parish priest sent Agapito to someone who took people to Texas, where Agapito had an uncle who worked in the cotton *pizca* (harvest). The boy left town and went north. Guadalupe was soon receiving letters daily; meanwhile, she helped out in the San Francisco barrio church, participated in patriotic neighborhood "queen" contests, and watched her tiny city grow.

To her great-granddaughter Doña Guadalupe recounted the news she received from Agapito: he had moved to Chicago to work in a meat-packing plant. They had hired him in Texas and paid his fare to Chicago. Agapito went with two friends, with whom he had formed a trio that played for small audiences in the Mexican barrios around San Antonio. Agapito explained to the Chicago anthropologists in 1925:

> Me vine huyendo de la guerra de allá, en La Piedad, cuando los federales mataron a un tío, y el señor cura me presentó con un señor que acarreaba gente pa' Texas. Ya acá seguí con la guitarreada y pus le entré al oficio del pan. Cuando me vine pa' Chicago a trabajar en la empacadora, me di cuenta de que la cosa estaba re fea: los morenos no nos querían, los polacos menos, quesque porque les rompíamos la huelga; a mí no me gustó nada la cosa, y como ya le hacía al oficio de la guitarra y del pan, pus me fui a ver a un paisano que trabajaba en una panadería de esos alemanes raros, quesque son judíos, y ahí me puse a trabajar hasta que el paisano y yo vimos que había harta gente que quería sus cemas de Numerán, de ésas bien migajudas, así que por las noches nos pusimos a hornear pan en el departamentito que teníamos, y por las mañanas lo vendíamos entre la paisanada. Luego mandé trai a mi mujer pa' enseñarle el jale y así con ella y otras comadres hicimos pan en casa pa' vender.[4]

Don Agapito learned basic English to get around; by 1940 he had survived the Depression and was the owner of a Mexican bakery in Pilsen. And, indeed, one day he mailed a letter to Guadalupe: "I'm sending money for the trip so that you can come here, I've asked a priest to marry us."

Doña Guadalupe told her great-granddaughter that against the wishes of her mother, the priest at San Francisco church, her father, and her friends she took the train and left, with the blessing of El Señor de La Piedad, the town's patron saint. It was a scandal. She knew it would be difficult to go back. But Doña Guadalupe never told her great-granddaughter what she told her interviewers in 1925: "[M]e mandó decir mi comadre Leonor, que ya tenía su tiempo en Chicago, que había mucha güera polaca acá y que pus el Agapito no les hacía el feo, verdad, y que ya el hijo del carnicero del barrio de San Francisco había tenido una criatura con una de esas polacas, así que me vine a Chicago, pus 'hora sí que por lo que era mío, ¿no?"[5] Agapito had told the anthropologists that the Polish women had "solid foundations" (good legs), but for marrying there was nobody like a Mexican woman. Besides, he had to teach the trade to his wife so that the business they were setting up would prosper.

During her years in Chicago, Doña Guadalupe celebrated Mexican civic and religious fiestas and spoke Spanish with everybody, although her grandchildren didn't respond in Spanish. Her great-granddaughter learned Spanish at the university, thanks to her interest in recovering her people's memory. Doña Guadalupe became a United States citizen in 1950. One son fought in the Korean War and received a medal for his excellent service. In Doña Guadalupe's home, therefore, the United States flag flew on July 4 and the Mexican flag on September 16. The walls were covered with memories that had no fixed fatherland.

Don Agapito learned the boleros that were played at the local cafés and record stores, but before long only the old folks listened to his songs. He took to composing corridos inspired by the one he liked so much, "Valentín de la Sierra." One of Agapito's corridos, popular in Pilsen in the 1940s, goes like this:

> De qué sirve saber mi oficio
> Si fabricantes hay de a montón
> Y en tanto que hago yo dos bolillos
> Ellos se avientan más de un millón
>
> Los hay más prietos que chapopote
> Pero presumen de ser sajón
> Andan polveados hasta el cogote
> Y usan enaguas por pantalón
>
> Hablar no quieren muchos paisanos
> Lo que su mamá les enseñó
> Y andan diciendo que son hispanos
> Y renegando del pabellón.[6]

Oh, well, one fine day, the great-granddaughter asked Doña Guadalupe, "Mama Lupe, what do you feel like, a Mexican or a *gringa*?" The old woman responded: "Ay, m'hijita pus qué queres que te diga si soy de La Piedrita, de noche la cabeza la tengo allá y de día se borra todo y estoy aquí, pus uno no se olvida de esas querencias de criatura, pero cuando voy pa' La Piedad ya no me hallo allá, todo está tan cambiado, y uno es el recordadero de los que uno quere, criatura del Señor, y lo que quero está aquí, m'hijita, mira, aquí estás ¿no?"[7]

"You wish you had never left La Piedad, right, Mama Lupe?" said Jacky, her head probably filled with Ethnic Studies courses. Doña Guadalupe responded, "¡Ay, no m'hijita¡, ¿qué estaríamos haciendo 'horita en el pueblo? ¿De criadas de los Álvares como mi mamá? ¿Gente sin coche y sin casa, sin educación? Ondi crees, no m'hija, lo de allá todito se me quedó como los rezos, puras recitadas de recuerdos, pero . . . pus aquí ensina juntos y bien . . . ¡Gracias Padre San Francisco! ¡Gracias mi Señor de La Piedad!"[8]

2

Juan de López y Lara was born in Mixcoac, near Mexico City, in the early seventeenth century. A descendant of Nahuatl-speaking indigenous nobility, Don Juan studied with various priests in Tlatelolco; he was never ordained. Instead, he taught holy Latin and cultured Nahuatl, while at the same time administering the small farms his family had in Milpa Alta, those fertile and well-tilled soils that produced vegetables to supply the growing Mexico City market. The farms produced very little income and lots of trouble: there were constant disputes with the Milpa Alta indigenous communities, whose residents claimed collective land use on the basis of centuries of working the land that Don Juan de López considered his personal inheritance. Don Juan spent his last forty years in litigation before the courts of New Spain, claiming the properties that, to his way of thinking, belonged to him due to his noble indigenous lineage and the edict that his majesty Emperor Charles V handed down in the sixteenth century in recognition of the privileges granted to the "de López" family for services rendered to the emperor and to Christendom. In any event, competition from the many indigenous communities, whose production was increasing in response to demand from the city, put an end to Don Juan de López's small business. The man died in relative poverty, in his home in Mixcoac, in the terrible year of 1692, when on top of poor harvests, hunger, and speculation, the news came from Mexico City that the rabble was rising up. He died the summer of that year, a few days after the riot, and never knew that the uprising had been put down not by the viceroy's palace guards but by priests who went out with the sign of the Holy Cross, calling for order and peace.

Don Juan married the daughter of a Spanish bureaucrat because, in spite of his noble lineage, he had no riches to offer. His wife, Doña Cleotilde, made up for her relatively low ancestry by being a creole descendant of the first wave of conquistadors. The couple's many offspring chose various professions: among them were priests of small parishes, officials who left no mark, colonists in the lands of Nuevo Santander, wives of bureaucrats, and a mystical nun who imagined that due to a divine gift she could speak the language of her ancestors—which she hadn't learned from her father— to communicate with Quetzalcoatl, who was none other, the nun claimed, than the Sacred Heart of Jesus transubstantiated.

To survive with so many offspring, Don Juan had to engage in law-suits against the indigenous communities that he considered enemies of his lineage and his rights, irreverent plebeians, penniless people protected by local priests. Only the dirt-poor Otomís from Mexico City disgusted him more, speaking that degenerate Nahuatl. He had good relations with the city's creoles, but he knew he was not considered their equal, not even by that wise man Don Carlos de Sigüenza y Góngora, who used to come to him with questions about the language of the indigenous people and the figurines that the wise expert on indigenous affairs collected. Don Juan thought of himself as a subject of his Catholic majesty, whom he had served faithfully, like his ancestors, the de López family, and only regret-ted that his privileges were endangered by local intrigues. The man was aware of his options: he was neither a creole nor a common Indian who could live on Indian *parcialidades* (community-owned barrios and lands), with his books, his readings in Latin, Spanish, and Nahuatl, and his circle of well-read urban friends. No, he was certain that he was meant to serve God in the best way possible and to study the institutions and the lan-guage of his ancestors in depth, all of which, in the long run, would dem-onstrate the intrinsic nobility of the de López family. His struggle was against the forgetting that would erase his nobility and his language.

What concerned Juan de López were books and literature. His library grew at the expense of his household and wardrobe needs. Among his childhood memories, Don Juan treasured the conversations his father had with various Nahuatl-speaking wise men, in which the name of Don Fernando de Alva Ixtlilxóchitl always came up. Now no one was left from that wise, Nahuatl-speaking generation, very few struggled to continue studying their ancestors and their language. It was a lot to ask that a single memory, Don Juan's, keep those of so many others alive. Those were bad years, in which Christian universalism had turned him—an hidalgo—into the equal of those irreverent Indians who were protected and egged on by priests and local chiefs, bilingual *principalitos* (little chiefs) who didn't really know the Nahuatl language: their bilingualism made it possible for them to intermediate and thus maintain their power. Christianity in America, Don Juan believed, had forgotten its creators, men of his lineage.

Though he wasn't a creole, like Don Carlos de Sigüenza, Don Juan also hated Indian pagan idolatry. But he didn't share Don Carlos's antiquarian curiosity. Juan de López didn't believe that studying the past would lead to erudite conclusions about the roots of the Mexican people—a term that Juan de López used only to refer to the history of the Triple Alliance (a powerful confederation formed by Mexico-Tenochtitlán, Tetzcoco, and Tlacopan in the Anáhuac Valley)—the last Mesoamerican confederation before the Spanish arrival. No, he believed that the study and promotion of the indigenous language and past would bring universal recognition of an equally universal culture and language, which explained why hidalgos like himself, just like the creoles, belonged to the natural category of *principales* in the kingdoms of his Catholic majesty. His was memory in the service not of curiosity but of restitution.

Don Juan spent his life studying these matters, lamenting the disappearance of the intellectual life of Nahuatl, and fighting for his properties. These efforts provided regular sustenance and made him what he was: a bitter and devout Christian, his majesty's subject, with remarkable knowledge of sacred history, Latin classics, pre-Hispanic history, and the imperial law of lands and Indians. He was more comfortable discussing the lost tribes of Israel or the last Aztec emperor than the fracas over Juan Diego. When he died, his children sold his books, which bore a strange ex libris made up of emblems of the crown of Castile and sacred Mexica motifs.

The last time a book with such an ex libris was discovered was in the Nettie Lee Benson Latin American Collection at the University of Texas. It was a volume from the collection of the nineteenth-century Mexican sage Joaquín García Icazbalceta, which the University of Texas had bought in the early twentieth century. A curious note: today some Texans descended from the de López family claim to be "chicanos de Aztlán," via the family line of Don Juan de López, whose son colonized Nuevo Santander. They claim to be bearers of Don Juan's memories and indigenousness. Given United States legislation on memory, diversity, and the rights and customs of the Native peoples of Texas, the descendants are now demanding the return of Don Juan's books and a settlement, because they, who embody the forgetfulness that Don Juan feared (they no longer speak Nahuatl or Spanish), claim to be members of a twofold minority: "Native American" and "chicanos de Aztlán" within the United States identity politics (where such lineage takes on meaning). They say that they pray to the earth goddess and not to Western gods. That is their *jale* (gig), not the mission that Don Juan de López so eagerly pursued.

3

Epifanio Martínez, El Chilchota, was born in the second half of the eighteenth century in Chilchota, as his nickname indicates, in the valley that is home to eleven Purépecha towns, namely, Urén, Tanaquillo, Acachuén, Santo Tomás, Zopoco, Huáncito, Ichán, Tacuro, Carapan, San Juan Carapan, and, what else, Chilchota. These were prosperous and Christian lands of indigenous peoples assimilated to the Bajío agricultural region, areas with large mestizo populations. El Chilchota, as is evident, was very proud of his origins; wherever he went, he demanded to be addressed by his nickname: El Chilchota. He was the bastard son of an Indian mother who never spoke Spanish and a cacique father who never gave his name or much of anything else to his son. El Chichota grew up poor, like almost everyone in town, but never hungry. His mother sold *corundas de ceniza*, a type of tamale, in the market where El Chilchota grew up, among the bloody sights of pork bellies and bull tongues, surrounded by the welcoming smell of *acociles* (freshwater shrimp), nopales, cilantro, and *papaloquelites* (herbs). He learned Spanish quickly while carrying bags for mestizos who went to the Chilchota market in search of local products, people from Zamora and La Piedad. This child cargo-carrier would end up leaving town, overwhelmed by misery, abandoned by a mother who died during the birth of her second child, but he would return to spend his last years as one of the town's small landholders. He died in the late 1820s, leaving behind offspring from Urén to Chilchota and a house full of treasures: old documents signed by kings and viceroys granting community-held lands to the "natives of the region who in the language of these people, faithful allies of his majesty, are called Xilxolca or Xilxota." Among his mementos were also torn uniforms from the royal army, flags from the Three Guarantees army and, the item most treasured by El Chilchota, a commemorative coin with the effigy of Agustín I, emperor of

Mexico—"mi mero patrón" (my true/real boss), El Chichota said at the end of his life to anyone who came to his doorway for a chat.

El Chilchota went first to Valladolid (Morelia). He felt trapped in Chilchota by the stigma of his illegitimacy, by his exclusion from political and parish posts, by the absence of any type of recognition in the church or in planning for the annual fiesta. The town's patron saint was none other than Saint James, the same saint venerated from Lisbon to Guanabara Bay. Nevertheless, El Chichota was not excluded from paying town taxes with his labor. Chilchota's Indian authorities were constantly quarreling with the owners of La Gavia hacienda, who claimed legal rights to village land. El Chilchota, a smart and ambitious kid, could not see himself following in his mother's footsteps or involved in the town's long quarrels; though he spoke Spanish, he could not read or write and had no land or title to defend.

In Valladolid he found shelter in what seemed to him an enormous market, where sturdy porters could always find work; besides, there was never a shortage of tacos, *atole* (a drink made from boiled maize), or good *charanda* (a liquor made from sugarcane). He became one more *lépero* (member of the urban poor) in the city of Valladolid until regular service for a client, the head groom of the powerful Iturbide family, took him to meet young Master Agustín. He worked in the home of the Iturbides and watched young Agustín grow; for his part, Agustín enjoyed El Chilchota's sayings and companionship. Little by little, besides being responsible for feeding alfalfa to the Iturbides' many pure-bred horses, El Chilchota became a kind of nanny to young Agustín. When Agustín went off to military school, El Chilchota became the trusted servant of the house. Of course he became a devoted Catholic, which the mistress of the house appreciated; when the uprisings led by Miguel Hidalgo and José María Morelos began, he served as a messenger among the best families of Valladolid, going so far as to deliver gunpowder from house to house, because after the massacre of Spaniards in Guanajuato, it was necessary to be prepared. First a defender of the king and the church, he became a defender of Mexico and its emperor.

His luck changed when Master Agustín had him called to Mexico City to serve in his new imperial residence. El Chilchota was given a uniform that was hard for him to wear—he was used to *calzones de manta* (the white trousers worn by Indians); moreover, his master granted him ranks that he couldn't even pronounce. Don Agustín took him on his military adventures in the southern sierras. The emperor supplied him with horses and mules that El Chilchota put to work transporting merchandise from Mexico City to San Ángel, Milpa Alta, Coyoacán, and Xochimilco. He was with his master on the day Agustín de Iturbide went into exile, but he didn't board the ship; Don Agustín asked him to stay and take care of his house in Mexico City. And there he stayed until the family members of the frustrated emperor returned to bury Don Agustín, after his execution in Tampico. El Chilchota then decided to go back to his town with the savings he had from his mules, storehouses, and speculation on grain during every uprising.

He bought plots of land from creoles and mestizos impoverished by the wars of independence and spent his days telling stories, chasing women, and working his land with the help of peons he hired in the markets of the villages in the ravine. As a small landholder, he was visited by the town councillors, who requested his support in the new struggle for land, now before Mexican courts. El Chilchota boasted about his contacts and his important friends in Mexico City. He sent a child messenger to Valladolid in order to ask Don Agustín's old head groom to hire a city clerk to copy the deeds to Chilchota landholdings in the chaotic record offices of Valladolid and Mexico City. The head groom, by then the closest thing to a member of the bourgeoisie in the city of Valladolid, did more for El Chilchota: he hired a shrewd individual, who, taking advantage of the bureaucratic chaos in the aftermath of the wars of independence, could take care of any bureaucratic task for a price. It didn't cost much to buy from him all the deeds issued by the Viceroyalty of New Spain for the town of Chilchota. And of course they became El Chilchota's prized possessions.

The town hired a notary to write a new defense of its lands against La Gavia hacienda. El Chilchota, of course, furnished the notary with ideas he knew by heart: the seventeenth-century deed read: "We, the natives of Xilchota, the real and faithful servants of your royal highness and may God keep your majesty in His holy glory, declare that being the natives of these lands, the lost tribe of Israel, and descendants of the faithful vassals who served your majesty in the conquest of the Indies for the greater glory of God and of your majesty, ask that you grant us as property the use of our lands." If that was what the documents said, El Chilchota suggested: "You, write this down: We, the natives of these lands, are the true Mexicans, the very first natives of these lands, and therefore we are the original and only valid protectors of the Mexican nation, and as a result the Mexican nation owes us."

El Chilchota died without knowing how the dispute was resolved. As an old man, he was heard talking with the porters in the market: "[E]n este mundo, chamacos, al único que hay que servir es a Dios, y ése con su copal y sus misas tiene bastante, y d'ahi pa' l real hagan lo que sea pa' arrimarse un su maicito" (In this world, boys, you only have to serve God, and He's more than satisfied with incense and masses, and apart from that do whatever you have to do to get your cob of corn).

4

Isaac Yacob Kaminski was born in 1900 in a village near Lublin, Poland. For more than half his life he was known as Jacobo Camino, the name he took as soon as he found out, on his arrival in Mexico City in 1919, that *veg* (path) in Yiddish was *camino* in Spanish. He could not have found a better name, he thought: he was merely *un camino*, a walk from Lublin to Warsaw, from Warsaw to Berlin, from Berlin to Hamburg, from Hamburg to New York, from New York to Mexico. The civil wars that came on the heels of the Russian Revolution, the Spanish flu, the agricultural collapse during World War I, and the consequent outbreaks of anti-Semitism had led him and his family to look for a way out in America. Some went to the United States, others to Brazil and Argentina. One fine day Jacobo, following in the footsteps of some distant relatives in New York, ended up in Mexico. He figured it didn't matter which port the ship called at, he would make his way to New York City. He made his own *camino*: he became Jacobo Camino.

Truth be told, Jacobo fled as much from exhausting work in the fields as from the flu and anti-Semitism. He grudgingly followed the rabbinical teachings of his paternal grandfather and learned Hebrew and Polish besides the Yiddish they spoke at home. He didn't want to be a rabbi like his grandfather and his older brother, more because of wanderlust than because he didn't agree with the teachings of the Talmud. Ever since adolescence, Jacobo liked to take on small jobs to earn a little bit of money, which he shared with his family, and also used to party and chase peasant girls of all sorts. Reading letters from relatives in America, he imagined himself trying his luck, leaving the village and getting his family away from the periodic famines and persecutions. In fact, he didn't plan it at all: recommendations from an uncle, the insistence of a cousin, and the possibility of visiting Berlin sent him down a path of no return.

When Jacobo reached America, the first news he received was that he couldn't go ashore in New York. He was not given permission to enter the United States—the immigration quotas were filled—but he was told he could go to Mexico, stay there for a time, and then try to emigrate to New York. Jacobo had no idea what or where Mexico was, but he and an acquaintance came up with an idea: the two of them headed for Mexico. On arriving in Tampico, they considered walking to New York, certain that nothing could be that far away from anything else in America. Soon reality set in, and they found other immigrants in the same circumstances in Tampico and met an acquaintance from Lublin who had an "in" with an industrial livestock man in the area. They were there for a month, tanning hides, until they heard from a fellow countryman in Mexico City who urged them to go there. He told them about the electric lights, the streetcars, the markets, and the prostitutes. "It's ugly, but here nobody will call you a *Jud*," the man wrote from Mexico City.

Jacobo got to Mexico City in late 1919, to Tacuba Street, where a mutual aid society for Jewish immigrants was just getting off the ground. There he received his first bits of advice and a little money to make it through those first days. Jacobo was surprised: the color and smell of the people, the hubbub, the poverty, the wealth, the great churches, and the modern automobiles. Soon he began to sell holy cards with images of saints door to door in the barrio of La Merced and surrounding areas behind the National Palace. On Licenciado Verdad Street he heard people speak Yiddish, Polish, and Arabic; soon he had a group of friends and a small business selling fabric remnants in La Merced. Customers called him *el alemán* (the German): "Momma!" shouted a little girl when Jacobo knocked on the door of a house, "here's the German asking for his payment." Soon Jacobo realized that in Mexico being called a German was better than the rude shout closer to the truth ("Here's the Jew, he says you should pay him!"). And Jacobo got by with his little notebook full of names and the few Spanish words he knew. When he managed to save some money, he left the small room in the neighborhood where he had lived and began to try to bring his family. But the fare was expensive, and his parents and rabbi brother were reluctant to travel.

Jacobo's fabric remnant business prospered little by little. Come to think of it, this was a miracle unlikely to be repeated: poor salesmen who extended credit to poor customers based solely on trust. And it worked, that was the miracle. In any event, for Jacobo the important thing was not business but marriage. Another miracle: he managed to marry a Jewish woman from Bialystok whom he met during his walks through Mexico City. It was never clear to Jacobo's children or grandchildren how Ruth (that was his wife's name) had come to the city. When Jacobo entered her life, she had been there for some time, working at jobs that Jacobo himself never spoke of. The only memory that for generations has circulated in the Camino family is the anecdote about the miraculous coincidence of a young man from Lublin meeting a young woman from Bialystok on Cuahtemotzin Street in Mexico City. (Cuahtemotzin was then known as a red-light district.) The couple got married in the new synagogue in the city center; they moved into a small maid's apartment on Bolívar Street. And Jacobo continued with his fabric business, with Ruth helping, even after the birth of their first child, who spent his first years among fabric for brides' dresses and leather for sandals, among the strident chatter of Gallegos (Spaniards from Galicia) and the sweet echo of Spanish spoken in different accents: Arabic, Yiddish, Chinese, and the plebeian singsong of the city that would later be stereotyped in the movie *Nosotros los pobres* (We the Poor, 1948).

The Camino family moved from Bolívar Street to a comfortable apartment in the Condesa neighborhood in the mid-1930s. And it was exactly then, when things were going well, Don Jacobo recounted, that two serious problems that would decide the rest of their lives "came home to roost": on the one hand, the dreadful news from Europe, the efforts to get his brother out and to save relatives and friends; on the other, a local campaign against Jews, Chinese, and Lebanese led by politicians on the right and left in Mexico City. The campaign died down little by little, though some days they didn't open the store for fear of the yelling, stone throwing, and looting. Jacobo and other foreign businessmen in La Merced managed to arrange a meeting with President Lázaro Cárdenas, who promised to protect them. He didn't necessarily keep his promise, but before long the petty second-rate politicians were gone, and Don Jacobo returned to his business and to his central concern: to convince his rabbi brother that the community in Mexico would continue speaking Yiddish and follow Jewish customs and that he himself, a cultured orthodox rabbi, was needed in Mexico City. Jacobo failed. He never saw his brother or the rest of his family again. As the only member of his immediate family who was still alive in 1950, it was forever clear that Mexico had saved his life in 1919 without his even knowing it. A tragicomedy of miracles.

Ruth and Jacobo had three sons, all three prominent in their fields—one was a businessman, another a scientist, and the last an architect. By the late 1960s the couple had closed their store in La Merced and lived in Polanco in a comfortable apartment paid for by their children. The frequent gatherings in old Jacobo's home were a potpourri of accents and views: old merchants, shopkeepers, and porters from La Merced who attended the parties organized by the Caminos, with whom Ruth and Jacobo shared their memories in the Mexican Yiddish of La Merced, while their grandchildren, dressed to the nines, held forth in another corner in their hipster Spanish, as though wealth were the destiny of their people, as though it had always been thus and would be forever. Each group at the parties had memories of its own private Mexico. Only Jacobo and Ruth could move freely between those Mexicos, incompatible in themselves, that met in the Camino home.

Jacobo Camino died in the early 1990s. He left a memoir written in Yiddish that a niece translated for the family. One passage in the memoir says: "We are Mexicans because we are survivors, and this land is of and for them, survivors, never forget that."

5

Joan Rivera i Montforte
Oral History Project
National Institute of Anthropology and History
Spanish exile
February 10–17, 1974

The interview took place in the home of Señor Rivera, 35 Emerson Street, Colonia Polanco, Mexico City.
[The researcher's questions are inaudible on the tape.]

[Inaudible question]

You see, I was born in the *zona alta* of Barcelona [upper Barcelona] in what they called there a *torre* [tower], one of those large houses of the haute bourgeoisie in the late nineteenth century, on Balmes Street, in old Sant Gervasi, in 1893. But, *niña*, before I go on, what you don't know is that I didn't flee to Mexico once, I did it twice. When I had just turned fifteen, my parents got what they had dreamed of for a decade, that is, an *indiano* [emigrant to America] son, a son in America, although Cuba was no longer an option, and I didn't go to Argentina (which was what they wanted) but to Mexico . . . and well, I left Barcelona in 1908, I fled—"juyí," to say it in the slang they use around here, I "juyí" [laughter] . . . so, the house in San

Gervasi, a big old house that was falling apart, you're not going to believe this . . . it had seen better days. It was on Balmes Street, back then a filthy trail of either mud or dust, depending on the month, and full of rats, fleas, and dogs regardless of the day or the hour. In that mansion, my father, Pere Rivera i Rovira, the family patriarch, ruled over grandchildren, daughters, sons-in-law, a garden, and all kinds of cumbersome ugly things, printing presses, fabrics, drapes, and dresses. Because, see, *niña*, my father was a very down at the heels bourgeois, and all he had left were his literary ambitions, his groups of friends close to the Catalan Renaixença movement [inaudible] . . . The hours he spent in *tertulias* [literary gatherings] and *jocs florals*! Do you know what those were? See, in Barcelona they were literary contests [inaudible] . . . Well, then, I'll get back to the subject and tell me if I digress too much and lose the thread of the conversation, yes. Don't be shy, get me back on course . . . well, as I was saying, my father had convinced me that I would be safe in Mexico from being drafted into the Spanish armies being sent to Spanish Morocco. But the entire house knew that I was going to Mexico to save the family . . . The *indiano* would send back money to restore the Riveras to their rightful place among the Catalan and Catalanist bourgeoisie . . . You see, my father had an enormous longing for the lifestyle of my grandparents, but they were ruined with what happened in Cuba . . . the old folks were Catalans and Catalanists, but they got rich as Spaniards . . . but . . . now I've lost my train of thought again, *niña* . . . Oh, yes, yes, I came to Mexico for the first time in 1908, and what can I tell you . . . if that was an exile, may they chain me to the Angel of Independence [monument in Mexico City] . . . ah, no, in 1908 it didn't exist yet, right? [laughter] . . . *mare de Deu de Montserrat*, if I were to tell you, that was an unforgettable awakening to adult life, what am I saying! It was an unforgettable experience of growing up, you know, *niña*, love, adventures . . . And I was but a lad of fifteen!

[Inaudible question]

No, I was only fifteen, I hadn't gone to school very much, the Rivera house had been my school, there I learned to read and to write in Spanish and Catalan, to recite poetry, to act, to recite the Catalan classics . . . listen, I still remember it: "Escolta, Espanya: la veu d'un fill que et parla en llengua—no castellana" [Listen, Spain: the voice of a son who speaks to you in a non-Castilian language]. And we ended the *tertulia* with "¿On ets, Espanya?—no et veig enlloc . . . ¡Adéu, Espanya!" [Where are you, Spain? I don't see you anywhere . . . Goodbye, Spain!][9] [laughter] . . . I won't translate that, *niña*, you will see that when we are done with these tapes you will be more fluent in Catalan than I . . . The writers and Bohemians who visited my father! . . . From the time we were children, my father had us act, recite, translate . . . I don't remember much about school and less about ideologies [inaudible] . . . No, *niña*, no, at that age one couldn't be on the left or the right, and of course I was the son of a Catalanist family, my father had been a member of the Lliga, one of the first nationalist organizations, and later I would also be a member, we'll talk about that, *niña*, . . . don't let me forget, about Esquerra Republicana de Catalunya [Republican Left], a party in favor of independence and the Republic . . . but for me to be a socialist or a Communist, ha!!! . . . *Niña*, as an unpresentable monarchist but brilliant *emprenyat*, as they say in Catalan, wrote—he and Josep Pla, *niña*, there were few like them—I mean that monarchist Julio Camba said that he couldn't have been a socialist because he couldn't afford it, he was always poor. I came from a sanctimonious family that was in fact totally bankrupt. The thing about Catalanism . . . I don't know, it could be that it was so as not to let go of the last tie that connected us to the well-born families of upper Barcelona, but ideology, ideology . . . hah . . . we had a trade, yes, printing . . .

[Inaudible question]

Yes, of course, of course, some of the old founders of the Lliga faithfully attended my father's *tertulias*, my house was a little center for literary and propaganda publications in Catalan, though the only wealth my father had was some of his friends. I learned the printer's craft there in the house on Balmes. My father, at the far end of the garden, in what had been a stable, had a small printing press that he used to print Lliga publicity, poetry and plays for the Diada de Sant Jordi . . . that's the Catalan fiesta, September 11 . . . the trade was useful the moment I set foot in the port of Veracruz, because there an acquaintance of my father's gave me two things, I remember that well: a train ticket to Mexico City and a letter of recommendation addressed to Santiago Bellescá, a Catalan printer who had an office in the city . . . you see memory is a strange thing, I don't remember exactly where the Ballescá workshop was, but I have engraved here in my mind, as if it were a landscape by the Mexican genius José María Velasco, the trip down on the train from the sierra of Veracruz and Puebla to Mexico City . . . Even today, the way the humid air smelled takes me back to that first impression of the unfamiliar vegetation, and those greens . . . but I'm boring you, *niña*, what was it you asked me? . . .

[Inaudible question]

No, as soon as I got to the Ballescá workshop, when the old man saw that I had no trouble operating the presses, he put me to work printing books [inaudible] . . . because Don Santiago had contracts for a lot of books from Genaro García, who was then in charge of the centennial independence celebration, and we worked day and night to finish the work on time. I lived in a small room on López Street, but the truth is that I slept very little. What I had left over after paying the rent I spent at night in bars, cantinas and . . . don't be frightened, *niña*, but I'm too old for lies . . . well, the truth is I spent time in the cheap whorehouses behind the National Palace . . . A man, *niña*, I had only just become a man! And, of course, I didn't have enough money to send anything back to Barcelona, but I had a great time, or at least that's what I thought. I slept little, worked a lot, and a couple of years went by like that, and it was a before and after for me. Look, *niña*, I was a boy with dreams and I went back to Barcelona a man and an idiot, that's the truth . . .

[Inaudible question]

The Revolution? . . . Now it seems clear to everybody that a revolution started in 1910, I was here in Mexico, *niña*, when all that *merda* began, and nobody heard about that, about a revolution, a revolution, not in 1910 nor in 1911. The first news of the rebellions I heard was at Ballescá's print shop. The old man said that it would pass, that we would keep working, that it wasn't the first nor would it be the last time, that it was like in Spain, just another uprising, that books had to keep coming out, that any government would pay for them . . . But he was smart, and around the middle of 1911 he decided to close his Mexican shop and print all the books he had committed to print from Barcelona. And that's how the years of my youth ended in Mexico, I returned with the Ballescás, because, to be honest, I was scared . . . and I don't regret it, but, but . . . like don Ramón María del Valle Inclán, but without all the comforts, just like him . . . Did you know that Valle was in Mexico City at the end of the 1900s? The cheapskate spent his time smoking marijuana and strutting around . . . So like him I came to Mexico but without Valle's father's money. That Porfirian Mexico was a school of sin for me and for the Marquis of Bradomín [Valle Inclán], but in 1912 I was already on my way back to Barcelona, and who could have known that I would go back to Mexico? But like Valle, I came back to Mexico, but I came to stay. Valle came only for the honors, more weed and whores . . . did you know? . . . he had an affair with Lupe Marín, the one who was Diego Rivera's woman . . . But where were we? . . .

[Inaudible question]

Yes, *niña*, but don't jump to the Spanish Civil War . . . when it began, in '36, I was almost forty, a lot of things happened before that, to me and to the country. When I returned from Mexico, the Barcelona that I had known still existed, but it grew and industrialized quickly; the monarchy seemed solid, but in less than a decade Miguel Primo de Rivera's coup d'état happened, a good thing for business, at least at first, but later . . . And finally we managed to found the Republic . . . a disaster, but I can't complain, those were important years for me. Between 1912 and 1936, I became a successful printer and publicist, I saved the house in Sant Gervasi, I married a niece, much younger than I was, but those things were done back then, *niña*, don't judge me . . . In 1932 I became a city councillor for Esquerra Republicana, and I also managed—why lie to you—to become a prominent member of the Catalan nationalist elite. Why not, I was a successful man on my way up. You see, the Republic, as chaotic as it was, opened new political spaces for people like me, from a family that had been trying to occupy a place that had been lost in Catalan society for a long time . . . My *chamba* [gig, line of work], as they say around here, prospered . . . I was one of the first to do modern publicity, posters, ads in the press, brochures . . . Do you know Anís del Mono? . . . No, right, well, it was a popular liquor and I worked on that publicity, which became an emblem of those years [inaudible] . . . rich, no, not rich, but well, we didn't lack for anything, you hear? nothing . . .

[Inaudible question]

No, *niña*, it wasn't Franco, it was General José Sanjurjo, Franco took over later. During the war in Barcelona things were really bad. Look, by then I was what Barcelona's anarchists and union people would call a bourgeois, and my wife was a Catholic who went to mass every day. Can you imagine us in Barcelona at a time when priests and businessmen were "taken out for walks," that is, killed, every day? . . . The Republican government, no matter how much they wanted to stop it, couldn't . . . Being in Esquerra Republicana helped me, so that they didn't take me for a walk, but it was clear that the nationalists [Franco's troops] would win, and when they did, we knew that things were going to be very bad for us . . . because we were Republicans, because we were Catalan nationalists . . . And so in late '38, I closed the business, and my wife and I left for France. In Perpignan, *niña*, the worst happened: my wife got sick with cancer, or that's when we discovered that she had cancer, because I have always believed that it began in '36, when she vomited a lot and was so pale . . . but, anyway, we were at war, it was difficult . . . and then in France, in the midst of so many refugees, with the great war about to come, a lot of friends exiled in France were taken to prison camps, others left to fight in the French resistance, I stayed to take care of my wife . . . it was horrible, *niña*, just remembering still hurts . . . Mercé, that was my wife's name, she wasn't even thirty years old yet, died on August 14, 1940 . . . but . . . but . . . just a minute . . . I get all broken up . . . that's what we old folks are like, *niña* . . . Well, I took off for Cuba with some acquaintances, but I hadn't been able to get much money out of Spain [inaudible] . . .

[Inaudible question]

Hatred, no, not vengeance either . . . When he was about to die, Paul Valéry said that hatred was most likely to end in error, bad taste, and vulgarity. *Niña* . . . there's nothing I despise more than bad taste and vulgarity . . . starting to hate terrifies me now . . . but when we arrived in Mexico, the hatreds that had driven so many of us out of Spain were repeated in exile. The Catholic Catalanists wouldn't talk to the Republicans; anarchists from all over kept on hating Communists. And then there was the hatred of the Mexicans, because, *niña*, there's now so much talk about love, a lot of oral history and testimonies and things like that, but at the beginning it wasn't like that, not even with General Lázaro Cárdenas . . . I remember the hatred that some Mexican intellectuals had for us . . . the insults we exchanged, because here in Mexico I went into partnership with a Cantabrian in a publicity agency, and as you can see from these shelves all around us, I'm a man of books . . . so I often got together with Salvador Novo, Mauricio Magdaleno, and Alfonso Reyes . . . And, of course, Max Aub, José Bergamín, Pere Calders . . . And there was a lot of gossip, *niña*, a lot of bad feeling . . . I don't hate anymore, and I don't love either. Not like in those years . . . Valéry was right . . .

[Inaudible question]

Would you like a cup of coffee? . . . I have a woman from Oaxaca here who is a great help in my old age [inaudible] . . . What? Ah, yes, you see, I came to Mexico City for the second time when I was more than forty years old, a penniless widower without children, and still a Catalanist. The first thing I did was to look for Catalans exiled in Mexico. I worked for the *Quaderns de l'Exili* with an excellent poet and novelist, Joan Sales . . . if you're not familiar with him, *niña*, you should read him, though I don't know if anything has been published in Spanish, remind me and we'll go upstairs and I'll show you Sales' books [inaudible] . . . what? Ah, yes, I digress a lot, don't I, but what I really like is talking about books . . . then I worked for Costa-Amic, another Catalan publisher here in Mexico, but before long I left the Catalanist circles, *niña*, not because it was impossible to reproduce the *tertulias* that we had had in Barcelona here in Mexico . . . There you have Pere [Calders], who wouldn't mix with anyone who wasn't Catalan . . . but *l'entrepà és l'entrepà* [a sandwich is a sandwich], as they say in Catalan, and you have to work hard at whatever you can get . . . and I went into business with a Mexican and a Cantabrian . . . we set up one of the first publicity agencies in the media . . . And you're not going to believe this, I married my Mexican partner's sister, Graciela Borges, granddaughter of Catalans! . . . She's at our house in Cuernavaca now, she can't stand the winter cold in this big old house, my *torre* in Polanco, though as you might imagine, she's much younger than me, *niña* . . . It had to be like that if I wanted to have children, there was no other way . . . I'm not complaining, she puts up with me shutting myself away with my books . . . and the gang of mad people who visit me . . .

[Inaudible question]

The business went well, *molt bè*, it got off the ground quickly, it gave me what my three Mexican children needed to live properly. I built this immense library for myself, I left the Catalan independence movement, but *niña*, I believe, and this is no exaggeration, that I have the largest library of Catalan literature outside of Catalonia, because I brought all of my father's books and I've bought what's been published in Mexico, Argentina, and Spain . . . because they say that Franco prohibits publishing in Catalan, but now I remember that I already told you that and let's go upstairs and I'll show you all the books in Catalan published in Barcelona in the last two decades . . . but, well, I definitely made enough money to do what I like best, converse and read, my friends are a *colla* [gang] of publishers, exiles, young Mexican readers and writers, and all sorts of bibliomaniacs [inaudible] . . . no, there's almost no one I can speak Catalan with here, my friends are people from all over . . . no, I don't go to the Orfeo Catalán here in Mexico often, . . . *niña*, you have to be very Catalan all the time there, I can do it for a while but it's not my calling, you know what I mean? [inaudible] . . . What? . . . Ah, Aub, he spoke everything, but his Catalan wasn't very good, and what point was there in speaking Catalan with Alfonso Reyes? Better to hear his delicious Mexicanized Spanish, his speech was full of mischievousness, but when he wrote he was almost classic [inaudible] . . . Write, me? No, no way! . . . Friends encourage me to put my *xarradas* [chats] or my thousands of anecdotes and ideas on paper but I haven't written three lines before I get the urge to read something good and I end up with a pile of books at my side and I wind up tearing the blank pages into strips to mark my favorite passages in books . . .

[Inaudible question]

No, nobody remembers me at the Orfeo Catalán in Mexico. We've discussed more Catalan literature in [my] big old mansion on Emerson Street than at the Orfeo in Mexico or Barcelona, but I don't allow purists to come in here . . . no, *niña*, I'm as passionate about my language as I am about Spanish or French. My English is bad, but look, look at that room: the shelves are filled with English poetry and novels. I can tell you, without a doubt, in the twentieth century there have been more and better novels and poetry written in Catalan than in the previous three centuries, but the new production is inseparable from the Spanish, the French, from world literary currents . . . We could talk about that for hours, *niña*, but . . .

[Inaudible question]

Yes, I've gone back to Barcelona a number of times, the first in 1967, to see relatives, to please my wife who missed more than I do a mythical Catalonia that no longer exists . . . I've gone several times since. The Barcelona that I've seen on four or five trips isn't mine. It's not that it's bad . . . *estic farto* [sic] [I'm tired] of all of these old folks here who complain about how much things have changed . . . What did they expect? And if we had won the war—and I don't know what "we" they're talking about . . . the Republican Catalanists . . . the anarchists . . . the Carlist Catholics—well, if we had won the war, would Barcelona have gone on being the same for all eternity? . . . Look, in spite of Franco or thanks to him and his alliance with rich Catalans, the truth is that the Barcelona that I've seen in recent years is a lot better than the one I lived in . . . more light, more color, more comforts, more work, more bread, more European, but also more *xarnega* [referring to descendants from the Spanish interior]. But, look, *niña*, when I meet my friends' children and grandchildren in private in Barcelona, the kids who grew up there aren't as radical—they want democracy, in our day it was revolution—but they're more nationalistic than we were when we were young . . . In Mexico I learned the one about two tits pulling more than two wagons. Normal, *niña*, normal. But if the flag pulls more than bread, something is wrong, *niña* . . . A sign that there is enough bread, and if that's the case, what's all the flag business about? Look, *niña*, flags are like saints . . . they all claim to perform miracles but if you don't pray to them they don't do anything, good or bad. With flags, as with saints, each in its place and to each his own, which is all a religious matter and nothing more . . .

[Inaudible question]

Let's go back, then, if you like, to the Mexican intellectuals. Look, *niña*, Aub laughed at Xavier Villaurrutia because he was a faggot. Salvador Novo at José Bergamín, well, because he was Novo, and Bergamín laughed at everyone because he was Bergamín. Don't believe those tales about brotherhoods among exiles and Mexicans . . . dogs are more brotherly, that is, stray dogs, because when have you seen the fancy ones talking to each other? . . . Here we did well in the long run, since there was no way for us to kill each other, though had there been, we would have gone on killing each other . . .

[Inaudible question]

What do I owe Mexico? Peace, potential, the chance to make a third life for myself, when I was already old . . . but I feel that the possibilities it gave me, it takes away from others . . . I became an exile here and millions from here became exiles in the United States. . . .

[Inaudible question]

Is exile hard? . . . Don't pay any attention to whining old Spaniards, *niña*; of course it's hard but it's not the lack of a country that hurts, it's not even missing some people, or a lost landscape—anybody can feel that without having gone into exile. For me it's not the exile that's hard but knowing that there is no possible exile from here. The Barcelona I knew no longer exists, nor does the Mexico I experienced in my forties, and there's no other way to live than longing for what is no longer nor will be . . . That's what hurts . . . Now there's a troubadour going around among the Catalanists—very good he is, very good—and he sings the one that goes "l'única seguretat, l'arrelament dels meus dubtes" [the only security, the rooting of my doubts]. That's it, that's what I feel . . .

[Inaudible question]

No, I won't leave, because nobody believes that Franco will die, that *torracollons* [*sic*] [motherfucker] is immortal . . . besides, my children, my grandchildren, my wife, my books . . . everything I have is here. I will die in Mexico, but don't expect to hear some cheap sentiment from me about how much I love this land. One shouldn't love the land, but one shouldn't be ungrateful either. I'm fully grateful to the Mexico that opened the world up to me when I was an adolescent, and for the Mexico that allowed me to reinvent another life for myself when I was in my forties and full of old tricks. I'll die here, because my children, my wife, my grandchildren are here. Dying here will be less painful. A Catalan poet, who never left Catalonia and died young of tuberculosis during the war . . . here in Coyoacán we published for the first time an anthology of his poetry . . . so, this poet wrote a line: "Més que el dolor sofert, el dolor que es prepara, el dolor que m'espera em fa mal" [More than the suffered pain, it is the forthcoming pain, the pain that awaits me, that hurts me].[10] I won't translate that for you. After our long *xarradas* this past week, I'm sure you understand, and if not, *niña*, as they say here in Mexico, *te lo afiguras* [figure it out] [inaudible] . . . Mexico is for me today, as it always was, a painkiller that causes some pain but relieves much more. This is where I want to die. If Franco dies first, I'll stay here anyway . . .

[Inaudible question]

Is there anything I want to add? About what? The war? Ah, well . . . I don't know, look, there's a character in a novel by Joan Sales, whom I got to know here in Mexico, a Catholic Catalanist I had never met in Barcelona—I think I already told you about him, don't let me repeat myself, *niña* . . . Well, this character that Sales created is delicious . . . Sagasti, I believe was the character's name in the novel . . . an innate storyteller of all sorts of mad stories and in the novel he appears on the frontlines in Catalonia, on the Republican side, fighting, though it's not clear if he flees to the nationalist side, if he gets bored with the speeches of anarchists, nationalists and Catalan nationalists, Communists and Communistoids, the fact is that he mocks everything . . . but he steals milk from the Republican side to take to his best friend's son. Sagasti is secretly in love with the child's mother, his best friend's wife, he wants to be a notary and believes that he ended up fighting for one side because the war caught him on that side . . . in short, I won't tell you the whole story, but I wish I had had Sagasti's boldness, but then I was a believer, not in Catholicism, but in Catalanism, until I saw the horrors on both sides, and I fled, like the many who fled from one side to the other on seeing the savagery of their respective groups . . . that was the war, a collective horror that nobody knew how to stop. Some won, the rest of us fled, physically or mentally. It's like, knowing the true nature of yourself, never looking in the mirror again . . .

[The transcription of the interview ends with the following note written in red pencil.]

Don Joan Rivera died in Mexico City on February 13, 1984. The National Institute of Anthropology and History (INAH) tried to acquire his library as a donation, but half was sold by Joan Rivera's widow to United States universities and the other half was divided by his children between the Orfeo Catalán de México and the Fundación Josep Irla of Esquerra Republicana de Catalunya.

[Illegible signature]

October 18, 1997

6

Pablo Pérez was born in San Juan Chamula, Chiapas, in 1962, spent periods picking coffee, worked in oil camps in Tabasco, and later returned to San Juan, only to set out for the jungle with some *compas catequistas* (friends who taught radical Catholic social thought) in search of land. He became a Zapatista in the 1990s, rose up to fight for land, and for a few years followed some friends who were close to the Zapatista leadership. Now he lives near Los Angeles and wires money to one of the Zapatista municipalities, whose funding comes partly from nongovernmental organizations and partly from remittances that Mexican emigrants send from the United States. In 1980 no more than 500 *chiapanecos* lived in the United States; in 2000 there were 6,000 and the number kept growing. Pablo is now one of them.

Pablo is not what in Chiapas is called an *indio*; nor is he, properly speaking, a *coleto*. He doesn't speak any variant of Maya Quiché, he's the son of hacienda farmhands, and was a farmhand for years himself. He finished primary school in San Juan Chamula, and when he heard *catequistas* talking about equality and land, he followed them, since the coffee and oil *jales* [gigs] were over. He saw an opportunity to get land in the Catholic revolutionary movement. For a while things were fine, though it was hard work cutting down the jungle and dividing the land. Then came harassment by the military, for the Zapatistas had become both a national-security threat and world media stars. There were the constant visits from foreigners and the international resources that tended to favor the "sexier" settlements close to highways and San Cristóbal but did not reach deep into the jungle where Pablo had his land. There he married a *guerrillera* and they had a son. Realizing that money and aid would never come, he began to look for a way out, precisely when the struggle changed from a leftist land movement into a mystical craze for the indigenous utopia and the Mayan religions.

One day, in San Cristóbal, as he was *pistiando* (drinking) with a *compa*, a Guatemalan who was passing through approached him. The drinking bout with the Guatemalan lasted two days; they talked about the North, about *polleros* and *coyotes* (human traffickers), about work, cars, money, and families; also about Mexican, Salvadoran, and black prostitutes and things like that. Intrigued by the conversation, Pablo asked his friend Jim—a young anthropologist from the United States who worked in Pablo's "community"—about the North. Jim discouraged him, told him that the North was horrible, that he would lose his identity and his customs and that what was important there was who had the best car and the best house; that the trip was dangerous and expensive. Soon the young anthropologist went back to Berkeley with his laptop and his iPad. Pablo still had the itch, his little plot of land, and was struggling every day to make ends meet, to buy medicine and milk for his son.

One fine day, another Guatemalan came looking for Pablo. He was a friend of the Guatemalan that Pablo had partied with. He invited Pablo to go with him to the United States, said he had already talked to a *coyote*, that it cost three thousand dollars, that he didn't want to go alone, that it would be easier with someone from Chiapas if the Mexican army stopped them. Using the deed to his land as guarantee, Pablo got money from an acquaintance in San Juan Chamula, who gave loans at high interest rates. He left with a backpack and a few names and telephone numbers. On arriving in Tijuana, he called Jim—after all, they had been buddies. Of course, Pablo didn't know that for Jim he was an informant and that the long conversations were part of a doctoral dissertation, not of a friendship. He informed Jim that he planned to cross the border the next day: would he meet him in San Ysidro? Jim, though disappointed in his informant, felt a moral obligation, so he went to meet Pablo at a gas station in San Ysidro in his little old Honda. Jim had to wait almost half a day, but Pablo arrived, yellow, tired, and with a Barça backpack. They got into the Honda and headed for Los Angeles.

There Pablo got in touch with various Mexicans, who, not being Zapatistas, were somewhat distant at first; but before long Pablo was standing on a corner waiting for work as a day laborer in the garlic harvest. There he met two other former Zapatistas, and together they went looking for work in a restaurant near Pomona. It was there that, two years later, Jim went to look for him with other anthropologist colleagues. Jim began an interview: Why did you come? What is your reaction to the strange, inhumane, and capitalist world of Los Angeles? Have you seen what the market does to Mexicans (obese consumers of cell phones)? Do you regret your decision? Do you think about your *guerrillera*? Were you an informer for Mexican military intelligence? Do you feel like a traitor to your people?
. . .

Beer in hand, Pablo tells them how hard it has been to achieve stability, but that at least language isn't a problem. Everybody speaks Spanish, but now he's taking English classes and they've promised to promote him when he learns a little bit more. He tells them that his Greek boss is an asshole but that he helps with the immigration police. He tells them that he's bought a *troca* (truck) with a buddy and that they're thinking of driving it to Mexico to bring back their wives. His wife refuses to come. Pablo wires money every month. Temptations? There are many, but a kid is a kid and he has to wire money so that he grows; what he wants to do is bring him so that he can go to school in California and learn English "right now when his little brain is tender . . ."

They say goodbye. Pablo has a gig working extra hours at night. He's paid his debt, and pretty soon he'll begin to build a house in Chiapas, in the outskirts of Tapachula, where his wife has found a piece of ejido land for sale. The anthropologists tell him that they'll put him in touch with Berkeley's Zapatista support group if he wants to contribute to the cause from the United States. Right now, Pablo tells them, he doesn't have time, but when he's finished paying for the *troca* and buying the rebar for the foundation, sure, "there are a lot of *paisas* [fellow countrypeople] who need the three thousand dollars for the trip."

ON LANGUAGE

Chapter 8

POLYGLOTISM AND MONOLINGUALISM

Spanish has been spoken in the United States for nearly two centuries and will be widely spoken for the foreseeable future. Nevertheless, Spanish and its corollary, "the Mexican," have long been the center of a vortex of fears and myths. The language is not officially sanctioned by any university or agency in any state of the Union, though there was no option but to sanction Spanish as one of New Mexico's languages, if only temporarily, when it was finally granted statehood in 1912. Spanish is widely spoken everywhere in a growing number of states; it is the most studied, least well learned second language of the United States. It is a second-class language that makes possible debates on "bilingual education" that are not about all children learning at least two languages but about some "alien" children gradually unlearning their ethnic oral tongue—which, apparently, does not require complex grammar or phonetic instruction. Spanish is the language of the largest minority, and yet a small percentage of this minority, if by minority we mean voting citizens, fluently speaks it or is fully able to use it as a written form of expression at all levels (academic, literary, professional). Most Ph.D. students in American history declare command of Spanish, though very few actually read it or speak it. But then again, who really needs another language to earn a Ph.D. in American history? Beside, we've been told, Spanish is what old German philologists called *mexikanisches Rotwelsch* (the argot of Mexican criminals), used by "rapists" and "bad hombres." All in all, what the City upon a Hill fears is that Spanish is killing English off.

Spanish, thus, is one of the world's most widely spoken languages, with a long and distinguished literary tradition, but it has no cachet whatsoever among mainstream United States literati. A foreman in rural Oregon or a physician in a community clinic in East Los Angeles should be able to mumble it, but not the erudite Princeton professor of English or American or European histories. What a destiny for an old language: it is the most feared language in the United States, yet it is the only one that is believed to be acquirable by either contagion or osmosis—it ain't German, for God's sake, no need to study it seriously. Even in Germany itself—with an educational system that guarantees the knowledge of at least two foreign languages—the recent popularity of Spanish over French as a third language among young people has enraged old German humanists. Recently a prominent German historian of World War I, unaware of my mother tongue, openly commented to me his *Wut* (fury): his daughter was learning Spanish, instead of French or Italian, in her Gymnasium; "Spanish is a mere Italian dialect, she can learn it in the streets," he told me.

Having the historical opportunity to sanction a polyglot society, United States literati and politicians opt to panic about the end of a myth: a monolingual country. Think about the logophobia expressed by politicians in California and a Harvard professor (Samuel Huntington) in the 1990s; the anti-French displays in the tragic aftermath of 9/11; or President Donald Trump's fear of "aliens" who command a larger vocabulary than he does, but in Spanish. Why this logophobia? I'm only a Spanish speaker, I don't intend to teach a thing to the English-only United States . . . other, of course, than its absurdity. To expose the absurdity of the situation, here are some stories of the coexistence of Spanish and English in the United States.

1

In the United States there is no one-and-only form of Spanish in the same way that there is no one-and-only form of English. All conceivable versions of both languages are combined and spoken simultaneously. This is an unprecedented and incredible linguistic and social fact. Many believed that America brought about the end of "proper" English. For Henry James, United States English represented a degeneration of "true" English as a result of too many influences, which explained "the imperfect disengagement of the human side of vowel sounds" (*The Question of Our Speech*). United States English had betrayed the roots of proper English with an indiscriminate use of the letter "r." Nevertheless, nationalist intellectuals transformed the French, German, and Spanish languages, or intonations of the same languages, into the spirits of new nations. United States English, thus, was made into the spirit of democracy. Like Borges's

"The Golem"—"[i]f (as the Greek affirmed in the Cratylus) the name is the archetype of the thing"—patriotic United States poets believed that all democracy, liberty, and equality were embodied, as Walt Whitman said, in "the honest words" of United States English: "Mississippi!—the word winds with chutes—it rolls a stream three thousand miles long" (*An American Primer*).

For American English, the solution to the dilemma of being either the ignoble abortion of an illustrious language or the true language of democracy was furnished by political and economic might throughout the twentieth century. The language hence became today's Latin and all other languages fear its influence and importance. The very history of philology experienced the gradual victory of American linguistics—from the relative marginality of nineteenth-century American philologist William Dwight Whitney (who engaged in public debate with German Oxford professor Max Müller to gain European recognition) to Noam Chomsky's reign as a king of modern world linguistics. But regardless of philological schools, English won. In the last part of the nineteenth century Der Allgemeine Deutsche Sprachverein aimed at finding German equivalents for French concepts—replacing such terms as *physiologie* with the immensity of *Menschenleibsbeschafenheitslehre*. Today's German has undergone a reform in order to adapt the language to the overwhelming presence of English terms. In Spain, in the late nineteenth century, Galician, Catalan, and Basque nationalists banned the incorporation of Spanish words into their respective languages. In 1935 Julio Camba—a brilliant, if reactionary, Galician writer—ridiculed the neologism of a Galician nationalist: if the expression "professors' findings" was *hallazgos de catedráticos* in Spanish, it was *hexádegos de cadeirádegos* in nationalist Gallego—which is musical but unnecessarily baroque. By that same token, in late nineteenth-century Mexico, the dandy Manuel Gutiérrez Nájera, known as El Duque Job, called for an official campaign against English terms in Mexican Spanish, suggesting that the growing number of U.S. entrepreneurs residing in Mexico City learn Spanish. He believed that they were "like Catalans: willing to risk it all, except their language" (*Manuel Gutiérrez Nájera*). But English won: recent canonical dictionaries of the Catalan and Spanish languages have admitted, after long debates, such terms as "piercing," "chat," "software," "cool," and "feedback." Moreover, the parlance of teenagers in many languages is English; the mark of class in all languages is fluency and good pronunciation in English.

Very few welcomed the dominance of English in the early twentieth century. Few were like the polyglot poet at the margins, Fernando Pessoa. "The problem with an international language is about going back," he wrote in 1920 (*A língua portuguesa*). "When we seek this type of language, we are not really in search of something new but rather of something we have lost." Pessoa dismissed the dream of a neutral artificial language (Esperanto, for instance) and declared English to be the triumphant world language. But his conceding victory to English was also a jab at nineteenth-century homogenizing desires. A real man, he said, can only be polyglot: "We concentrate on Portuguese as if this language should be everything; we should not forget, however, that it cannot be more than half of everything ... Using English as the scientific and general language, we will use Portuguese as the literary and particular language ... In order to learn we will read English; in order to feel, Portuguese. In order to teach, we will speak English; Portuguese for what we wish to say" (*A língua portuguesa*). Indeed, Portugal, India, Spain ... all have been Babels of some sort; language pluralism has undoubtedly been contentious, but it has never been an insult as it is in the United States.

English has never been a single language, however; nor has it ever been the only language spoken in the United States. Spanish has been as "American" as *la tarta de manzana* (apple pie). In the 1910s Aurelio M. Espinosa, a New Mexican philologist, showed the rich variations of New Mexican Spanish in tandem with philologists from Spain, Mexico, and Argentina; he collected *romances* from old Spanish oral tradition in the United States. For by the end of the nineteenth century Spanish was as much the language of the southwestern United States as it was of La Mancha and Castile, where the same old *romances* were found. In turn, H. L. Mencken studied the borrowings from Spanish in the English language and had no fear: English would reign, but Spanish had affected English irreversibly (*The American Language*).

Of course, the problem with Spanish in the United States is that, unlike German, Yiddish, or Italian, it just does not go away. Over the years it has become easy to accept German and French influences in English; anyone can be a connoisseur and the dullest person can be said to have a Weltanschauung; the use of Yiddish words is as New York as the *New Yorker* magazine. The influence of Spanish, however, is seen in "no way, José," "guerrilla," "cojones," and "sombrero." Every day new mouths cross the border carrying alien words, and no wall can stop illegal trafficking in words. Despite the fears of invasion by alien words, Spanish in United States mainstream culture remains "fiesta," "siesta," and "cerveza"—a language of janitors, caciques, aliens, a repertoire of words to be used here and there in an ethnic comedian's gag or to deliver commands to nannies and gardeners.

When an "English only" campaign was launched by the governor of California in the early 1990s, the idea presumably was that by decree all sorts of Spanish and Chinese speakers could be left without a voice. And yet who actually speaks the language that Daniel Webster, among others, "Americanized"? Not Mexicans, of course, but not Chinese, Japanese, or Vietnamese either; nor is it spoken in poor African American, Italian, or white neighborhoods. When Samuel P. Huntington (*Who Are We?*) raised fears based on the widespread use of the Spanish language vis-à-vis the American language and "creed," what kind of English did he have in mind? East LA English? I suppose that would not have counted as English for Professor Huntington. Then again, perhaps he was thinking of Tamil or Bengali English, widely spoken in the United States, or maybe Texan English. Or perhaps he was actually referring to the parlance of Nigerians. Hard to say. It may very well be that English is only spoken properly in certain enclaves of the Boston area. And in President Trump's anti-Mexican and anti-immigration crusade, the lack of command of English is a criterion for the exclusion of undesirables. Command of what English? President Trump's English? True, that wouldn't be much to ask.

Spanish has also counted on its "guardians." During colonial times, not speaking peninsular Spanish meant political exclusion, and purists in various countries fought battles against the "Americanization" of the Iberian languages. The Hapsburgs were great pragmatists and forced Indian towns to pray to the Christian God but not to speak Spanish. Friars learned various indigenous languages; some Indian nobles and black intermediaries became bilingual (in Spanish and countless Indian and African languages). This pragmatic bilingualism explains the survival of various indigenous languages until the twenty-first century, creating a New World of Christian polyglots. During the eighteenth century, the Bourbons were centralists, as good French modernizers, and did try to impose Spanish. However, they had less than a century to accomplish it. They indeed defeated some Catalans in revolt (1714), but they did not totally succeed in their project of linguistic homogenization.

The nationalizations of Spanish were gradual but conclusive. In 1874, when the Real Academia Española de la Lengua opened an outpost in Mexico City, Mexican philologists reported on the need to save Mexican Spanish from a threefold evil: Spain's snobbish disdain for *mexicanismos*, the vast influence of French, and the growing presence of English barbarisms. And yet from the times of Sor Juana Inés de la Cruz (seventeenth century)—who played artful word games using Spanish, Nahuatl, and African cadences—to the nineteenth century, Spanish was nationalized in Spanish America in variegated fashions. Ignacio Manuel Altamirano—a bilingual, Nahuatl-Spanish intellectual—made linguistic-nationalist efforts. Logophiles such as Andrés Bello, Rufino José Cuervo, Juan Bautista Alberdi, and Domingo Faustino Sarmiento made local and global Spanish endeavors. Central Mexican Spanish became one idiom, Argentine Spanish another, and so on. However, thanks to great efforts to monitor and protect "high" Spanish, the written language, despite variations, remains more or less homogeneous (linguists estimate a 94 percent level of compatibility among all written forms of Spanish). However, guardians of Spanish still watch over the proper development of the language, making sure our great "treasure" survives all forms of *mestizaje* and English influence.

These guardians, however, subsist today mostly in *academias* in Mexico City, Buenos Aires, Madrid, and other cities. To be sure, they would not last a day in Los Angeles, Austin, Chicago, Santa Fe, or New York, because Spanish has entered a new era in the United States, its 1,002nd—to paraphrase Antonio Alatorre's wonderful history of the language, *Los 1001 años de la lengua española*. The Mexican, European Spanish, Nicaraguan, *potorro* (Puerto Rican Spanish), Argentine, Portuguese, Guatemalan, Venezuelan, Colombian, and Mixteco varieties of Spanish all coexist with various English languages and others in the United States; they are shaping the "how to say . . ." of tomorrow for both Spanish and English speakers.

We may believe that our languages matured for centuries, until one fine day the distillation process ended with a "one-and-only" true vintage English and a "one-and-only" true vintage Spanish, which we carry forward as two monolithic blocks. We might believe that the language of the cold northern European archipelago was in the making for a long time until it emerged as pristine, practical, and beautiful modern English, better than agglutinating German, a new English language infected by verbose French and Latin yet alive and different from imprecise and wordy Romance tongues: a language that is here to stay and forever to be the same.

In Madrid we can be certain that the triumphant tongue of Castile, like Alonso Quijano, El Quijote de La Mancha, will defeat the new dragon,

English, as it apparently defeated Arabic, French, Portuguese, Catalan, Euskera, Nauhatl, and Quechua. We may choose to believe that the victorious blocks of Spanish and English were transported to the United States and the rest of the Americas as solid ice. In reality, just like ice, languages are made of water, currents of liquids that have never stopped flowing and transforming. Even if guardians carry on thinking that they are preserving a solid substance, in truth what they jealously guard is water: an evasive, dynamic, healthy, and ever-changing stream of words and meanings. The cult of monolingualism is a desert to this stream.

Advocates of English only and Spanish purists continue to play a role, but the truth of the matter is that other characters, other perspectives, are necessary to deal with what is going on nowadays in North America. On the one hand, there is the need and the opportunity to make Spanish a first-class language in the United States; on the other, there is the prospect of reviving a certain type of intellectual for the well-being not only of our words but especially of our knowledge: no longer monolingual luminaries but also polyphonic teachers.

Languages will keep evolving in an unpredictable fashion in the United States. English-only proponents will be very busy; fans of Spanglish or some form of ethnicization of the Spanish language will have lots of material to ruminate on. But what would happen if state universities, say, in Texas and New Mexico, were to become major bilingual global centers, in which students and professors, regardless of their ethnic background, would discuss, teach, learn, and produce literary and academic work, in all fields, equally and without distinction in both English and Spanish? Why would it be such a big issue if successful politicians, regardless of their ethnic origin, had to be able to speak and write Spanish in Chicago, Los Angeles, or Miami? What is the problem with having bilingual politicians and intellectuals? To be sure, serious multilingualism, as in Canada, the Netherlands, and the European Union, produces all sorts of political, technical, and bureaucratic difficulties. But so does the obsession with monolingualism. Beside, as it happens, Spanish is everywhere in the United States and things will only get "worse," due, as it were, to an original sin in the cartography of the City upon a Hill. In this context, the monolingual obsession is the closest thing to cultural anorexia.

The change can start at the level of intellectuals and scholars who should abandon their monolingual fears and start considering Spanish as more than an ethnic language that speaks of fiestas and siestas. Intellectually, we cannot underestimate the importance of polyphonic individuals, who, though perhaps lacking one specific fixed language, are at the same time free to cross-pollinate, without fear, carrying meanings from one current to another: experts in reasoning from all angles. But monolingualism has become an unwritten canon in mainstream United States intellectual and academic life. Parochialism reigns, and even recent trans-, post-, and global trends exist only in English and thanks to English. To restrict Spanish clusters of knowledge to ethnic academic ghettos is a natural complement to the fear of this language that is spoken everywhere in the country. The gibberish of monolingual fears feeds the periodic nativist rumbles.

Every language has benefited greatly from polyphonic voices; for instance, it would be difficult for contemporary English to repay its debt for growth in lucidity and succinctness to writers, philosophers, and other intellectuals like Joseph Conrad, George Santayana, Vladimir Nabokov, Czeslaw Milosz, and Joseph Brodsky, along with many South Asian writers who have used English as their prose vehicle, though with many other languages in the background of their thoughts. In Spanish, can we calculate how much of the revolutions in the language of Rubén Darío and Jorge Luis Borges came from their saying too many "un-Spanish things in Spanish"? Fernando Pessoa's choice of Portuguese meant that some of the greatest poetry ever produced in the twentieth century was written in that beautiful language. We owe this simply to the polyphony of this poet educated in South Africa. Paul Celan said that poets can only tell the truth in their mother tongue (*Selected Poems and Prose*). And yet the high standards of truth and beauty that Celan achieved in his incredibly concise but conceptually dense German poems were unachievable without his polyphonic and tragic existence.

In an environment that favors monolingualism, these writers might seem to be useless snobs—and snobs many of them were and are (though no more nor less than monolingual luminaries). But their importance relies precisely on their ability to learn from the many intonations of various languages. They could be as snobbish as Santayana or as ironic as Cervantes, who mocked the low and highbrows of various peninsular languages. They could laugh at today's academic jargons—today's versions of *novelas de caballería* (chivalry novels). In a world that is shrinking, with the fear of languages on the rise, these luminaries become indispensable, as does the need to de-ethnicize the Spanish language.

(Dear reader, a version of these reflections was rejected by a mainstream United States cultural journal—which will remain unidentified.

Rightly so, I am sure, for my essay lacked research, quality, and precision ... But I was told by anonymous readers that my essay had great potential for an *ethnic* journal. I rest my case.)

2

To understand the crossed history of languages in the United States and Mexico, I offer a story that might seem to be pure invention. The reader will decide. I want to tell a story of parallel lives that mitigates monolingual fears.

In 1863 Jorge (George) de Santayana was born in Madrid, the son of a Castilian father and a Catalan mother. Until eleven years of age, he spent his childhood in Madrid, Ávila, and Reus. He learned how to speak like any other child born to Spain's nineteenth-century petty bourgeoisie. We can imagine that he understood his relatives' Catalan; we know that he wrote Spanish. At a very young age, he tried his hand at poetry and wrote a short novel in Spanish while he was also learning English with British teachers. At twelve, we find him in Boston, living among an aristocracy in straitened circumstances, relatives of his mother's first husband and the father of George's beloved sisters. In Boston he relearned English and adopted it for written expression, a choice that he held to until his death in 1952.

In that same year, 1952, a man named—the reader may believe this or not—Sergio "Atila" Guerrero was born in the city of Chihuahua. Until he was twelve, he grew up in the poor barrios of that city, surrounded by an ever growing number of brothers and sisters. From his mother he learned the brave, outspoken Spanish of the *raza* of northern Mexico. When he was thirteen, he crossed the border alone. He settled in East Los Angeles and began to become polyphonic: he spoke the language of his mother and his siblings and more or less wrote it. He learned English and the Spanish of the barrios of East Los Angeles. What's more, he was perfectly fluent in all of them, becoming the star student of the barrio's high school and a leader on his block. At eighteen, he was just another Chicano. He spoke with, and wrote to, his mother in his first language; his mother wanted Atila to go back to Chihuahua to work at the new Hilton in that city with his fluency in what she believed was English. But Atila wrote poems, he was a Chicano *lletraferit* (wounded by letters),[1] but he expressed himself in a Spanish full of *haigas* (*haya*) (have, has), *ensinas* (*así*) (like this/that), and *ensinotas (precisamente así)* (just like this/that). He also knew how to fire volleys of insults with that mixture of the various Spanishes and Englishes of East Los Angeles. He thought he spoke English, the one and only true English. Until his death in 1992, he never forgot his mother's language or that idiom spoken in East Los Angeles.

In 1882 George Santayana began his university studies at Harvard. His father and sister had taught him the refined Spanish that he was fluent in: he understood and was comfortable with works by Miguel de Cervantes and Francisco de Quevedo; he learned Greek and Latin. At Harvard he wrote satirical poems at the slightest provocation, in an eloquent baroque English that his Harvard classmates were unable to place. What was George? British? An English-speaking German? Or simply an eccentric commonwealth millionaire? Santayana at Harvard, like Atila at Yale, came face to face with liberal America, loving and hating it; he accepted that liberal tolerance reigned, "but as you are tolerant of all the kinds and sizes of shoes in a shop window." He held tight to his carefully constructed skepticism:

> [T]he liberal minds were thirsting for a tyrant. I, being a materialist, cynic, and Tory in philosophy, never dreamt of rebelling against the despotism of nature and I accepted having feet, ugly and insufficient as they might be, because it would be much worse not to have them. But as to shoes, I have and mean to keep a free mind, and would be willing to go barefooted, if it were convenient or if it were the fashion. So I believe, compulsorily and satirically, in the existence of this absurd world; but as to the existence of a better world, or of hidden reasons of this one, I am incredulous. (*Middle Span*, vol. 2 of *Persons and Places: The Background of My Life*)

For Santayana, the *Encyclopaedia Britannica* was an indispensable instrument of acculturation. In those years he kept writing letters to his father in Spanish and took summer trips to Ávila, where his father, de facto separated from his mother, lived until his death. In Ávila and in Reus, Santayana was still Jorge, son of Don Agustín de Santayana, the former Spanish government official in Manila. When George finished his BA at Harvard, his father asked him to apply for a job in the Spanish Ministry of Foreign Affairs, where they needed truly bilingual Spaniards. Instead, Santayana traveled to Europe, encouraged by his teacher, a certain William James. He lived in Germany and tried to write his thesis in German, but by then he had made a decision: his language for written expression would be the mixture of versions of English that he had crafted. Thus it was that a Spaniard, like various Russians, Austrians, Poles, and Germans, became one of the twentieth century's most successful English-language prose writers. He was polyphonic in his English, so that he could say, as he stated, "plausibly in English as many un-English things as possible" (*The Philosophy of George Santayana*).

In 1969 Atila Guerrero was accepted by Yale University, thanks to one of the first recruiting programs in the poor neighborhoods of Los Angeles. The reader might doubt this, but believe me, he was one of the first Chicanos to attend Yale. He arrived convinced that he spoke English perfectly and that only his last name and appearance gave him away in the midst of so much whiteness. But soon he realized that the languages he spoke were no help in his new life. He decided to learn English better than any of his classmates, to become so fluent that with a turn of phrase he would be able to reveal not just his own courage, intelligence, and rage but courage, intelligence, and rage in their most intrinsic nature. He achieved the ability to intimidate, brag, and flirt in the English of Yale. I saw (though the reader is free to disbelieve me) the *Oxford English Dictionary* that Atila had treasured since his time at Yale. Its pages were folded, underlined, torn. This was the rule: the first time he looked up a word, he underlined it, and if he needed to look it up again because he didn't recognize or had forgotten it, he underlined it again, this time with greater emphasis. If he had to look it up a third time, he ripped out the page. Strangely, this seems to be similar to the method suggested by legends about Santayana's last years. They say that on a bench in a Roman park, in the early 1950s, an old man could be seen reading and ripping out each page after he had read it. The rumor is that he was reading Plato and that he knew that life wouldn't give him time to read him again.

Atila was a fast learner: by his fourth year he was writing essays and poems in high English, filled with elegance and precision and taking care with words as only someone foreign to them can. On top of that, he learned how to behave at the aristocratic parties of his well-born classmates: he spoke correctly and insulted without giving offense. He didn't know, however, whether he wanted to join the world of his classmates or put an end to it. Quoting Tennessee Williams ("Desire and the Black Masseur," in *Collected Stories*), Atila said, "[W]hen desire lives constantly with fear, and no partition between them, desire must become very tricky; it has to become as sly as the adversary."

But he also added another language to his polyphony while at Yale, from another world: the English of New Haven's poor black neighborhoods. He explained it like this (believe me): "The academic title Yale conferred on me required that I look for warmth far from the coldness and the foreignness of scholarly surroundings. I found refuge in the city of New Haven and its black people . . . It was then that my chameleon-like characteristics began to bloom." After leaving Yale, Atila was able to travel without a passport through various keys of the English language. He said: "I was proud of being able to participate in a congress, get involved in a discussion about how Agamemnon lay dead at the entrance to Troy in a poem by some English poet. But I was doubly proud about being able to party until late at night on Dixwell and Congress Avenue. Those avenues were affectionately known by their black residents as 'Dixieland' and 'The Congo.'" However, he was still fluent in his mother's language, and he called her frequently. Besides, he learned *potorro* as easily as he caught on dancing. In the mid-1970s Atila was a foreigner among foreigners in New York: a Mexican, Chicano, from Chihuahua, from Yale, black, a poet, a yuppie, homeless, a salsa dancer and especially adept at the merengue. He was a product of the seventies who had tried everything and everyone. One day he met a woman, and as Santayana would say, not about Atila but about Oliver, the protagonist of his novel *The Last Puritan*: "He thought, like Don Quixote, that it was his duty to be in love." So Atila got married. There's no reason for the reader to believe this, nor am I going to overwhelm you with the whole story, but the marriage lasted less than a year.

By 1890 Santayana had returned from his postgraduate studies in Germany. He understood German but thought it would be too time-consuming to write his doctoral dissertation in the academy's High German. He returned to Harvard and finished his dissertation under William James's mentorship. By then Santayana's polyphony was so evident that it became a lesson for the cultural backwater that was American academic life. By 1900 Santayana was a professor in Harvard's philosophy department, where he shared an outstanding reputation with his teachers William James and Josiah Royce. His fame as a philosopher and essayist grew. But success seemed to bore him. He became completely fluent in the language of Boston, of Harvard, of the academy. He felt empty, because for him the United States was a vacuum, not only physically, but "the moral emptiness of a settlement where men and even houses are easily moved about, and no one, almost, lives where he was born or believes what he has been taught" (*Character & Opinion in the United States*). In the early 1930s he wrote to his sister: "I am sick of America and of professors and professoresses . . . I am pining for a sunny, quiet, remote, friendly, intellectual, obscure existence" (*The Letters of George de Santayana*). He felt American only because of "long association" and sent his letter of resignation to Harvard, after twenty-three years of service, from France. He lived in France, England, Italy; he traveled constantly to Spain; he was moved by ideas and also by men. As Atila says about a character in his unpublished novel "The Other Side of the Lighthouse," the world is trapped in its "definitions of woman and man," "and I was perceived as a man and did not wish to be trapped by definitions." Nor did Santayana.

In 1980 Atila began a career that would take him far. He became a journalist. During his trips to Paris, he not only became fluent in French but got fed up with cosmopolitanism. I ask the reader to trust me when I say that Atila felt lost at the end of an avalanche of delirious loves, ending always in a return to his friendship with a man from his youth, the perfect accomplice, former rival, former lover, former university classmate: a talented black musician whom Atila found murdered in the musician's apartment in New York. He felt the tremendous sadness that comes with the loss of innocence: "innocence doesn't exist until it stops existing." However, he made therapy of his work and rose to such an extent with his ability in so many languages and sensibilities that he soon found a place in the Olympus of late twentieth-century communication: television. He had a great career that led to a Grammy award—believe it or not—for his coverage of the Falklands War and travels through the world: New York, Paris, London, Buenos Aires, Rio de Janeiro. Atila, the polyphonic man from Chihuahua, Los Angeles, New Haven, New York, Paris, and Mexico, became a United States citizen at the invitation of President Ronald Reagan.

One day, however, at the height of his television career, he decided to leave all that, to go back to school to be what he had always wanted to be: a poet, a writer in all of his languages. But one was lacking: the Spanish that he read in Lope de Vega as well as in Alejo Carpentier, in Francisco de Quevedo, and in José Revueltas. He left everything and went back to the modern cloisters of knowledge, a prestigious university in his California, the land that he, like Santayana, thought of as "civilization on a holiday" (*Character & Opinion*). He wanted to learn the tessituras of Spanish that had escaped him and to write in all of them, because, he said, "when Angels learn to write, the heavens are threatened." But he ran into the purists of the language: Mexicans, South Americans, and Spaniards who, being ignorant, warned that Atila *no habla español*. The lords of the

Latin American booms, parochial monolinguists, humiliated him for his "errors" in Spanish. But not for long: Atila learned that Spanish and managed to say marvelous "un-Spanish things" in Spanish. This was his last victory, but a victory nonetheless.

In 1936 George Santayana published his roman-à-clef, *The Last Puritan*. The novel is about the life, career, and premature death of Oliver Alden, a novelized Santayana who died in a tragic accident only a few days after the armistice that brought World War I to an end. But Oliver had a puritanical sense of duty and, just before leaving for the war, reflected: "I have been a conscript all my life: a conscript son, a conscript schoolboy, a conscript athlete, a conscript soldier." Oliver had to learn the English of America, like Santayana, like Atila. Although he learned it, says the novel, "it always remained a foreign language to him, as did common American speech in general. He didn't hate it; sometimes it made him laugh." Like Atila, Oliver also knew passion, in this case, in the form of the captain of his father's yacht. But his passions brought him down because of his puritanism. As Atila later explained in an unpublished poem, "sometimes / passions are glaciers / that drain frigid moments / into our hearts." The language of *The Last Puritan* brought Santayana not only fame but fortune. It became one of the best-selling novels in the English-speaking world. William James wrote to George H. Palmer (April 2, 1900) that Santayana was a lesson in "moribund Latinity" applied to North America: "I don't think I ever knew the anti-realistic view to be propounded with so impudently superior an air. It is refreshing to see a representative of moribund Latinity rise up and administer such reproof to us barbarians in the hour of our triumph" (*The Letters of William James*).

In 1990 Atila Guerrero finished his roman à clef "The Other Side of the Lighthouse." The reader might think that I'm making this up, but for those who will grant me the benefit of the doubt, I tell you that the novel describes the life of Segismundo, an Atila torn by honesty. The novel begins with *El siglo de las luces* by Carpentier: "Hacia el Oriente se erguía, enhiesta y magnífica, vislumbrada por los ojos del entendimiento, la Columna de Fuego que guía las marchas hacia toda Tierra Prometida" (toward the east there rises up, erect and magnificent, glimpsed by understanding's eyes, the Column of Fire that guides marches to all Promised Lands). This inspired one of Atila's poems, "The Lighthouse," about seventeen young men in a train car. "Where is the light, one asks." And the one who's made the trip before says: "in the serpent's eyes." They are "necessary and unloved labor." When the train crosses the border, the serpent has begun digesting the men. Only one survives: "he will take the train down south to tell the next seventeen men where to find the lighthouse in the north."

Atila's novel is about what exists on the other side of the lighthouse: poverty, intelligence, struggle, and, above all, a deep and gradually growing doubt about everything; that is, the skepticism of a wise and poly-phonic chameleon who has moved through a variety of lands, in different tessituras. But Atila's novel is proof that, as Santayana said, "Scepticism is the chastity of the intellect, and it is shameful to surrender it too soon or to the first comer" (*Scepticism and Animal Faith*). Unlike Oliver in *The Last Puritan*, Segismundo in "The Other Side of the Lighthouse" doesn't die but ends up paralyzed, orphaned by so many languages, so many people, frozen and yelling, "Oh, girl! Oh, girl!" like a character in a Toni Morrison novel.

To many critics, Santayana was a magician in the English language, as they said, because of his Spanish origins. For Bertrand Russell, Santayana was a petulant Spaniard who didn't believe in the genius of a single Anglo-Saxon or German. For some Spaniards, like Miguel de Unamuno, Santayana was no more than another Englishman with a Spanish name. That's the high price you pay for being polyphonic. Santayana himself never regretted his love for Spain and the Spanish language, just as he never regretted his love for the United States and its language, but, he said, "My love for Spain and America is manifested by living there as little as possible" (*Character & Opinion*).

Many considered George Santayana to be insufferable, a pedantic genius, whose shoes, Russell says, were always impeccably spit-polished. Atila Guerrero—and if the reader has believed me up to now, there's no choice but to believe this last bit—was blessed with a lucid intelligence and also a Santayanesque pedantry. Even on his deathbed, he told his mother how spectacular he had looked during his final poetry reading. When he was living in California, Atila went out into the street in search of beauty. He looked for enchantment in the landscape, in people, in speech; he hunted for appearances, bodies, phrases, sayings. And he won people over with his gift for words. Atila inhabited language in the way Raimundo Lida said Santayana did: "understanding an idiomatic expression . . . is knowing what to do and what to say in its presence and that knowledge is much deeper than the imaginative echoes that might come with it" (*Belleza, arte y poesía en el estética de Santayana*).

The body is what understands, said Santayana. Atila, like Santayana—who once refused to meet with Ezra Pound because he only wanted to see "people and places that suggest the normal and the beautiful: not abortions or eruptions like E.P." (*Persons and Places*)—thus refused to see and speak to those he called "the Romans": the prototypical tanned students of the rich university where he studied, in monolingual white California.

Polyphony is irony's natural partner. Santayana and Atila found it with ease. When a quarrel arose about the proper place for an oil painting featuring James, Royce, and Santayana at Harvard, Santayana made an ironic remark about the democratic North American spirit and the ego of philosophers: "Whatever metaphysical egotism may assert, one cannot vote to be created" (*Character & Opinion*). Atila, in turn, when we spoke seriously about the usefulness of remembering and memory, ended up mocking me beautifully: "The pearl is the memory of an intolerable suffering. Ask any oyster." In summary, to exist, for Santayana and for Atila Guerrero, was to go on constructing, with irony, cruelty, and intelligence, *obras maestras* (masterpieces): their own lives. The two conceived the scene in this way, but which of the two wrote this long, and yet somehow short, cruel, and ironic description of life lived as an orgasm?

And I suck patiently—and impatiently—I wait for my fantasy to fulfill itself in whose orgasm? Mine or his? I think of what else I should be doing to better myself to conquer those innermost desires that seem to be quenched time and again only momentarily by a phallus I do not really want and, tend to believe, not exactly need. Nevertheless, I continue to explore the ridges and valleys covering this obscurity hidden since birth by clothing and shame . . . loss of obscurity which rules mankind: God. Yes God. Is it not He who is kept behind altars, never seen but felt everywhere? . . . I go up and down, swallowing, forcing tears out of my eyes . . . exciting my cerebral fibers to a frenzy . . . pleasure, anxiety, trust, adventure, lust, faith, love? No! These words describe only other people's frustration, not mine. My sole purpose here is the debauchery of this young man who will soon be old like I am now seeking perhaps not as consciously but as actively the same thrill. Mea culpa, mea culpa, my head bounces up and down, up and down this inverted chimney . . . mea culpa, I protest, I have sinned, I have pleasured . . . so I punish myself . . . I flog my throat with this relentless passion. My heart is touched each time I gag down this tasty stick of flesh . . . I have sinned, St. Genet . . . I whip my tonsils, my ears plug up, my toes curl, I perspire, I undo my inhibitions, for the walk across the river of manhood—this manhood, his and mine—has taken me to a point of no return, of no concern. Concerned I am, with my apparent self-inflicted humiliation, but more so with ravaging this beautiful specimen of youth not yet gone my way . . . His legs begin to tremble . . . I look up and see the look of grief and loss of control . . . ecstasy on his face. But after this, I know you will leave me and never think of me again . . . return to me now! Return to me that I may have you now and forever! He begins to writhe to the rhythm of my musical lips . . . I sing, I moan, with expectation. A thug in my house, a street urchin, has me by the throat and I am helpless . . . Return to me! Return to whom? To what? Return to me . . . His soul explodes and I catch it in my loneliness. He straightens his clothes and leaves with a curt "I'll see you" under his breath. I remain in my room drowning in my past and present rationalizing that I am only a conduit for the transfer of energy and the elimination of excess heat. ("The Other Side of the Lighthouse")

The lives of Santayana and Guerrero are fused in death, the first a victim of the usual cancer, the latter a prisoner of the then-new cancer, AIDS. Until the end of his life, Atila loved Chihuahua, his mother, his brothers and sisters. But he died at Stanford, the university he had chosen to relearn his Spanish. He still greeted his mother with *Oiga, uste* (Listen, mother). I remember him glorying in his polyphony during gatherings with elite Mexican students at Stanford. He would approach groups of dressed, coifed wives of Mexican students from the business school, made-up to the hilt, and would talk to them as though he were a wetback from Michoacán. The women were perplexed, who had invited this janitor to a party for high-class Mexicans? Then he would approach another group of junior businessmen from Monterrey; he spoke to them in a Caribbean accent, while telling them that he was a Mayan Indian from Chiapas. For those young people from Monterrey everything to the south of Linares is Chiapas, so they believed him. Later he walked up to a group of potential presidential candidates, Mexican students who were sons of the Mexican political system, and spoke to them in perfect Chicano. And the potential presidential candidates asked one another: who invited that Chicano who didn't even know how to speak good Spanish? But then he launched himself into a group of master's degree students in engineering, and he spoke to them in elegant, sophisticated Spanish, claiming that he was a famous Mexican writer invited by Stanford. As the gathering went on, the rumors grew: questions flew back and forth, everyone wondering what this janitor or Chicano or Mayan Indian or respected intellectual was doing there. When some brave souls approached that strange character in red sneakers to clear up the confusion, Atila responded in the most refined English: "I beg your pardon? Forgive me, but I do not speak Spanish." That's how polyphonics amuse themselves.

To conclude, between 1987 and 1990, Sergio Guerrero heartlessly edited and commented on my papers in English. He, who could read my thoughts in Spanish, taught me how to write English. He changed my life. To him, eternal gratitude. Before teachers like him, one is always a student of words, a modest apprentice of worlds, as I always was in the presence of Sergio "Atila" Guerrero.

Note: The reader may believe me or not, but years ago I donated the copies of Sergio Guerrero's manuscripts that I owned to the University of Texas Nettie Lee Benson Latin American Collection. Sure, I might have written them myself, just to create an imaginary character—after all, that's why Sergio taught me to write comme il faut in English. The reader may have a look at the manuscripts and decide.

Chapter 9

AMAR QUERIENDO COMO EN OTRO TIEMPO

LANGUAGE, MEMORY, AND BOLEROS

Sé más refranes que un libro, y viénenseme tantos juntos a la boca cuando hablo, que riñen por salir unos con otros; pero la lengua va arrojando los primeros que encuentra, aunque no vengan a pelo.

(I know more sayings than a book, and so many come all at once to my mouth when I talk, that they fight with one another to get out; but the tongue throws out the first ones it finds, though they have nothing to do with what I'm talking about.)

SANCHO PANZA IN MIGUEL DE CERVANTES, *El ingenioso Hidalgo Don Quijote de la Mancha*

There is a distance where magnets pull, we feel, having held them back. Likewise there is a distance where words attract.

KAY RYAN, *The Best of It*

Time and again I've been warned: in these postmodern times it's impossible to love in the same way the way I learned to love—that is, through the old Mexican boleros and rancheras: "Seeeñores . . . seeeñores . . . , los familiares del cadáver me han confiado, para que le diga el duelo" (Gentlemen . . . gentlemen . . . , the relatives of the corpse have entrusted me to speak at this wake). Known in its day as bolero love,[1] it's extinct, that love that spoke of *hastío* (ennui) and *frenesí* (frenzy), all in *azul* (blue), that tearful love filled with affected flattery that was also erotic—so erotic!—but prudish at the same time. Once upon a time there existed a sort of love whose irregular gerund was *cursilando* (being corny).

On behalf of those of us for whom "to love" is *amar queriendo como en otro tiempo*,[2] I want to honor the knowledge contained in that language and that seduction, that *amor de mis amores* (love of my loves) that *sangre de mi alma* (blood of my soul) . . . that living *amarrado al recuerdo* (tied to memory) of the lyrics of boleros and rancheras popular in Mexico City between 1920 and 1950.[3]

I speak here of my memories of these ways of loving and not of my own ineptness in matters of love—I'm beyond repair. But just to illustrate the point: more than a decade after our time together, a certain She, *la que hubiera amado tanto* (the one I would have loved so much), kindly asked me to sign a copy of a book I'd written. Without much thought, my pen activated the automatic *amar queriendo como en otro tiempo*, which is hate—*el odio es amor triste* (hate is sad love)—but it is also love—*milagro de la vida* (the miracle of life). It is also the mechanism that has rewired a hypothalamus subjected to heavy doses of dated boleros and rancheras. The dedication that I wrote said simply: "A aquel, aquel amor . . ." (to that love, that love . . .), because that's what came to my mind—a bolero by Agustín Lara ("Aquel amor"). I stopped there, thank God, because the bolero goes on to say: "aquel amor . . . que marchitó mi vida" (that love . . . that wilted my life). As luck would have it, in the 1990s very few could decipher the message, maybe a handful of eighty-year-old taxi drivers in Mexico City addicted to El Fonógrafo (a radio station whose motto was "music linked to your memories"). She, the one I loved, did not share those memories. Thus, without the aid of notes or Google, I'll now let my memory bring to mind boleros, and we'll see what happens when the bolero and I "nos hacemos de palabras" (literally, "make ourselves of words," meaning confront each other).

Memories of My Memory

In 1920 as today, all loving in Romance vernaculars mysteriously but certainly goes back to the medieval troubadours—"Ay mi senhor, assi moir' eu! / Como morreu quen amou tal dona!" (Oh, my lord, thus I die, as one who loved that woman) (Carolina Michaëlis de Vasconcellos, *Cancioneiro da ajuda*)—or to the Romantic movement; also to the singers of epics and balladeers of the peninsular languages: "Sospiro lo sospirado, / que sospiré muchos días, / suspiro desemulado / Las llagas antiguas mías" (I sigh what I have sighed, / which I sighed about for days / I sigh in secret / over my old wounds: *Cancionero de Lope de Stúñiga*). However, I simply want to emphasize a recent and transcendental turning point in the innumerable historical continuities and breaks in feeling and expressing love: the popularization of the phonograph and the radio.

In 1929, Mexico City alone had twenty-five radio stations. XEW, "the voice of Latin America from Mexico" (the radio station's tagline), started broadcasting in 1930. When love's griefs could be sung, recorded, and broadcast urbi et orbi, every person's voice became an echo of the chorus of a loving chatter. Entire populations contributed, some more, some less, either by composing or singing or just by feeling themselves able to follow ways of reasoning that were as universal in their moral as they were implacable in logic: "es natural que mi cariño huérfano de besos busque dónde estar" (it's natural that my affection, orphaned of kisses, looks for somewhere to be: Agustín Lara, "Por qué negar"). There you have it, a loving en masse that led tacky *boleristas* to call the bolero "the sediment of culture" (as César Portillo de la Luz used to say in his concerts). (By the way, surely *boleristas* did not know it, but prominent early twentieth-century Spanish philologists, such as Ramón Menéndez Pidal and Américo Castro, talked of *sedimentos* [Celtic, Iberian, Latin] in the forming of the Spanish language.)

In light of this, I really have no need of Henri Bergson or Gaston Bachelard to make myself clear: I'm referring to the first massive occurrence of the same instance experienced simultaneously by people in all walks of life—an instance that, in addition to being experienced as collective consciousness or unconsciousness, was repeatable at any time, anywhere. People could listen to the radio at home or play the two sides of a long-playing record time and again on those baroque consoles, altars of the national "we," or on ever-cheaper record players. What's more, in the city anyone could request a rendition of one or more songs from the troubadour on the street or in the streetcar or from the omnipresent guitar players in cantinas and restaurants: sing me this or that fragment of the Esperanto of love that everybody understood and could repeat by heart.

In self-referential fashion, popular songs express the possibility of accessing this instantaneity. That is, if there is thinking about thinking, some songs also sing about listening: "toquen otra vez 'La que se fue'" (play "The Girl That Went Away" one more time: José Alfredo Jiménez, "Tu recuerdo y yo"), "Guitarras, lloren guitarras" (Guitars, Cry, Guitars! by Cuco Sánchez), "Guitarras de media noche" (Midnight Guitars by José Alfredo Jiménez), "oiga usted cómo suena la clave, diga usted cómo suena el bongo" (listen to the sound of the clave, tell me about the sound of the bongo: Agustín Lara, "La cumbancha"). Heard right, these sounds answer

Ludwig Wittgenstein's riddle: "Can anyone believe it makes sense to say: 'That's not a noise, it's a colour'?" (*Philosophical Remarks*).

It seems to me that this language of love was not experienced as a lesson but rather as complicity, namely, the deep connivance of secrecy (foreplay, eroticism) and commonness. People all felt that they were inventing that language just by speaking it, just by guessing at its twists and turns, just by loving or by talking about love. And no one stopped making love or talking about it.

The "I" and the others knew the lyrics to the songs, apprehended them, understood what they were for, when and how to use them. Repeating one of those love tunes was reactivating the instantaneousness that two, ten, or a hundred consented to share. Other than lighting a candle to a saint or paying homage to a king, this language of love constituted the first occurrence in history of such massive mnemonic simultaneity. There was nothing particularly Mexican about it, except that Mexico City was among the three or four great capitals of this first collective instantaneity in Spanish. In English, various generations voiced and echoed, "Romance was a thing I kidded about / How could I know about love / I didn't know about you" (Duke Ellington, "I Didn't Know about You"). In Spanish the reflex was automatic and massive: for everybody and anybody at all times and practically everywhere, "conocí a una linda morenita" (I met a pretty brown girl) was followed by "y la quise mucho, por las tardes iba enamorado" (and I loved her a lot, in the evenings I walked around in love: Armando Villarreal Lozano, "Morenita mía").

The metaphors, hyperboles, and similes of the bolero and its neighbors became individual instances, unique, indivisible, but only at the moment of the practice of love. That is, when loving, a man or a woman could feel the here and now as if experiencing a private bolero. Mentally they made the instantaneity that the songs created, in private and public spaces, their own and unrepeatable, and without even reciting the words: "besos mordelones" (biting kisses), "bocas cual diminutos corales" (mouths like tiny corals), "ojos iguales a penas de amores" (eyes like the sorrows of love). (Oddly enough, though they militantly shared the heterosexual consensus, boleros and popular songs were almost always adaptable not only to the female or male voice but to any sexual preference, just like a Shakespearean sonnet, whose object of desire can be interchanged without altering the rhyme.) In short, the collective instantaneity always preceded the person, for the same reason that there is no language that is not social.

But that language of love so universally shared, once embodied in a memory, once a habit of being (Bergson), produced a consciousness that I believe gained an existence beyond words and music. This is like Wittgenstein on the guitar: words were the evidence of love, words that were simultaneously intimate and social conventions: the "I" who loves not only says and hears loving words but also sees, feels, and experiences what the other person expresses through language that exists in spite of language. Let me put it this way: I can repeat thousands of those old love songs by heart, due to a childhood vice that is of no importance here. Let me just say, with Themistocles and Rubén Darío, that I can't remember what I want to and I sometimes remember without meaning to. With the passing years, I've stopped listening to and repeating some of those tunes, and I often experience what the early nineteenth-century French physician Jacques Lordat said about aphasia: "I had to respect the fact that the mind's inner functioning could dispense with words" (*Exposition de la doctrine médicale*). Because the songs I remember are music and poetry that form mental bundles made of evocations released by the notes and the chords, by the sensations unchained by sonorous adjectives, bright colors, poetic images filled with sensuality and cliché. All that is also inevitably attached to places and smells that belong to the moment when the songs were first fixed as bundles in the mind of every lovebird the world has ever known.

I recognize these bundles as sentiments that I cannot express in words, because they aren't linguistic, but their evocation corresponds, undoubtedly, to lines from some bolero that I haven't heard or sung in a long time. In other words, I don't remember, but I feel. I evoke the sensation, I feel it in all of its intensity, but I can't remember the lyrics to which it corresponds. For days on end I try to remember the stanza so as to understand, so as to put into words what in any case is a living, conscious experience. This is knowing something that has no name. Of course, I'm an "errante trovador que va en busca del amor" (roving troubadour wandering about in search of love: Eduardo Márquez Talledo, "Nube gris"), but I'm not that old-fashioned: when I don't remember all the lyrics, I go to Google, like every savvy intellectual of our day, but how do I look for something that can't be expressed in words? For days on end I'm filled with a sensation whose musical-poetic reference I cannot find. When I finally remember the words—and I still am able to recall them, although the day will come when I am no longer able to find them—the experience becomes more certain but also more mundane. It has a name, date, smell, flavor, and a why and when. This is ordinary knowledge, with a name and location. But why explain so much; an old popular bolero, with traces of tango, or a tango with traces of bolero, has already said it:

Seré en tu vida lo mejor
de la neblina del ayer
cuando me llegues a olvidar
como es mejor el verso aquél
que no podemos recordar.
(I'll be in your life the best
of yesterday's mist
when you come to forget me
like that best of all verses
that we can't remember.)
(Virgilio Expósito, "Vete de mí")

We long for the verse that we feel is more eloquent. But the verse is no longer made of words. It was and is poetry. The problem is that by 1920 poetry no longer existed as massively shared memory, if it had ever been everyone's consciousness. The popular romantic song became the closest thing to *the* poetic consciousness of a city, a nation, or a language. Not even poets as popular as Amado Nervo, Gustavo Adolfo Becquer, and Juan de Dios Peza were really memory en masse, unless they were lucky enough to be translated into a popular song between 1920 and 1950.

Thus, thanks to technology, the instantaneous became collective knowledge in unison with individual lived experience. Loving became a question of the verb *ser* (to be) for *being* then and there; a question of the verb *estar* (to be there) for being "polvo pero polvo enamorado" (dust but loving dust) (from Quevedo's "Amor constante más allá de la muerte," but also a bolero, "Amor constante"). But something more than technology nourished the power of knowledge—the epistemological power, we pedants say—of the popular love song from 1920 to 1950: namely, *cursilería* (tackiness, corniness, kitsch). Better yet: the inevitable corniness that results from intellectualizing the basic instinct to fornicate, even a little bit. Apart from the reproductive mandate of the species, the rest is literature, long and dense, about a mammalian subspecies that for millennia has not resigned itself to unceremoniously ovulating and ejaculating. *Cursilería* arose, arises, and spreads every time one or more of those involved in fornicating decides to open his or her mouth other than to moan, either to procure sex or to editorialize coitus. Once again, there's nothing especially Spanish or Mexican here. The popular song in English and every other language comes from that millennial editorializing about coitus or its absence. And so we have the delicious corny and erotic suggestions of

Cole Porter ("Some Argentines, without means do it, People say in Boston even beans do it, Let's do it, let's fall in love"). Better yet, there's the Porter of love, who, though suggestively homosexual, is no less corny when mixing high and low culture and high and low sexual positions ("You're the Top"):

> You're the top!
> You're the Coliseum.
> You're the top!
> You're the Louvre Museum.
> You're a melody from a symphony by Strauss,
> You're a Bendel bonnet,
> A Shakespeare sonnet,
> You're Mickey Mouse!
> . . .
> But if, Baby, I'm the bottom,
> You're the top!

In terms of *cursilería*, the only novelty about the bolero and its derivatives in those yesteryears was that for the first time a historic version of corniness was consumed universally—a mixture of Victorian moralizing, nineteenth-century romanticism, popular eroticism and blasphemy, and the first avant-gardes. I'm not referring to a literary current, but to a way of talking about, feeling, and experiencing love; a way that at one time was a literary current. I believe that this way can be called coyness—the English term that, unlike any Spanish word that comes to mind, brings together timidity, modesty, sin, desire, flirting, and sensuality (as in Andrew Marvell's "To His Coy Mistress": "Had we but world enough and time, / This coyness, lady, were no crime"). Because in essence all of those old romantic songs dealt with copulation and nothing more. But if even today we can't copulate without the disguise of romantic love, of coyness, what can we expect of love during that extended nineteenth century that lasted, in popular Spanish, until well into the 1950s?

Nowadays, soon after we pay attention to the lyrics of those songs, their *cursilería* floods us with tinsel, the badly matched bits of music and poetry, all having to do with the simple instinct that we call in Spanish *follar, coger, pisar, chingar, planchar, tranzar, comer, yacer*. To fuck. In fact, it seems to me, though I can't be certain, that all of that was already corny in its time: it was always meant to be so. Because in nineteenth-century modernity—in the face of which the pretension of believing ourselves post- is absurd—everything to do with love was *cursi* or else it wasn't love. It could be erotica, ethics, sexology, or pornography, but not mundane love. In that other time, "I want to fuck" was said like this:

> Si no fuera a pedirte tanto,
> yo te pidiera vivir de hinojos,
> mirando siempre tus tristes ojos,
> ojos que tienen, ojos que tienen
> sabor de llanto.
> (If it weren't asking you too much
> I would ask you to let me live on my knees,
> looking always into your sad eyes,
> eyes that have, eyes that have
> the flavor of weeping.)
> (Guty Cárdenas, "Ojos tristes")

Asking for so much, giving so much, is all about sex. Let's imagine our great-grandparents making the suggestion, finding solace in the offer or in the asking, in the obligatory poetic instantaneity of a shared code based on giving to whoever asks in the right way, which is what the bolero was. That is, if you were to give me sex, I would not only accept but praise your coyness, because I paint you with the eyes of a saint, of inert sensuality that isn't inviting anything, though it wants everything, because your tearful eyes are those of a good woman, not lustful and lascivious, and because timidity and modesty are more arousing.

The instantaneity I'm talking about was the exchange of fleeting, shared sensuality, and it was, it had to be, *cursi*. Yes, because romantic love is corny, but also because the bolero is militantly hackneyed—a pretense of elegance that was not, even then, elegant. But also because, when in the chemical state of falling in love, few were or are Charles Baudelaire or Stéphane Mallarmé or Giacomo Leopardi—who at the height of the romantic century renounced love (what foresight!) in order to be profound, real, and thus pessimistic. Nothing is further from the bolero and its kin. There could be hatred, and even a lot of pessimism, in boleros, but only within the hate/love, happiness/sadness binary that arises from the essential faith in absolute perfection and happiness. Not Leopardi but boleros, which can be philosophically penetrating, but only because they don't try: it's unintentional philosophy. Leopardi's paradigm of profundity and abandonment sounds like this: oh happy one "a cui fu vita il pianto! A noi le fasce / Cinse il fastidio; a noi presso la culla / Immoto siede, e su la tomba, il nulla" (for whom lament was life / boredom wrapped us / in our swaddling clothes; / and nothingness guards our cradle and our tomb: *Canti*) This is the way the bolero faces life's uncertainties:

> ¡Ay cómo es cruel la incertidumbre!
> . . .
> ¡Ay . . . esta amarga pesadumbre!
> Si ella merece mi dolor o ya la tengo que olvidar.
> Si la vas a juzgar, corazón,
> nunca pienses que ella es mala
> si es valiente y te comprende
> no la pierdas corazón.
> (Oh, uncertainty is so cruel!
> . . .
> Oh . . . that bitter sorrow!
> Does she deserve my pain or must I now forget her?
> Heart, if you're going to judge her
> never think that she's bad
> if she's brave and understands you
> don't lose her, heart.)
> (Gonzalo Curiel, "Incertidumbre")

We feel profundity when we read Johann Wolfgang von Goethe's "Herz, mein Herz, was soll das geben?" (Heart, my heart, what's the meaning of this [feeling]?), but why? Because of what's been said or because it's Goethe and he's German? A bolerized tango says it like this:

> Uno sufre hasta entender
> Que uno se ha quedado sin corazón.
> (One suffers until understanding
> That one has been left without a heart.)
> (Enrique Santos Discépolo, "¡Uno!")

Yes, Joaquín Pardavé's bolero went a little too far by comparing a woman to a hyena: "tu pecho de mujer, nido de hiena" (your woman's breast a hyena's nest: "Falsa"). But Friedrich Schiller had already done that: "Da werden Weiber zu Hyänen / Und treiben mit Entsetzen Scherz" (Then women to hyenas growing /Do make with horrors jester's art: "Das Lied von der Glocke").

An older tango made it clear—bear in mind that in matters of memory and popular song the bolero was the short story, the tango the novel:

> Primero hay que saber sufrir,
> después amar, después partir
> y al fin andar sin pensamiento.
> (First one has to know how to suffer,
> then to love, then to leave
> and finally to go on without thinking.)
> (Virgilio Expósito, "Naranjo en flor")

Lope de Vega, in delightful Spanish but with another kind of coyness, expressed love's riddles:

> Juntos Amor y yo buscando vamos
> esta mañana. ¡Oh dulces desvaríos!
> Siempre mañana, y nunca mañanamos.
> (Together Love and I go searching
> this morning. Oh, sweet madness!
> Always tomorrow, and we never wake up together.)
> (Lope de Vega, *Sonetos*)

The bolero was less profound but not less playful:

> Quién me roba tu amor
> si lo tengo guardado.
> Quién me roba tu amor
> si tu amor es robado,
> si tu amor es mi vida,
> si lo tengo guardado.
> Quién me roba tu amor
> si tu amor es sagrado.
> (Who can steal your love from me
> if I keep it safe.
> Who can steal your love from me
> if your love is stolen,
> if your love is my life,
> if I keep it safe.

Who can steal your love from me
if your love is sacred.)
(Agustín Lara, "¿Quién me roba tu amor?")

Lope and his enigmas:

Que vele o duerma, media vida es tuya:
si velo, te lo pago con el día,
si duermo, no siento lo que vivo.
(Whether I stay awake or sleep, half my life is yours:
if I stay awake, I pay you for it with the day,
if I sleep, I don't feel what I live.)
("A la noche," in Lope de Vega, *Rimas*)

The bolero and its enigmas:

Porque te vas mi bien
tan deprisa no gozas mi agonía
Si la noche se espera todo el día
espera tú también.
(Why are you leaving me, my love,
so quickly, you can't enjoy my agony,
If the night can wait all day
you, too, can wait.)
(Álvaro Carrillo, "Un poco más")

Instantaneity, then, disseminated and produced by radio and phonograph, sustained in the *cursilería* that is the open secret of love. In the coy version of those years, love was possible thanks to a prolonged Victorian morality that demanded wordy propositioning, roundabout ways of asking for sex, modesty and sensuality in women, and, above all, collective memorization. *Cursilería* was not only the great leveler in matters of love; it was also the field of battle on which the moralism of the period was broken, violated, and twisted—all in the natural attempt to return to instinct, to free sexuality. Thus, it was a corniness for which vengeance and hatred were possible:

Pensaba que tu amor
habría de serme fiel
No contaba yo

con que fueras mujer
Sinónimos son hoy
Mujer y veleidad
Tan parecidos son
que suelen ser igual.
(I thought that your love
would be faithful to me
I didn't take into account
that you were a woman
Synonymous these days are
Woman and fickleness
So similar are they
that they tend to be the same.)
(Agustín Lara, "Pensaba por tu amor")

Or even better, this one, in the deep voice of Veracruz's *cañaveral* (sugar-cane field), that is, Toña la Negra's rendition (oh please, fellow academics, don't make a big deal of her race and gender; indeed, she was Antonia [Toña] and she had dark skin—and so what? she was a goddess):

De mujer a mujer
Usar podría de mis recursos
Como tiene que ser
Lo cojo en mis brazos ardientes
Con besos de muerte
Lo estrecho con fe entre mis brazos
Y lo hago sentir
Que de mujer a mujer
La lucha haremos
Y así triunfaré con él me quedo
De mujer a mujer.
(Woman to woman
I could use my resources
As it should be
I would take him into my burning arms
With kisses of death
I would hold him very tight between my arms
And I would make him feel
That woman to woman

you and I will fight
And I will win and keep him
[I tell you this] woman to woman.
(Esteban Taronji, "De mujer a mujer")

This is corny, yes, but without modesty, without frills, hard and rough. Baroque corniness served to express the crudest insults and passions, without need for explanation, within a shared code of sins. Some examples:

[mujer] Sabes de los filtros que hay en el amor,
tienes el hechizo de la liviandad.
([woman] You know of love's filters,
lasciviousness is your enchantment.)
(Agustín Lara, "Mujer")

 Vende caro tu amor, aventurera
Dale el precio del dolor a tu pasado.
(Adventurous woman, put a high price on your love,
Let suffering be the price of your past.)
(Agustín Lara, "Aventurera")

Prefiero una y mil veces que te vayas,
porque de ti no quiero ni la gloria.
(I prefer a thousand and one times that you go
because from you I don't even want glory.)
(Juan Pablo Miranda, "Mil congojas")

Me embriagaré, sediento de placeres,
en la pagana copa de otros labios.
(I'll get drunk on my thirst for pleasure
In the pagan glass of others' lips.)
(Guty Cárdenas, "Para olvidarte a ti")

Thus, through technology, *cursilería* boosted the mnemonic strength of old popular romantic songs shared across generations. But above all songs could be retained, could be memorable and unforgettable, thanks to musicality in three keys: rhyming verses, simple catchy harmonies mixed with images, and the uncanny strains produced by coupling. Songs' lyrics were full of verses drawn from the legacy of *modernismo*, crafting radiant, if simple, metaphors that easily but surely stuck in people's memories. Old romantic popular songs appropriated the sophisticated poetic extravagances of such *modernista* poets as Amado Nervo, Rubén Darío, or Julio Herrera y Reissig. To put it in English, it would be like Lord Byron's language becoming the slang spoken by urban masses. By speaking it, each individual could embody the sublime eloquence that nevertheless was totally passé by the 1930s. This out of sync, upside-down gentrification of words could sound like this:

> Un cruel puñal con arabescos de oro
> Llevo en el pecho hasta la cruz clavado,
> Una bella mujer a la que adoro
> Allí pasando lo dejo olvidado.
> (A cruel dagger with golden arabesques
> I carry in my chest buried to the hilt
> A beautiful woman I adore
> Left it there in passing.)
> (Guty Cárdenas, "Un cruel puñal")

Or this:

> Ya estaba olvidado
> mi amor fracasado
> y llegaste tú.
> Bordando el pasado,
> como en un dechado de raso y tisú.
> Divina sorpresa
> que dio a tu belleza
> fragante y triunfal,
> la suave promesa
> de un amor que empieza
> como un madrigal.
> (My failed love
> was already forgotten
> and you came along.
> Embroidering the past,
> as in a satin sampler
> stitched in gold and silver thread
> a divine surprise
> which charged your beauty

with joyous fragrance,
the gentle promise
of a love that commences
like a madrigal.)
(Gonzalo Curiel, "Sorpresa")

Now, the popular songs that began to be called rancheras after the introduction of the radio were something else. This type of popular tune had
another source of words to mine: the old anonymous ballad tradition that
had circulated in different parts of Mexico for centuries. We could even
go as far back as the Spanish *romancero*, which inspired versions of the
old *romances* "El francés" and "La delgadina" in Mexico's popular rancheras. The ranchera also benefited from the global logophilia of the nineteenth century, which involved many Mexican collectors of popular songs
and *romances*. The ranchera's first phonographic divas, Lucha Reyes and
Concha Michel, soaked up those collections. Be that as it may, little by little
old traditions, particularly rural ones, got mixed up with urban boleros—
as was the case in the works of such prominent songwriters as Manuel
Esperón, Tata Nacho, and, finally, José Alfredo Jiménez. They left behind
what was no longer theirs: the freshness of country ways of speaking, the
mistaken but revealing syntax and spelling of people who could, for example, talk about forgetting and remembering with simplicity but also
with an almost neurological objectivity: "quisiera olvidarte" (I would like
to forget you).

y no hacer un recuerdo de ti
y no hacer un recuerdo de ti.
(and not make a memory of you
and not make a memory of you.)
("Me importa poco")

It doesn't say *y no recordarte* (not remember you), it twice says: and not
making of you that precious thing: *un recuerdo* (a remembrance, a
memory). Or listen to this grievance—which Goethe would have taken
credit for had he understood it: "Ingrata mujer perjura /le robates la ter-
nura / a mi pobre corazón" (Ungrateful, perjuring woman / you stole the
tenderness / from my poor heart: "La pulquera"). Old rancheras tell their
stories in few words (only the tango is prolific), but their language gives the
impression that there is no hurry. For example: "cuando se estaban peli-
ando / pues que llegó su padre de uno, / 'hijo de mi corazón, ya no pelies

con ninguno'" (while they were fighting / it happened that the father of one of them came / child of my heart, don't fight anymore with anybody: "El hijo desobediente"). The father scolds his son, and the son submits this sweet response: "sólo le pido a mi padre / que no me enterre en sagrado / que me enterre en tierra bruta / donde me trille el ganado" (I only ask of my father / don't bury me in blessed earth, / bury me in brute soil / so that the cattle will walk over me).

There's no lack of irony in rancheras; they borrow wit from the Mexican or Mexicanized Spanish book of sayings: "no soy monedita de oro pa' caerle bien a todos" (I'm not a gold coin to please everyone: "No soy monedita de oro"). Or when a simple man gives a rural policeman an unfriendly look: "¿oiga amigo qué me ve? / la vista es muy natural" ([the policeman says] hey, buddy, what are you looking at? / [the man says] seeing is only natural: "Corrido de Arnulfo González"). After an exchange of bullets, the policeman responds: "le dijo: oiga no se vaya / acábeme de matar" (he told the man, hey! don't leave / finish killing me). The point is that this old popular genre that we call rancheras today was no less eloquent than the bolero but drew its eloquence from quite different sources.

The bolero and its appendices *anacó* (popularized and vulgarized) highbrow literary *modernismo*, absorbing the product already digested by nineteenth-century rhetoric, without needing to recur to Greek or Roman mythology or to a single erudite citation. It is *modernismo* as common sense. But two or three pieces in my head are—so to speak—footnoted. For instance, the almost-anthem of Puerto Rico by El Jibarito, Rafael Hernández:

Borinquen,
la tierra del edén,
la que al cantar
el gran Gautier
llamó la Perla de los Mares.
(Borinquen [Puerto Rico],
the land of Eden,
which in his verses
the great Gautier
called the Pearl of the Seas.)
("Lamento Borincano")

It is as if the song were footnoted: "Théophile Gautier, XXX, p. X."

A more recent bolero that I recall in the tearful voice of Daniel Santo quotes J. M. Vargas Vila, a very successful Colombian novelist in the 1920s:

Cada vez que me dices que no me quieres,
en mi mente se transforma y se perfila
el odio que tenía a las mujeres
el colombiano a quien llamaron Vargas Vila.
. . .
y que sólo hay que gozar de los placeres
que nos brindan una mujer o la bebida.
. . .
No sufre el corazón, no hay alma herida,
del sabio es la razón de Vargas Vila.

(Each time you tell me that you don't love me
my mind materializes and shapes
the hatred for women felt by
the Colombian they called Vargas Vila.
. . .
and one should only enjoy the pleasures
that a woman or drinking provides
. . .
The heart should not suffer, there should be no wounded soul,
wise is Vargas Vila's truth.)
(Daniel Santos, "Vargas Vila")

All in all, the truth is that I have a hard time remembering others like these. It was customary to assume as our own language all of that linguistic enchantment without paying attention to sources. That said, the fact is that songs were not memorable because of their erudition but because of their contagious word games. The lyrics of the songs followed rhyme schemes and harmonies that were more or less simple, with repetitions and choruses like mnemonic games:

Tipi, tipi, tin, tipín, tipín
tipi, tipi, tipitón, tipitón
Todas las mañanas frente a tu ventana
Suena esta canción.
(Tipi, tipi, tiptín, tipitín

tipi, tipi, tip tipitón, tipitón
Every morning at your window
Sounds this song.)
(María Grever, "Tipi tipi tin")

Pero habla, habla, habla
Hasta que quedes vacía de palabras.
(But talk, talk, talk
Until you run out of words.)
(Álvaro Carrillo, "La señal")

Noche tibia y callada de Veracruz
Canto de pescadores, que arrulla el mar
Vibración de cocuyos que con su luz
Borda de lentejuelas la oscuridad
Borda de lentejuelas la oscuridad.
(Veracruz's warm and still night
fishermen's chant, that the sea lulls to sleep
Vibration of fire beetles that with their light
Embroider the darkness with sequins
Embroider the darkness with sequins.)
(Agustín Lara, "Noche criolla")

The simple rhymes followed minor keys that invariably changed to major, three or four notes on a musical staff, but with tempos that could vary depending on where and when the lyrics were sung. That explains the ease with which songs were memorized and adapted to different places and circumstances. If you listen to the first versions of "Amor perdido" by Agustín Lara (1920s), you'll find the same lyrics, the same chords in versions from the 1930s and 1940s, sung by María Luisa Landín or Toña la Negra. But the tempo and cadence are completely different. In the 1920s the influence of the Caribbean, Yucatán, and the foxtrot inspired Lara to come up with a faster tempo, between the *son bambuco*, a Yucateco and Caribbean musical genre, and the Spanish *copla*. But over time the bolero slowed down; it seems that sensuality is more itself in slow motion, a laziness that incites the most sinful of daring thoughts in the long pauses between one word and another. Experience this, for example, in the cavernous lasciviousness of Elvira Ríos or in the nasal concupiscence of María Victoria (Google them).

In the 1930s boleros picked up tempo midway through the song but were always on the slow side. When trios began to interpret boleros, the tempo and cadence varied in the intricate vocal arrangements and arabesques between one bar and another, from the extremely slow phrasing of the Martínez Gil brothers ("Chacha, miiiiii Chacha linda" [Chacha, myyyyy pretty Chacha: "Chacha"]), to the faster, even tropical feeling of Los Panchos ("Me voy pa' l pueblo, hoy es mi día" [I'm going to my hometown, today is my day]: "Me voy pa' l pueblo": Los Panchos, original by Marcelino Guerra Abreu). And when the big orchestras turned the rumba and the Caribe into an epidemic, the old boleros left their sluggishness behind—they were sung fast and rhythmically (as in the version of "Amor perdido," accompanied by fast drumbeats and trumpets, which included this definition of love: "fue un juego yo perdí / esa es mi suerte / pago porque soy buen jugador" (it was all a game, I lost / that's my luck / I pay because I'm a good player).

All of these, for the generations that grew up with them, were no more than unconscious mnemonic resources, which left that vast amatory bulk permanently installed in the brain. Words, adjectives, verbs, metaphors, hyperboles, symbols . . . an unconnected variety that switched on, consciously or unconsciously, during many daily activities. In Mexico's scientific press, between 1880 and 1950, we find the adjectives and logic that come from *modernista* poetry and boleros. In 1899 physician Francisco Martínez Baca, in a study of the tattoos sported by criminals and military personnel, described the eroticism of tattoos relying on the prosody and literary images that later became amatory common sense via boleros. The tattoos' eroticism, he thought, responded to the fact that the "reproductive sense, put to sleep by the lack of action, is exalted by recollections, and thus demands the fulfillment of physiological functions, which, if unsatisfied, further excite the imagination, awakening desire and increasing [sexual] appetite" (*Los tatuajes*). In turn, Dr. Guillermo Campolla Núñez in the 1940s considered love a toxin, in these terms: "I do not admit that Adam was expelled from his earthly paradise as a result of temptation: it would be easier to admit that Jehovah, kind as ever, would forgive the sin; but the toxin [love] ruled him from the first moment, and Adam surely preferred condemnation to renouncing the use of the toxin" ("El amor es un tóxico"). Indeed, either science spoke boleros or the other way around—there was no way out. Moreover, the rhetorical and metaphorical repertoire provided by bolero sociability could be felt in legal and patriotic prose, but let's take this no further.

However, the unconnected assortment of memorized logical, rhetorical, and metaphorical resources made connections through the command: *amar con sentimiento* (to love with feeling). And then all those resources took on meaning and found their outlet:

> Ven que mi cabaña con la luna pintaré
> Contando las horas de la noche esperaré
> Piensa mujer que te quiero de veras,
> Piénsalo, piénsalo bien.
> (Come, I'll paint my cabin with moonlight
> Counting the hours of the night I'll wait
> Think, woman, that I love you for real
> Think about it, think about it a lot.)
> (Agustín Lara, "Piénsalo bien")

And allow me to throw out this last one just because:

> Por tus ojazos negros llenos de amor
> por tu boquita roja que es una flor
> por tu cuerpo de palmera lindo y gentil
> se muere mi corazón.
> Si me quisieras figulina de abril
> mi vida entera yo te daría a ti;
> si tus labios rojos yo pudiera besar
> me moriría de amor.
> (For your big dark eyes filled with love
> for your little red mouth that's a flower
> for your pretty, charming palm-tree body
> my heart dies.
> If you would love me, April figurine
> I would give you my whole life;
> if your red lips I could kiss
> I would die of love.)
> (Juan Arvizu, "Damisela encantadora," originally by Ernesto Lecuona)

I Live without Living in Myself

The sociology of the bolero and its kin has already been done well.[4] In 2010 Carlos Monsiváis died, one of the bolero's last native speakers, the last great Rosetta Stone who could translate the bolero into social analysis and society into a bolero. Monsiváis's science and weapon were his excellent memory, in itself infected by the symptom I've been describing. I will not go into any more details from the outside (society) in (memory), but rather from inside out.

It turns out that mine is an untimely life; the memory of which I speak should not have been my own (as a Mexican born in the 1960s). My consciousness is divided: one part remembers and speaks not in the language I learned from my grandparents, but in the language that they must have had in their memories. Another part retains what it was appropriate for me to remember, given my position in time and space. Untimeliness produces innumerable anxieties in matters of love, but that's my problem, and at some point I'll recount it or I'll sing it in a bolero. But untimeliness has served me as an excuse to explore more fully—as though I could see my language outside of myself—what philosophers, poets, and neurologists have been examining for some time; that is, the very experience of consciousness. I explore it by focusing on the human phenomenon par excellence: embellishing coitus with all sorts of mental resources. I focus, thus, on love and the way it is spoken. Untimeliness in my memories has furnished me with sufficient intimacy, because it's my own memory, but with large doses of strangeness because it's a memory that doesn't correspond to my life span. It's a memory within my own memory, which is gradually losing neural connections inside me, but above all through brains other than my own. Like a scientist who inoculates herself with a serum she's discovered, I explore in myself the encounter between memory and consciousness thanks to the anachronism that is my own memory.

A cup of tea and a madeleine unleashed the craft and the vice of memory in Marcel Proust; he found that pleasure always occurs in the past tense. But fiction or not, it was his own life, not his grandparents'. I've made use of love, and of the language in which I learned it: the old popular romantic song. I suppose an old mathematician could reconstruct his mathematical sociability and feel nostalgia for that first delight in the logic of a theorem, for the reasoning that occupied his thoughts for decades. I imagine, thus, that the mathematician can at times experience the sensation of his mathematical consciousness as though it were outside of himself, not his own language—even though it is—but the history of his discipline, something of which he is part, which he has constituted and been constituted by. But that sensation lives outside of him like a spatiotemporal consciousness that is essentially shared by only a few others, but relived as his own each time that he is the one thinking. This type of consciousness is activated involuntarily in the mathematician or the hackneyed troubadour, with a familiarity that borders on automatism, until one fine day that consciousness reveals itself to be strange, foreign, moribund. For the "I" gains a degree of independence from us as the "I," which is a small "we," gradually dies. Death, of course, ends everything, but that's not the problem. The real dilemma is the stochastic of forgetting. An old Mexican corrido has already said it all: "la muerte no mata a nadie / la matadora es la suerte" (death doesn't kill anybody / luck is the killer: "Corrido de Felipe Ángeles").

What I fear is not anachronism but forgetting. What intrigues me is more than nostalgia, *saudade*—that old Portuguese term that at once connotes past, present, and future; memory, melancholy, homesickness, and hopefulness. Sometimes I think the modern popularity of what Cyril Connolly (*Enemies of Promise*) called "Proustian onanism" is due to the fact that *À la recherche du temps perdu* gentrified a common human mania: *saudade*. In turn, the rapid evolution of neuroscience, from Santiago Ramón y Cajal to Oliver Sacks (as it were, two great novelists of *saudade*), is Proustian onanism as science. It's fine to make art and science out of *saudade*; it's like legitimizing, say, crying at times for no reason through sonnets or through a study of hydraulics. When we live, as I do, with a memory and a language that are on loan from another time, the melancholy we feel for what's lost must be somehow feigned; it's *saudade* for a past that was never really mine. It's a sham, of course, but similar to the feigning of a poet (Pessoa) who feigned so completely that he feigned pain; pain that he actually felt.

Boleros, as a default format for loving, allow me to conceive hopes with no real reference point, and thus I experience a maudlin consciousness working automatically within me and in spite of me. Unlike a childhood memory, however erroneous, which exists only in reference to a real experience, my bolero-driven recollections have no more backing than the mechanisms of *saudade* in their pure state. Memory remembers because it remembers, yearns because it yearns, and eventually forgets because it is in fact selective forgetfulness. In effect, think of *saudade* as a trace of our neural evolution that allows us to both identify and preserve hope, thus defeating forgetfulness, if only temporarily.

Nevertheless, *saudade* is not good for much else. It's the vice of *ensimismamiento* (self-absorption), and it's dangerous—it can lead to depression and death. I should, of course, try to block the mechanism (*saudade*) without deleting the many songs that I carry in my head. Maybe I should try to turn those songs into simple data. Then again, no sooner do I try than I hear a bolero whispering: "y ahora que te voy olvidando / siento que está llegando otra nueva canción" (and now that I'm forgetting you / I feel a new song coming: José Antonio Méndez, "Otra nueva canción"). It's hopeless. When I try to deactivate *saudade*, its sad and useless language of hope, I find myself feeling *saudade* for the innocence and hopefulness of my previous attempts. Better to sing myself another bolero: "y si pretendes remover las ruinas que tú mismo hiciste / solo cenizas hallarás de todo lo que fue mi amor" (and if you try to remove the ruins that you yourself made / you will find only ashes of all that my love was: Wello Rivas, "Cenizas").

There's no cure. I'm always the rememberer, the *palabrado* (one articulated or named) by the language I possess and that possesses me. Love is the memory of pleasure, which in itself is so fleeting that it can truly be no more than that, memory. My memory retains a passé language capable of producing passion that is not truly my own. On evoking such passion, my memory seeks not to confirm its truth but to revive what can only be past. And thus, to the sound of boleros, I re-create the shudder of supreme human intimacy, which I call to mind in the form of an unforgettable embrace . . . but with a woman I've never met.

Chapter 10

WICKED TONGUE (EXTRACTS)

I here transcribe stories about Don Ignacio Merlina y Rapaport, an old exile from the Spanish Civil War, informal teacher of a circle of inexperienced young Mexicans, who in the 1970s frequented his house on Río Guadiana Street, right next to the Paseo de la Reforma, Mexico City. After speaking at some length with the survivors of those *tertulias* (literary gatherings), I have decided to transcribe what memory can retrieve from the sea of Don Ignacio's precepts. He was a gentleman allergic to any kind of academia, who had no disciples and neither fame nor fortune, a rara avis who, with his library, made a good living. His odd lifestyle aroused no envy in any renowned scholar or intellectual either in Spain or Mexico. As brash as he was, Don Ignacio remained aloof and unknown throughout his life.

Memory can't be trusted, it imitates itself, so I relied on friends' notes as well as Don Ignacio's own, if only to compare recollections and keep a minimum of fidelity. I am grateful to Don Ignacio's family, who generously gave me access to his notes and library, with the condition I not reveal the location and fate of Don Ignacio's legacy or anything about the personal life of our dear *mestre*, a promise I fulfill to the letter. This, dear reader, is why I must excuse myself for not naming the sources of my quotations.

Erudition

Don Ignacio Merlina y Rapaport, a distinguished bibliophile and man of extensive but disordered memory, provided unusual philological services upon request. His specialty was finding the usages of words and concepts in Spanish from the moment such language was first printed. Another service he offered was looking for the Spanish-language equivalents of all sorts of human knowledge. For, as it happened, mainstream European and American scholars found it necessary to liberate the Spanish side of what was ratified as *essential* erudition, even if it was mainly for the purposes, of "English only" wisdom. If Harvard needed a quotation to decorate philosophical speculations by, say, William James, Henri Bergson, and Rabindranath Tagore, Don Ignacio responded by return mail with long quotations about neuronal connections from Santiago Ramón y Cajal. He used to send the original Spanish quotation in red pencil and a translation to the language that was required, often English, in black. If the request was for a parallel to Edward Gibbon's irony, he sent translations of the Italian writings of the Nuevo-Hispano Francisco Xavier Clavijero. What most delighted Don Ignacio was to send poetic echoes for French, English, German, or Italian rhymes. He had compiled detailed indices, by word and subject, of everything, from the old Iberian *xarcas* (verses in a mixture of Arabic and Spanish) and the Gallego-Portuguese verses of Alfonso el Sabio, to the Spanish, Argentine, Philippine, Mexican, and Paraguayan Romantics. If Berlin or Princeton asked for something similar to Paul Celan or Wallace Stevens, he would respond with lines from Antonio Machado, Jorge Luis Borges, or lesser-known poets from the Río de la Plata or Andalusia. He earned decent money without having to leave home. He didn't make use of any kind of electronic gadget, just books, paper, pencil, and memory. He rarely bought a new book; the most recent in his library had been published in 1970.

And thus erudite essays in English journals began to include quotations from the Spanish. Miguel de Cervantes, José Ortega y Gasset, and Jorge Luis Borges were no longer the only names that brainy intellectuals from Europe and the United States knew how to pronounce. One day Don Ignacio received an unheard-of request: he was to find an echo for a paragraph in English that included neither the author's name nor any other reference. When Don Ignacio asked, they informed him that the text came from the "path-breaking mind" of a famous English-speaking expert in literary theory whose "epistemological" contributions were countless, a late follower of Martin Heidegger and of post-this and post-that studies, realms that Don Ignacio found not only unfamiliar but indecipherable. The paragraph in question was long but had only two sentences, thirty-five commas, eight parentheses, five hyphens, an infinity of gerunds, lots of adjectives made into nouns (through the overuse of the English suffix "-ness"), and two verbs whose functions were unclear both in their respective sentences and in the paragraph. Don Ignacio looked for a parallel in something by Baltasar Gracián and in a verse by Luis de Góngora; in a long sentence by Azorín (José Martínez Ruiz), in a certain enigma by Sor Juana, in some *esperpento* (grotesquerie) by Ramón María del Valle Inclán, and in the equivalent by Ramón Gómez de la Serna. He found something a bit similar in a philosophical text by an unknown nineteenth-century Peruvian thinker, but nothing that seemed like the paragraph he'd received, at least in form. However, Don Ignacio's memory had its resources.

The following is found on page 123 of an article published by a famous literary-theory scholar who won the annual Modern Language Association prize for the best essay in the field of critical narrativity:

> [W]hat I aim at complicating is the ethnocentric narrativity of suffering in Western literature which essentializes sadness through the hegemonic maligning of female alternative pain through the juxtaposition, that is, through the dominant sexual performativity of male phallic pain—seen as coitus negation or coitus interruptus whereas it is simply female resistance—vis-à-vis the invisibility of women's capability of multi and post (and/or)gasms. Non-Western, non-canonical notions of pleasure furnish us with narratives of non-invasive eroticism—or should we say not belonging to a penetration-centric Western episteme. A simple but thick line from a non-Western mestizo, Alfonso Reyes, puts this negation in his counter-hegemonic alternative view of Afro Cuba, in which the mockery of Western Orientalism becomes the affirmation of Cuban black desire:
>
> No es Cuba—la que nunca oyó Stravinsky
> concertar sones de marimbas y güiros
> en el entierro de Papá Montero
> ñáñigo de bastón y canalla rumbero.
> (It's not Cuba—the one that never heard Stravinsky
> composing marimba and percussion sounds
> at the burial of Papa Montero,
> a ñanigo [black man] with a cane and a *canalla* rumbero [very good dancer].)[1]
>
> But an anonymous Afro-Cuban *danzón* condensed this narrativity of post-phallocentric notions of suffering through un-Western traditions of coyness and solicitation of coitus, alas with hyperbolic reference to divine powers—perhaps derived from the rich voodoo Cuban tradition:

¡Ay Fefita por Dios, no me hagas sufrir!
¡Ay Fefita por Dios, no me hagas sufrir!
(Oh, Fefita, for God's sake don't make me suffer!
(Oh, Fefita, for God's sake don't make me suffer!)[2]

Writing

With the Grim Reaper whispering in his ear, Don Ignacio Merlina y Rapaport began to reflect on the irony that had earned him a living for decades: selling in English what he had read, written, and thought in Spanish. "Thinking and writing in Spanish," he used to say, "is a form of trifling exhibitionism." Because, he explained to us,

> Of this there is not a shadow of a doubt, *nens* [boys, children]: to the planetary literati, what is thought and said in Spanish counts for little or nothing. Writing in the language of Castile means finding contentment in speaking to and among the tribe, without any hope of escape from the jungle. Whoever writes in Spanish within the confines of Anáhuac should consider himself to have been well served if he is read by two or three intrepid readers in Madrid or Barcelona. Let the poor scribbler in Spanish be certain of this: that he writes only for those in his own linguistic neighborhood. In the valley of Anáhuac we gaze at our navels, in Barcelona they see only their own, and even more so in New York and London.

It's not that Don Ignacio was a Spanish logopatriot, like those whom we Mexicans and Argentines have to thank every time we open our mouths, or like those who consider it a betrayal of the fatherland when a Spanish speaker thinks and writes in one of the chic languages of the intellectual firmament. He used to tell us: "Given the choice between falling into the logopatriotism of the bureaucrats at the Spanish embassy [here in Mexico City], or that of the great peninsular philologists, or that of some of the Catalan exiles here in Mexico, I would rather fall into the void." No, Don Ignacio wasn't one of those. He himself made a living by writing in English and French, by expressing in those languages what he thought and read in Spanish. But, he said, "I learned some languages late in life. *Clar* [of course], I could have made a career as a thinker and writer in Catalan, but the blackboard and the school desk [always] win: I was educated in

Barcelona, in Spanish, and at home languages rotated depending who was with us. Every day we spoke Spanish and English, the only common language between us and the Romanian cousins who came to live with us; Catalan if grandparents from one side of the family were present; and German, Spanish, or Portuguese if it was the other side. I could have reeducated myself to write in Catalan, but by then my conviction that I existed on the margins had already grown fat, so why bloat it further?"

Beyond any kind of logopatriotism, Don Ignacio thought and wrote in Spanish with immense dignity. He didn't seem to be bothered by his marginality; he was a dealer in marginality: he sold little dictionary entries and quotations, windows into a universe considered so insignificant that the English-speaking world seemed satisfied with a few quotations selected by Don Ignacio.

Back in the 1970s, when our Mexican university professors still defended a kind of leftist *afrancesamiento* (francophilism) against vulgar, capitalist, imperialist English, Don Ignacio didn't lose any sleep over the preeminence of English. He assumed it to be our epoch's destiny:

> For Dante, [Luís de] Camões, and [Luis de] Góngora, writing in vernacular was to think a bit in Latin, a bit in sundry unfixed *romanischen Sprachen*; for [Rubén] Darío, [José Maria] Eça [de Queirós], and [Joaquim Maria] Machado de Assis, to write in their Romance language was to smuggle thoughts in French. And for a long time now, writing good essays, good thoughts, good literature in Spanish has been impossible without loading up on English reading. *Nens*, never forget it, we are marginal, not *gilipollas* [idiots]. Borges and Pessoa, by way of English, were to their respective languages what, by way of French, Darío and Queirós were for Spanish and Portuguese. No need to be shocked. We have to write our Latin vernaculars and our English in our good Spanish. That doesn't free us, we'll still be intellectual nullities, but this is our destiny in thinking and writing today in Spanish. The alternative, a purist attitude immune to English and enemy of Catalan and Mexican Spanish and other local languages, is intellectual anorexia. And, to be sure, it is a lost cause.

For Don Ignacio, living on the margins had its advantages when it was done right. He believed that monolingualism was the patrimony of English-speaking luminaries: "on the margins, nobody even picks up a pen in a single language." And in any language, he told us, "the exact, life-changing word" is always in short supply.

In what language has the most stupidity been written? Clearly in Chinese and English, that's simple statistical frequency. But it's fair to assume that in all languages, proportionally speaking, the same large number of *burradas* [idiocies] have been written. In every one, lucidity is scarce. Conclusion, *nens*, as they say here, "no semos" [an archaic Spanish form of "we're not," common in rural Mexico] any more lucid or more asinine, but indeed "semos" invisible to the mainstream of world thought. Those who are visible have the advantage of having their best points and their sillinesses known and appreciated. For invisible ideas, what difference does it make whether they are *gansadas* [nonsense]? Nobody will look to us for a single clue, for the same reason that the majority of the Spanish-speaking intelligentsia doesn't look for clues to anything in Romanian or in Japanese or even in Portuguese or Catalan. We commit, without a second thought, the same crime that is committed against us. And when we try to free ourselves from the sin, we do so via our new Latin, English.

The problem, he said, was not only the lack of command of this or that language. In England and in the United States many entrepreneurs, physicians, and teachers speak Spanish, Don Ignacio used to tell us. And he then told stories of Jewish writers in the old Austro-Hungarian Empire whose mother tongue might have been Polish, Yiddish, or German but who always wrote in High German: "I think that Joseph Roth, an Eastern European, a Galician, could halfway express himself in Polish or in Yiddish, but he always wrote drunk and in German, he who would have liked to be the son of an Austrian count rather than an Eastern Jew like his father, whom he never knew." Why? "Lineage."

Nobody looked for anything important to read in Yiddish or Polish, just as today the planetary intelligentsia looks to Spanish only for data, news, little useful things to document barbarity or folklore, never ideas or profound thoughts. The assumption is that if something is *encara* [still] not in English, it is because it does not deserve to be read. Recall that English friend of Fernando Pessoa, a gentleman who lived in Lisbon for many years, spoke Portuguese and read the city's newspapers. But he asked his friend Fernando to translate some of his poems into English; he wanted to read them. Why, Pessoa asked, if that *besugo* [fool] was fluent in Portuguese? And I remember the response that Pessoa wrote in English: "Because Portugal is his office, not his home, though he lives there, and he would as soon think of reading a Portuguese book for pleasure as of diving into a ledger for excitement."[3]

In effect, there is "no escape" from the marginality of writing in Spanish or in Portuguese. That's what Don Ignacio thought.

When the *chamacada* (a Mexican word for a group of young people) that gathered at Don Ignacio's house started moving away to study in England, France, and the United States, he recommended that we write as much French or English as we could. He wanted us to write in those languages but "never stop writing in Spanish, even if only long letters written as exercises for your fingers and neurons; even if you only write personal divertimentos, please do write in the language that until now has taken you in as its own." Writing academic reports or essays like the ones he received in English, he said, is a matter of technical proficiency. "Writing, what is truly called writing, in another language will be difficult for you, but you must do it, not for the good of the foreign language but for the benefit of your own tongue. After writing in another language, your own will never be the same, for better or worse."

> Writing in good English won't save you from marginality. There are more obstacles ahead: not even a press in Barcelona, one of those famous ones, will dare to publish an essay on, say, [Émile] Zola or [Heinrich] Heine written by a Mexican. Resign yourselves, *nanos*, marginality is, first, inevitable, and second, delightful. Talk to the tribe, if anybody outside listens, fine, if not, fine. Embrace English, make it your Latin, but let your vernacular be your being, your inhabiting this slice of time and space that it has been your lot to live.

Don Ignacio added more counsel when we began to return from our studies abroad or stayed on to live our lives in other languages. One afternoon, during summer vacation, sitting in his library, he came out with a handful of mimeographs—the old smelly kind with the ink that came off when you touched them. With a mocking smile, he passed them out to us. "So that you do not forget either me or the punishment: writing in Spanish." I transcribe here the text, entitled "Writing in Spanish":

> 1. Do not be translators. Your only intellectual duty is to think for yourselves ([Immanuel] Kant). It is unnecessary to write in Spanish, well or badly, merely to disseminate what international luminaries have sketched out. For that, there is English. Have something to say, something well thought out, which pushes your language to its limits, which shows your full citizenship in the various tones of the marginality to which you are condemned. Writing thus

is building for words "un su huequito,"⁴ so that they resound beyond the here and now.

2. Be local out of necessity, but never a localist, willingly or unwillingly. Nobody can write in Spanish without the local echoes of a city, of a neighborhood. But don't assume that the language of Chueca or Coyoacán is all there is to Spanish.⁵ And please do not join the ethnographic armada by talking like the people, which always turns out to be a frozen version of the language of one people, the people from here or there. Each word has its own wisdom and flavor; if you don't feel each word in full, you might as well write user manuals or academic reports in English. You can only enjoy the wisdom and the flavor of the local if you find the way to transcribe not the Mexicanism or the Catalanism or the local *lunfardo* but instead the knowledge and the feeling that the words convey.⁶ If I write "no se crea, mister, el esfínter cagaticio aprieta mejor,"⁷ in order to capture the stories of transvestites that a cabbie here once told me, I would have to write a paragraph to explain the flavor, the delicious obscenity, the class connotations, and the ambiguities demanded by the back and forth of everyday Mexican rhetoric.

3. There it is, *nens*, you have to write in more than one Spanish. All of us, due to social class and geographical origin, ordinarily write two or three [different] Spanishes. But our linguistic marginality doesn't excuse us from knowing as many Spanishes as possible. It's not enough to read Spanish, Peruvian, and Argentine authors. You have to hear the words in situ, travel, live in other Spanishes. You will always be automatons of your own languages, but a little bit of foreignness with words makes them more alive, more in possession of themselves.

4. Any language can be wordy, but behold: wordiness has been a lasting sin in Spanish. Writing in Spanish should be an act of contrition: we are and we have been wordy, through our own fault, through our most grievous fault. Bequeath every word its due existence, every adjective its weight. That brings us to the nub of the matter: those who write in Spanish should keep, at their writing table and in their minds, a pair of scissors—indeed, gardener's shears for merciless pruning. (The same could be said of those who write, say, in French, but who am I to say it?)

5. Assume there is a poem, an essay, or an unpublished novel that is wonderful, which can be expressed only thanks to the resources that Spanish offers.

If so, it's because that Spanish includes centuries of attempting to say the unsayable in Spanish, readings in many other languages, and because it already includes the very awareness of a long experimentation. Experience your language in its whole present-day breadth and its whole historical depth. You must turn off the automatic pilot of every element of your language, manually try, experiment, and then get rid of the scaffolding, leave in ink on paper only the essence of the endeavor, your endeavor. Nothing else. Do not overwhelm with erudition and do not leave your language running on autopilot.

6. Writing in Spanish will not save you from marginality. That is your penance and your blessing. But this much is certain: inhabiting the margins without knowing all of their corners is not to be marginal but *pendejo* [stupid]. To take up your pen believing yourself to be a secret Hegel in Spanish is as foolish as believing that there exists an alinguistic essence that can be expressed either in household Spanish or in computer English. If you want to nest in the possibilities that your language offers in its vast marginality, read poetry. Regardless of your chosen rhetorical domain—novels, history, science— reading poetry helps . . . In Spanish, in English, in whatever language you can. For it's in poetry where words unveil their secrets. There are plenty of manuals for using languages (dictionaries, grammars); ah! but the only manual for being echo and voice, master and innovator of languages, is poetry.

7. Languages, like nations, have shed too much blood. And what languages need is less blubbering and more hands on deck. Spanish is an imperial language, *¡i tant!* [of course], but the language of a decrepit empire. If we were Catalan or Basque or Nahuatl or Quechua speakers, we could try to resist imperial impositions; it's not easy, for Spanish is marginal in the world of ideas but imperial in its domains. And what if a lot of Basque and Catalan and Nahuatl today is Spanish written in Basque, in Catalan, and in Nahuatl? If these are your languages, write them, let them live and prosper. We Spanish-speaking logophiles will try to read all of that as far as we are able. But do not forget Spanish: you will always be welcome into this other, somewhat greater, marginality. I'm not saying that you should learn Spanish, there's no need, you already know it; I'm saying that you should resign yourselves, as so many others have, to writing in your languages, including Spanish, which isn't anything terribly complicated and grandiose. Or don't: learn instead to master English in all of its splendor, which is another imperial imposition but less down at the heels. In any case, remember: with language, less blubbering and more hands on deck; writing is neither a historical nor a genetic *fuero* [privilege]; it's a craft learned through long hours of ass-breaking labor. Here is the clue: brain ready, butt flat, get to writing and off the jeremiads go. Language is a craft, not torture.

8. Writing your era's Latin does no harm. Write English, it's what these times mandate; it's a nuisance but also offers great advantages. If as a Spanish-speaker you replace Spanish with English, consider yourself well served. That would mean either that you write well in English or that you have nothing much to say. Neither of these options is a tragedy, neither for you nor for any language. But take note, do not assume that by writing in English you are no longer marginal—that depends on who you are, where you write, how you write, what you say. As happens in Spanish or French, academic or literary fame often comes from parroting. Parroting in English is brilliant, but it is still parroting. In a hundred years, of this you can be certain, nobody will read 99.9 percent of what is today written in English, Spanish, or German. Returning to Spanish, your marginal existence in a plebeian prose, is only worthwhile if you aspire to think and write like that 0.1 percent who will be read in one hundred years, even if you fail. True failure is not trying, especially at the margins, in Spanish.

9. Rule for Writing in Three Parts: (a) if you don't read, don't write; (b) don't read just to write; (c) never write more than you read.

Vocation

[Recording transcribed from "Books: Vice and Craft," a lecture delivered by Ignacio Merlina y Rapaport at La Casa del Lago, Chapultepec, Mexico, April 15, 1974]

I am grateful for the invitation and I begin without further ado. Books call to mind, on the one hand, straightforward nouns—paper, ink, publishers, libraries, and bookstores; on the other, verbs: to read, to write, to research, and to think. About the former we will speak another day, if the opportunity arises. When I refer to the latter, I'm talking about vices and crafts. And this is where I will take you. I will be brief.

[Here's my watch (inaudible) . . . well that's it, one must flee, as from hunger, when somebody of the Iberian persuasion—*peninsular* or *indiano*—begins to make improvised use of language without a watch at hand. "Don't kill me with a tomato," Ramiro de Maeztu said to the Spanish Cortes; just shut up, Don Ramiro, shut up. And he didn't shut up (laughter) . . .[8] Later he was killed by anarchists or Communists, but, well, that wasn't the lesson I wanted to pass on (laughter) . . . but, behold, always keep an eye on your watch, don't trust yourselves, the language of Castile is a curse: once we start, there's no power on earth that can shut us up.]

Books have always been the common denominator among poets, novelists, historians, scientists, essayists, and teachers. Even before neurology and scientific history and sociology or even the craft of the novelist existed, all the practitioners of these realms were members of the guild that bought, stole, loaned, read, wrote, and treasured books. Until very recently, that guild always had very few members. Not only because leisure and money were indispensable to belonging to such a guild, to enjoying the vice of books, but also because, after all, why? What is the sense in being bookish? No one in his right mind would adopt a vice that might bring a little fame but almost always leads to hunger and insignificance. One of these addicts, a poet, Manuel António Pires, confessed to his books: "E só nós sabemos / que morremos sozinhos / (ao menos escaparemos à piedade dos vizinhos)."[9] That's it, that's all you can get from books.

We know the names of those who became famous as a result of their book vice, just as we know the names of Giacomo Casanova and the Marquis de Sade, but not those of the thousands of failed Don Juans. Only antiquarians and useless scholarly types—those are your other specimens of the bookish lineage—know the names of the many anonymous readers who, in the middle of a lost town, say, in the province of Girona or in a hacienda in the state of Hidalgo, had libraries and simply read because they read. We have no idea whether they wrote or not. Their writings have not reached us or they are so rare that they are impossible to lay hands on. The vice of books was expensive, yes, but not as bad as the vices associated with horses, drugs, jewels, political positions, women, or men. Besides, when Latin reigned, it was common for a reader in Amsterdam to know what volumes another was reading in Toledo or Oporto. In the nineteenth century book addicts ordered from catalogues, they had agents who procured French, Spanish, German, Mexican, and Italian books. There were not a lot of books, and the important ones, for members of the guild, were essential.

Well, there is nothing brilliant or interesting in what I have said so far. And yet today it would seem that the vice of books is a professional activity with millions of practitioners. It is assumed that newspapers, radio, television, universities, schools, literary magazines, cafes, and gatherings like this one are filled with members of the guild of the vice of books. What's more, for some time now, there has been a battle to belong to the old guild: universities are filled with experts in literature and poetry, in history and sociology, who claim to be the true heirs of the guild. They insist that they are the ones who truly read, who think seriously and professionally, who do rigorous research, who write the real books. They disdain the journalist, the dilettante, the person who deals with books without having a diploma. At the same time, those outside universities—self-taught, stubborn readers, literati, essayists—disdain the specialization, the obscure prose, and the useless erudition of academics. They claim that books are theirs and theirs alone.

I'm not the one who gives out the book addict ID cards. I am only saying that there are no borders separating the university, the academies, and those outside. A lot of professionals inside and outside the university own their craft, with or without degrees, competent people indeed, who earn their daily bread with paper and ink. That is their trade, like people who sell cars or oranges or who castrate pigs or skillfully slide their knives over the surface of the gyro spit to make us "tacos al pastor" [inaudible] . . .

Thus, there are many more professionals of the book than there are persons completely hooked on the vice of reading and its consequences. Small wonder that those truly possessed by books were the very epitome of human degeneration in the late eighteenth century. They were considered obsessive masturbators, sick, and depraved, and they were shunned. Reading and thinking in tandem are done *just because*. They can provide an income—I make a living from it—but I cannot recommend it as a career. To reduce the guild of the book to a professor who reads to prepare for class or to write a competent academic article in order to get a promotion, or to an opinion maker who manufactures clever editorials with a cigarette, a cup of coffee, and *The Oxford Book of Quotations* at his side—a volume that is to the vice of reading what onanism is to Don Juan's vice—to reduce the guild of the book (that perversion that is at once a curse and a blessing) to these tasks is like reducing writing to shorthand typing.

The pointless guild of books and its milieu—research, discovery, knowledge, lucidity, language—have lots of fans but few true members. But being or appearing bookish has become a profession, like that of stand-up comedian—which isn't being Miguel de Cervantes, or Voltaire, or Mark Twain—or like the "merolico" [street vendor of traditional medicine] on Tacuba Street—who doesn't aspire to be Louis Pasteur or Santiago Ramón y Cajal. Books as a profession can bring fame, prestige, and money. There are many like that who read or write one or more books to make a living and become famous. But to be a book person, to be part of the confraternity of the vice, is something else, certainly not to be recommended, because belonging to books isn't living, reading, and thinking; it's reading and thinking, period. That is living. A vice. I repeat, as they say here, "¿a quién chingados le interesa la manda esta?" [who gives a fuck about that?]. Who chooses to be disabled or schizophrenic? We confuse life and books as a result of some genetic defect or childhood trauma, or because of lack of love or social skills or as a divine punishment. The Portuguese poet Jorge de Sena said that it is as difficult to know how to live as it is to know how to read, but, and I quote de Sena, "vivir, mesmo ignorando, afinal é dificil, e nem sequer uma questão de gosto. Gostar de ler é que será difícil—o que não ofende ninguém."[10] Exactly, for, if there were a way, as there is for those attached to alcohol, to *des-librarse* [get rid of the vice of books], quite a few would be believers and prophets of the treatment. But there is no cure, and once infected, no one harbors any hope of relief.

I have said that the adepts of the vice of books are few, and they are repugnant. It remains to be said that because of their squalidness and their scarcity, they are indispensable. They are bees for the pollen of knowledge of the human condition. For that reason, and only for that reason, it would be worthwhile to separate the wheat from the chaff, inside and outside of universities and academies. But today that's almost impossible: so many occupations have grown up, so many pretensions around books.

I propose that we do an experiment that would provide a solution for variable *n*: the precise number, name, and quality of those degenerates I've been talking about. It would also be a fine public health measure because, as they say in Catalan, *no és de rebut* [it's unacceptable] that those losers are walking around, mixing with decent, well-meaning people. The survey I propose has been conceived *a la mexicana* because here in Mexico—and you must excuse the audacity of this foreigner—those who flaunt books live next door to those who flaunt power. And the experiment is this: that the Mexican state do what it often does—that is, grant scholarships, subsidies, prizes, and honors to everybody who claims to be a book person. Scholars and intellectuals, thus, could apply for the "Voz y Eco Nacional" [National Voice and Echo] grant and award, let's call it, which would include, say, a monthly stipend for life equivalent to one hundred times the minimum wage, an assistant, a national prize, numbered seats in the Academy of Language or History or the academy in the applicant's field, and national ceremonies upon turning fifty, sixty, seventy, and (should it be necessary) eighty and ninety years of age, in addition to the well-known posthumous honors, guaranteed burial in the Palace of Fine Arts, the National Auditorium, or the Estadio Azteca—*según sea el sapo la pedrada* [according to the fame of the deceased] [inaudible] . . .

The only requirement for nominees, as I was saying, would not be a doctoral degree or a certain number of pages published or citations in academic or literary publications. The nominee would simply be required to promise—in a document signed before a notary public—never again to read a single book and under no circumstances to pick up a pen or touch a keyboard. For purposes of our experiment, the number of "National Voices and Echoes" would be inconsequential. The eureka moment would come when we counted and determined who hadn't applied for the grant, who had persisted, instead, in the vice of reading, thinking, and writing. Indeed, we would have come up with a reliable solution for variable n—the number, name, and quality of those possessed by books and their milieu. I suspect that this variable would be a small number, but its value would be incalculable.

Once the constituents of variable n had been revealed, all that would be necessary would be to isolate them and to read their work if they write. (An act that would disqualify us from applying for the "National Voice and Echo" prize, but, oh well, there are worse dishonors.)

Thank you.

Lletraferit

It might have been because he was old or because he was a man—and a man of letters, at that!—but in fact Don Ignacio Merlina y Rapaport had a strong proclivity to talk about himself. An unreconstructed *mamón* (pretentious person) he was not, but he was an enchanting egocentric who easily fell into his favorite subject: himself. More than anything, Don Ignacio was a *lletraferit* (he used to say it in Catalan): wounded by letters, by the word, by knowledge, and by the cheap vanity of intellectuals.

He did listen, though often awaiting excuses that would trigger stories about his own life and readings. "Life unfolds in many places, but in truth it only occurs in one's own head," he told us, "that's all there is to it: thinking is a form of onanism." Maybe because of my youth or God knows why, but I did believe in his generosity. His egotism didn't bother me. I visited him in order to listen and learn, bouncing my ideas off of his and seeing what happened. Maybe words become a wound because *lletrafer- its*, by necessity, have to put up with a lot of other unbearable *lletraferits*. In my youth I didn't care, I reached for the knife to be wounded as quickly as possible.

This wasn't the case for X, one of the faithful participants in the gatherings on Río Guadalquivir Street. She was a brilliant, cultured young woman who, yes, was as big a *mamona* as they come and used to mock Don Ignacio's egotism. Once, when we had left Don Ignacio's library, as we walked along the Paseo de la Reforma to the Chapultepec metro stop, X went on and on: "I told you so, it's all about him, he uses us like a mirror, he doesn't listen, he constantly repeats himself." With time we would all become *mamones*, but in those years X's comments hurt me deeply, not because I believed in Don Ignacio's benevolent empathy—I suspected that there was something to X's criticism—but because I wanted to be- lieve in the existence of disinterested intellectual camaraderie. I wanted to believe in plain and simple human empathy. As long as the sense of intellectual communion reigned among us, I didn't feel denigrated as Don Ignacio's mirror.

At this point I better settle scores before saying more about Don Ignacio. Hardly twenty years old, X already thought of herself as a future Nobel Prize winner or, at the very least, as the next Carlos Fuentes—as she herself said in so many words. To be sure, it's debatable whether to be another Fuentes represents a lack or an excess of ambition, but in those years, among her friends, her ambition seemed to us to be too much. Be that as it may, X did not lack intelligence, so her concerns didn't seem banal to me. I did wonder whether intelligence was possible without ego- centrism. *Lletraferit* = pretentious asshole? Little did I know then that I would eventually become a professor at the University of Chicago, *mamón* among *mamones*.

X was fully aware of her own intelligence, and she was a shameless pedant. She had no problem with that, and why should she? As far as she was concerned, modesty in someone who sees a little beyond the obvious indicated a failure to overcome Christian humility or else it wasn't mod- esty at all, just plain stupidity. But our life trajectories reveal more than my recollections: Don Ignacio died unknown, and X went on with her life, convincing herself that a series of positions in our country's cultural institutions and a couple of novels that were nothing to write home about added up to the Nobel Prize she'd promised herself. As for the rest of the confraternity's members, we all won our own shares of pedantry, *sense por* (without fear), as Don Ignacio said. One had some success as a professor, another became a somewhat famous "opinion maker," another a rich businessman, and yet another a modest writer. That's about it. X was neither more nor less than any of us, but in those years she already had the self-esteem that the rest of us wouldn't achieve until much later.

Let me return to Don Ignacio. One day Don Ignacio's and X's egocentrism put our meetings on hold. I don't remember the specifics, but I retain the vivid image of Don Ignacio perorating about himself and some profound matter. In the midst of that, X arrogantly asked him something like whether he could tell us about it without talking about himself. And that's when all hell broke loose: Don Ignacio became more Iberian than ever; he interrupted X's arguments as though we were at a gathering of soccer fans in a café in Barcelona and mocked X's ignorance and vanity. It was truly unpleasant, unheard of in our meetings. I don't know whom I blamed more, X for the provocation or Don Ignacio for this reaction that made X the winner. The rest of us kept our mouths shut until sepulchral silence signaled that it was time to leave.

For two weeks we begged X to apologize. She refused, and not without reason. Nor did we have any news from Don Ignacio during those weeks. Three or four weeks later X called a meeting in her house for one of those displays that we foppish wannabe *lletraferits* put on; that is, she wanted to read us extracts from the political novel that she was writing. And it was then that she took out the letter: a sheet of paper carefully folded and covered with Don Ignacio's slanting, wandering handwriting. According to X, the letter had arrived within a week of the incident; it had been delivered by a taxi driver. X explained that she hadn't said anything because she had waited to meet with Don Ignacio in private, which had happened that same morning, the day she had planned to read us her novel. She said that things had been cleared up, that Don Ignacio was waiting for our usual visit, on the usual day at the usual hour, and that the old man "had understood my position." And then X began to read her novel to us . . . We weren't interested in her novel. We spent the night analyzing the letter word for word and extracting every detail of the meeting from X. Some of us made copies of the letter; I recall rereading it many times, fifteen years ago, and again five years ago, and when I found it to transcribe here:

Dear X:

Mea culpa, X, *mea culpa*, indeed, everything is about me. That can be explained.

As for the other matter, my reaction, it is clearly unforgivable. I should not, I repeat, I should not have submitted you to my Iberian charm. Do not forgive me now, forgive me tomorrow, when you see yourself doing the same in response to the irreverence of a young woman, who, wanting to talk about herself, makes you see that you speak only about X. So forgive me tomorrow, if you can. For today, understand me.

Catulle Mendès, a forgotten French writer admired by Rubén Darío, wrote some advice for a young man who wanted to be a "man of letters," *vol dir lletraferit*. The kid, *pobret* [poor boy], wanted to publish some bad poems and Mendès advised him to give up the idea. "Don't be stupid, there's still time to save yourself," he said, "it's not a life, the one we [men of letters] live, it's a poem or a novel or a play." There you have it, X. Mendès and I, dedicated to ruminating reality, digging in the brain matter we carry about, confuse thinking with living. "Ah," said Mendès, "all the glories that thirty years of work might have brought me I would give in exchange for crying warm tears for an instant, while realizing that I am crying."[11] Imagine, X, just crying without the possibility of narrating. Because, X, the wound of the *lletraferit* gets wormy with vanity, it bleeds from the impossibility of achieving truth and lucidity. Often the wound also sickens the letters themselves (in general, *lletraferits* produce cancer in words, which unnecessarily reproduces them, losing their intelligibility).

Dear X, let's agree that you and I are just that, *lletraferits*, as in self-absorbed, as in the constant thinking that we are thinking instead of living. Whether I am a successful *lletraferit*, or if you as *lletraferit* will become a famous novelist, essayist, philosopher, or intellectual *a la mexicana*, it doesn't matter, we are *lletraferits*; that is, riffraff who, rather than seeing and feeling, see that we are seeing and feel that we are feeling.

I won't bore you, I'm sure you already know them all too well, I mean, the theories about what was once upon a time called the soul, today consciousness. I don't know if there are indeed two brains rather than one: the first, just like an ant's, sees, feels, and reacts; the second, perhaps only in humans, bears witness to the first brain's seeing and feeling. Worse, the second brain makes storytelling out of everything, creating the sensation of the "I" who lives, knows, understands, strings together, argues, narrates. I don't know if there is any way to prove these fanciful ideas, but I don't know myself in any other way than the constant, unstoppable narrative that rumbles in my head, a play without intermissions, not even when I sleep, and whose protagonist is always the same—me and, at the same time, not me. To be sure, I realize that the ongoing play in my head is all storytelling; strictly speaking, it is not my life, but at times I can perceive it as though it were outside of myself—only because the "I outside" disguises itself as a scene in the unrelenting storytelling that I carry within me.

I imagine that every human being, you and I, and the cabbie who will deliver this letter, witnesses his or her own mise-en-scène every day, a drama that is usually innocuous—nothing memorable happens—but can at times be tragic or comic. But it is a play put on for your own consumption and entertainment. There's no audience: you are the only spectator, playwright, and actor. A punishment, *potser* [perhaps].

I suppose that, while I write this, the bricklayer who's leveling the pavement and listening to *cumbias* outside my window is putting on a play in his head, one that has something or nothing to do with the "piragua" [small river boat], *tachonada de luz y de recuerdos* [trimmed with light and with memories], the "piragua" of the Guillermo Cubillos mentioned in the *cumbia* the bricklayer is listening to. Maybe the scene that is now running through his head is erotic or maybe it has something to do with childhood memories suddenly brought to mind by odd shapes on the pavement. There's no way of knowing. If I go outside and ask him about his narrative, since he's not—lucky him!—a *lletraferit*, he will take me for a *tocat del bolet* [madman]. If he were to try to narrate the scene, he would realize that it is difficult. He knows the scene by heart but does not have the skill to recount it. The scenes are his, and his alone, they were not meant for sharing. If he could, would he want to stop the scene to take notes, to rethink dialogues, edit them, make them tragic or comic, like this or like that until they sounded good? Would he want to repeat the internal scene time and again, never really knowing which was more real, the scene itself or what indeed was actually happening to him?

The same is true of us, but our vocation is the internal theater, replaying the show over and over again; that is, pure egocentrism. There is nothing to be done about it. The bricklayer's hands and biceps betray his craft; our delicate hands reveal at a glance that we've never picked up a hoe or a shovel. Ah! But we have calluses on the human tissue that produces the internal theater. Our ego, X, has developed a tumorous mass because of the unconstrained reproduction of the cells that rethink things. The result: a persistent rethinking akin to refried beans. As we would say in Mexican, *así de chinita tenemos la conciencia de la conciencia, se para sola, la muy pelma* [untranslatable but meaning more or less we are annoying, forever conscious of being conscious, so much so that our consciousness seems alive and kicking].

This does not necessarily imply that it is a good workout for the intellect. No. There are, of course there are, engineers and mathematicians who go beyond this fixation with the internal theater and whose intelligence cannot be doubted. Ours, without necessarily being intelligent, is an obsessive consciousness of consciousness. We live on this, to read, and by reading to write, and by writing, to grant meaning to what perhaps wouldn't need meaning if it were a matter of simple biological survival.

In sum, my dear X, you, I, anyone like us—we are one and the same obscenity: *lletraferits*. Now, add up my years, and then *ja l'hem cagat* [we've screwed it up]. That's a lot of years to have lived like this. I don't have, I am had by thousands of scenes that repeat themselves over and over. Some rest forgotten and recur at the slightest provocation, others mix with new experiences or with my readings, and after having evoked them so often I don't know what I have experienced, what I read, what added to my true experience of the world. The worst part isn't the scenes scrambling up there, where "pelo fue," "donde calavero,"[12] but the obsession with recounting them, putting them together, editing them, rethinking the content and possible consequences. And so that's it, X, what's to be done? My most expeditious human empathy is the automatism of listening to you, processing what you express, clearing a path in the forest of my internal scenes that, in a flash, pounce, wanting to clarify what you are saying to me.

And hence you perceive that I talk about myself; I trust the scenes I compose before you—certainly, full of me—are about you. If you say "fear" or "illusion," my unrelenting tumor pulls from here and there remnants of stagings drawn from my world experience or my readings or from the many times I have tried to think "fear" and "illusion." Let's see if you understand me: my talking about myself is a clumsy and frustrated attempt to feel "fear" or "illusion" with you. Have no doubt, when it comes to listening, I do listen, not out of generosity, but necessity. My cerebral calluses demand clues to rethink, relive, the scenes that otherwise would run in circles around their own monotony. From you and from the others, that's how I learn. Or, dear X, do you think that you know my tricks better than I myself do? It's not you, it is I who am the most bored with myself. And yet, let it be known, Ms. X is right—it's all about me.

Do please realize this is how I make my living. That *futut* [fucked up] tumor of rethinking grants me either my innocuous form of human empathy, or it grants me ideas, scarce but welcome, for an essay. The tumor allows for the conjecturing of philosophical arguments, it makes sense of cultural or political experiences that change the very experience of those who read our open-air searches in the theater we carry within.

In effect, we are a bunch of insufferable *pelmazos* [bores], ego in its pure state, we're our own puppets and puppeteers. We are *lletraferits*. But we are not all the same. In my case, what I have set up in my head is, I don't know ... *qué vols que digui* [what do you want me to say?] ... a vaudeville. I'm very aware that it's a show and that it's both an ode to and a mocking of myself. There are *lletraferits* who take up the show they carry inside with sovereign seriousness. Go in that direction, and voilà: you will become what you have promised yourself. As for me, I don't bring my stories to the table to show off, not even to see myself before myself. My tales just come out because they come out, because I can't pronounce absolute truths about "fear" or about "illusion." Believe me, "mimismeo" [I speak a lot about myself], that is, I explain myself so that on seeing me playing my cards, you, in my vaudeville, find your own, and find other truths about "fear" or "illusion." Nothing more.

And so, dear, young friend, do not bother exposing me, I'm already taking care of that; I'm the buffoon of my drama, whose background choruses, well heard, reveal my envy—of your ambition, of your youth. The dwarf of my drama also exposes your buffoonery—you seek the opportunity to prove yourself as a *lletraferit*, and you are too confident that your internal theater is vast, but you don't realize that you have not lived enough to tell it, you lack experience in the telling. My buffoon is in equal parts vain and insecure, unable to stop the anxiety to know or to understand you or anyone else. He is also clumsy, so I cannot take myself too seriously. This may be simple need for human and intellectual empathy, and I do require it: I need you. I seek, though unsuccessfully, for my show to help you understand the play that you are putting together, so that one day you won't remember which scene, a thousand times repeated, was your own and which was mine. Because the fact is, my young *lletraferit*, that you will not escape from the prison of words.

Finally, X, before and after words there is always silence—which, come to think of it, produces "fear" and "illusion." It's good to know that silence waits for us there, ready to encompass us, but let's leave it waiting a little longer, let's keep trying to achieve intellectual communion.

But silence could not follow my Iberian verbal abuse. Because, dear X, whatever happens, let courtesy reign; among human attributes, it is the only proven gift. Its corollary, forgiveness, inflated by Christianity, isn't indispensable, but believe me, it brings us closer to escaping from ourselves.

Yours,

Ignacio

Archive

"The condition of the archive is the constitution of an instant and a place of authority": this was the quotation, in French, for which Don Ignacio Merlina y Rapaport had to find a Spanish paragon. Because all of a sudden he received various requests for Spanish equivalents to the uses of "archive," in English and French. The use of such a trivial word gradually multiplied among erudite theories in English, and it wasn't very "cool" not to include a Spanish voice in the matter. "Who would have thought," wondered Don Ignacio, "*háceme vuelto la cabeza nalga*,[13] now it turns out an ordinary word ('archive') is causing illnesses ('le mal d'archive'), and wordy phobias (archive as a metaphor for power, synonym for everything said, for everything to be said, the sayable and the unsayable, and an example of the mere possibility of saying). What had the poor little old word done to the professors? For archivists have enough *feina* [work] and consolation through their patron, Saint Benedict."

Don Ignacio carefully reviewed the many requests he kept in his filing-card box under the label "El coñazo del archivo" (The big time archive fuck-up). And he realized that none of the requests came from the natural source, that is, from historians, who are to archives what agave is to tequila. *El burro no pide orejas* (A donkey doesn't ask for ears), he thought. But, clearly, in various disciplines the word "archive" had outgrown its own semantic epidermis. It was no longer that Latinism borrowed from the Greek ("according to the Royal Academy, ἀρχεῖον—*arkheîon*, related to office, residence of the magistrates"); it was no longer simply the name of an "ordered set of documents" or "the place where they are kept" or the "action or effect of archiving." The word, in short, had turned into a mega-metaphor, or that's what Don Ignacio believed: "just like simple nouns with an uncontrollable metaphorical tonnage—'night,' 'blood,' 'heart,' and 'moon.'" Don Ignacio couldn't believe it: "they're getting their knickers in a knot over an insignificant word used by notaries, a term that has long been the property of witless bureaucrats and boring historians."

From the various requests, Don Ignacio deduced that "archive" had turned into a metaphor for various things: the power to select what to preserve, the power to decide the order in which things were filed, therefore synonymous with the deliberate exclusion of other records that weren't saved; also a simile for system, rules more or less inherited and accepted. That is, archive had come to be the power to legislate what is sayable and unsayable. From the multiple quotations in English, French, and Italian, Don Ignacio deduced this much, and also a clear pejorative tone: "Now the word 'archive' is an insult, something ugly and wicked," Don Ignacio explained to me. It's not that in Spanish "archivist," "archive," or "to archive" had ever had an agreeable flavor; "archive suggests boredom," indeed, but the word did not have what it took to say: "Listen up, you, fat slob, idiot . . . archive!"

Among the new connotations of the term, in addition to evil, Don Ignacio intuited something like optimism ("logophilia, that's it: someone controls the sayable because power is secretly 'archived' in language"). An optimism disguised as pessimism ("logophobia: they seek to escape from language, but not with silence, with words and more words"). The optimism is such, Don Ignacio thought, because it dresses the idea of "power" in coherence and direction ("too much to assume"). Thus, said Don Ignacio, the "archive turns out to be, first, a will and then an order, and therefore it commands, rules, archives, catalogues, and establishes the laws of memory and forgetting. Damned confusing!"

For Don Ignacio, the matter presented the following logic: an archive, what any ordinary person calls an archive, is a building, a depository for documents, in which some managers impose an order—this is to be saved, that isn't. Such an archive becomes an *archivito* (little archive) if seen as an anecdote of the big archive, language, which is bigger and more powerful than any building. Don Ignacio believed that in matters of language "it's hard to point out the person or thing imposing order and coherence." And Don Ignacio wrote this note to himself:

> In a nutshell: in the *archivito*, a bureaucratic convention, an order, classifies possible pieces of evidence that prove or disprove a historical argument (this happened or this didn't happen). That order is the accessible, if dictatorial, key to an amorphous mass of information that would otherwise be inaccessible. The order is a dictator, yes, but does anyone believe that anything is visible in an archive without some trace of a guide? Now, it's the big archive (everything that's been said, known, and remembered, whose major personification is language) that establishes the logic for reading within and beyond archives. However, explaining the mammoth archive, language, pointing to its owner or owners, is a fantasy as great as being able to exist outside of language, the big archive; is it possible to live free of the chaotic chains of language, in an unconjecturable orality without rules?

At the end of his notes, Don Ignacio wrote: "The semantic metastasis of the word 'archive' is not a sublime liberation conquered from outside of archives; it is simply proof of the seductive, if incoherent, power of the big archive, language." Unlike the philosopher or the literary critic, Don Ignacio thought, the common archivist knows that the archive's apparent order hides innumerable unexpected and undesirable consequences. "Who controls fortune, the good or bad luck of finding something unthought of, the serendipity intrinsic to archives?" For Don Ignacio, documents led to unheard of and uncontrollable stories, tales even beyond the suspicions of the power that ordered the archive.

In the end, said Don Ignacio, "the *feina* is the *feina*" (work is work). He had to earn a living. So he began to send ironic quotes from Tirso de Molina. In English he wrote to his clients: "In the manner that you want to make use of the word 'archive'—as a summary of everything and nothing, as a supreme will and no will—the term has been wonderfully expressed in Spanish by an old poet who, in describing an aged and garrulous woman, said (please notice the italicized words from which, in due time, you may also want to extract a lot of rhetorical juice in your insightful academic prose)":

> *Epílogo* de los tiempos
> *almacén* de las arrugas
> archivo de las edades
> y *taller* de las astucias.[14]

To prolong his secret mockery—and since they paid him per quotation— Don Ignacio also sent a reference to a gaudy, unknown Mexican writer who, Don Ignacio explained to his clients, "was not Homer but had a very telling name: 'the Messenger,' Telésforo Ruiz. In describing Mexico City's central plaza, Telésforo wrote the poem 'Las acabadas en al,' which nicely serves your intentions to prove that 'archive' is a word that cozily resides in the vicinity of power":

> El palacio nacional,
> antes virreinal,
> y el congreso federal
> comisaria general
> la sala presidencial

tesorería general
y el archivo general.[15]

With bills to pay, Don Ignacio included in the package something from *La musa callejera* (1883) by Guillermo Prieto, a critique of positivism and an affirmation of Don Guillermo's romanticism:

> Hoy que el alma es contrabando
> e impera lo positivo
> no queda sino el archivo
> para el que está viejetando [*sic*].[16]

Don Ignacio also sent a more enigmatic quotation ("nobody will understand it, but let's see what they do with it"). He explained to his clients the origin and the vicissitudes of the Moor Abenamar in a Spanish *romance*. He told them, with a bit of Gramsci and another *miqueta* (tiny bit) of Raimon, that the good Moor was "authentic testimony of *gent que anomenen classes subalterns*."[17] "What could be more 'other' than a Moor from La Morería whose songs come from the oral tradition?" (He didn't tell them, of course, that the ballads had been collected by "archivists" of words, reactionary and "hegemonic" philologists like Ramón Menéndez Pidal and Pedro Henríquez Ureña: "Why bother those who want proof of non-'archivability' with archives?"). He wrote to them: "Asking a favor from a Moorish captain—who in Granada fought against the troops of the Catholic Majesty of Castile—Abenamar addresses said captain":

> Claro espejo de las almas
> temor de los enemigos
> fuerte muro de Granada
> espejo de la milicia
> archivo en que mi esperanza
> vive, y todo mi contento,
> causa de todas mis ansias.[18]

Taking advantage of the quotation ("archive in which my hope lives"), Don Ignacio pulled a wild interpretation of the archive out of his sleeve. Of course, the apocryphal text that Don Ignacio sent neither rhymed with the academic use of the term nor was it a real quotation to be found in Spanish literature (but Don Ignacio said, "How much alleged evidence from archives is no more than a result of the invention to which the archive is an invitation?"). Without batting an eyelash, Don Ignacio charged for the quotation as though it had come from the work of an obscure Mexican writer from the early twentieth century, whom he baptized Ángel María Tonatiuh González, for better foreign consumption. Don Ignacio told me that the quotation was never included in English-language texts. But, by return mail, Don Ignacio received a question from a famous literary theorist from New York: "Was Ángel María Tonatiuh an indigenous woman?" Don Ignacio responded: "I am afraid not, as far as I know, *he* was a mestizo poet and, as a matter of fact, an archivist at the National Archive of Mexico. However, it was public knowledge that Mr. González was ostracized by the literati because of some of his overtly homoerotic poems." Don Ignacio said that you had "to throw a little more hot sauce on the taco, so that the client would bite." And in response to the New York critic, Don Ignacio added irony in the form of a question: "My esteemed Professor X, now you know: González was a *he*, and both an archivist and a writer, so he was neither Ms. Rigoberta Menchu nor Monsieur [Jacques] Derrida. And by the way, do you have any reference to a visit by Monsieur Derrida to a real archive? I would be very interested in learning about it."

In short, here is the bizarre, apocryphal text:

Oh, archive, cell of my certainties, carrying case of my body that broadens and shrinks to the rhythm of the uncertainty of what is stored; oh, archive, dumping ground of treasures and of universal and ecumenical garbage, imitation of the cosmos, my chaotic paradise. Ashamed as you are to be the repository of the tangled past, you flaunt touches of order and discipline in your name. But, home of mine, you are the very epitome of the "garbage" universe, synonym of "all," "anarchy," and "waste." Your power is the least of it. The core of it is your eternal and inevitable essence: chaos.

Garbage is possibility, it is finding, it is discovery, and it is evidence. My dearest, "finjamos que somos felices, triste pensamiento, un rato" [let's pretend that we are happy, sad thought, for a while] and that you could be either like a mind that remembers all or like a people that discard nothing.[19] If you were all memory, without catalogues, without hierarchies, memories alone, nothing more and nothing less, you would be omnipotent wisdom, but how would you make yourself heard? With what coherence, in what order would you recount everything, since an everything at once is like nothing? And if you were that, a sponge of all that has been lived, when could you tell the past, busy as you would be with the torment of accumulating more evidence merely due to the imperative of existing, of being archive?

If you were like a people that treasures everything, we would find in you material that demands to be reborn, something to reuse, new life for death, for garbage, for the past, for forgetting. But if you were like that, you would end up burying every reborn thing under the new garbage that would never stop being delivered to you, container of my soul. But you are not like that, my archive, no, no way! You store in your chaos, and in your pretentious desire for order, the hope of granting meaning to the past, to the present, to the future. You archive that possibility. And there is no way to get out of you, oh archive, "yo también me confundí, / cuando te vi, basura me volví" [I was also confused, / when I saw you, I turned into garbage].[20]

There's no escape, you are in command, but, archive of our memories, there is no foreman in you who lasts and reigns. Because there is only one God in the archive: chaos. Archive: more chaos today than yesterday and less than tomorrow; an inexorably lost battle against chaos; therefore, a catalogue of human megalomanias (traces of one who would control the uncontrollable). Also, you are an inventory of subversions, a secret index of orders and disorders, of worlds yet to be discovered, asylum of the solitary, the historian, the archivist, who converse with documents in an attempt to hear "entre las voces una" [one voice among the voices], anarchical echoes coming from outside, from within the archive, from the many boxes and folders, from the historian's imagination.

To preserve is the key, but not everything is in the archive. In your possession, archive of mine, there is the enigma of chaos and order, which, like good and evil, do not exist one without the other. Archive, my home, preserve my consciousness of archiving and of being archived by your divine chaos, whose dominion death does not defeat but rather fills to bursting.

ÁNGEL MARÍA TONATIUH GONZÁLEZ, *Memorias de trastienda*,
(Mexico City: Talleres Gráficos del Archivo Nacional, 1904, p. 220)

Palabrear

[Handwritten notes, with the heading "for MA's workshop," undated. I haven't been able to determine either the notes' context or the identity of MA. *Palabrear* means "to talk," or living both with and for words.]

Reflections on writing, old age, and, why not, exile . . . That's what I've been asked to talk about today. The invitation seems to allude to my personal trajectory; MA asked me to talk to you about me, that's the truth. But the truth is I don't write, *yo palabreo*, and thanks to exile, not because exile has granted me a unique clairvoyance, but because it allowed me to live into my old age *i prou* [and that's all]. There you have it, we've already covered one of the subjects. Let's move on.

I belong to a generation that has already seen its *maestros* die. As intellectuals, our national and international insignificance comes merely from the fact of having grown old. At one point or another, it becomes our turn to occupy the *maestros'* chairs, whether we deserved to or not. It is our turn simply because it is our turn. And here I am, talking as if I were a *maestro*.

As an old man, I suppose it's my turn to impersonate a flower and take my place in the vase with the other flowers. In a way, the time came for me to be what my generation dreamed of: the bosses with ink and books, only at the cost of becoming what we promised never to become. You young people, of course, know what I'm talking about, don't pretend that you don't. As you're listening to me, you think: we, the young cohorts, will never be like this old man who's talking to us today, because he's not as famous as we hope to become. This old man, you all think, is not even as important as the other old man who organized this talk. In your eyes, I'm sure, that man is famous, but also—I don't know—reactionary and piggy in the game that all of us are playing. I don't want to spoil your afternoon, *nens, nenas*, but I leave you with this: if you do not all entirely succeed in living by the pen, you will say that it was because of the betrayals of some *maestros* who filled your paths with stones. If, instead, you become the stable's next muleteers, it will be because you have become *los maestros*; that is, you will be the ones putting stones in others' paths, something you thought yourselves incapable of doing. To achieve the happiness of *palabrear*, I recommend that you select and honor good *maestros*. Then again, to achieve tangible success in Mexico, I advise you to set your sights on a good patron. Whether indeed he is a *maestro* or not, who cares?

Myself, thinking of my *maestros*, I only object to their dying. I feel more of a farce, and more alone, when I see my own *maestros* depart. This is the metamorphosis I am experiencing: from ambition into simulacrum, with nothing in between. Old age will save us from simulacrum, for sure, but not before rubbing lots of embarrassment in our faces, like this ridiculous situation I am explaining to you altruistically. But meanwhile, let vainglory come to us; loneliness, too, like a flower, knowing it is a mere weed, struts its charms. But we are, and you'll be, mundane herbs brought to flower by the sun of old age. And by being orphaned . . . And by the mediocrity of an intellectual environment that makes bouquets out of old weeds . . . And by a present that, in order to seem eternal, demands insignificance. This makes us feel special, when we are no more than the tired occurrence of the biological form of "our turn." Well, I trust I have now exhausted one more subject. Let's come to a stop.

What is left for us, old people, is irony. But it is just another mask that does not necessarily save us from insignificance. Oh well, seen with honest eyes, the enigma is cruel: your turn to strut on the stage comes when you're no longer able to surprise yourself. My words are bored with themselves, with the posturing, with the irony they've shown off for decades. I ask my words to articulate the anguish that their lack of precision and their incapacity to take risks causes me—they are so themselves. They always follow the same routes. They disobey. Their monotony importunes me, they don't astound me . . . you see, this is what they say, listen to me, I merely articulate platitudes.

My words could reveal themselves and say that in fact it is not their fault I do not know how to express what I feel; or, better, they could make me realize that I neither feel nor think anything because they, my words, are the long and short of what I think and feel. They could speak—that's what words are for—about being martyred in order to embody brevity and exactitude. But it is clear the torture has been useless: there are no tangible results. What I write conveys neither the silent void nor the precise word that melts or creates a great enigma. That's why I do not write, I word: *palabreo*, I search for, play, entangle, traffic with, twist, and buy words.

Jules Renard's *Journal* strikes me as a monument to the lost battle for brevity and exactitude, a rehabilitation treatment for the meaninglessness of writing. It appears with absolute clarity, in his entry for March 17, 1890: "I do nothing. I am more aware than ever that I am good for nothing. I feel that I will come to nothing, and these lines that I write seem childish, ridiculous, and even, and above all, absolutely nothing." Renard thought he still had the possibility to recur to hypocrisy. For him, it was necessary to pretend that the bad moment would pass. "I will have hope again," he wrote, "[I will have] more courage to make a greater effort." It seems that his words were meant to atone for their uselessness, while he certainly desired to get out of them in order to say something more than the weight of not feeling lucidity. Hope will return, Renard believed, but "nos espérances sont comme les flots de la mer: quand ils se retirent, ils laissent à nu un tas de choses nauséabondes, de coquillages infects et de crabes, de crabes moraux et puants oubliés là, qui se traînent de guingois pour rattraper la mer" [our hopes are like the waves of the sea: on withdrawing they reveal a mountain of loathsome things, foul seashells and crabs, reeking moral crabs abandoned there, that drag themselves on their sides to return to the sea]. Indeed! These wordy confessions—my own, for instance—only serve to reveal those crabs, but they also evince a minimum of sagacity: the awareness of the insignificance of writing. You will say that it is not much, but believe me, it counts for something as soon as one tests the weight of the generational stable. Because the *maestros* have gone.

And yet, that minimum intelligence is, per Renard again, "water that flows unused, unknown, there where a mill has yet to be installed." In short, trust me, I am trying to say, to think, but *palabreo, palabreo* [I word, I word]. "Ay," Luis Rosales said, "si fuera fácil / desempalabrarnos" [if only it were easy / to unword us].[21] Yes indeed: "si fuera fácil."

Many thanks, and much luck to you all.

NOTES

Chapter 1. The Laws of History

1. A Mexican popular saying drawn from Herod's historical cruelty: "Ley de Herodes, o te chingas o te jodes" (Herod's Law: Either you're screwed or you're fucked).

2. Antonio Machado (1875–1939), "Proverbios y cantares," *Poesías completas*.

3. Oscar Wilde, "The Ballad of Reading Gaol": "And all men kill the thing they love, / By all let this be heard, / Some do it with a bitter look, / Some with a flattering word, / The coward does it with a kiss, / The brave man with a sword!"

4. Jorge Luis Borges's "Funes el memorioso," in *Ficciones*.

5. Fray Luis de León (1527–1591), "Vida retirada": "¡Qué descansada vida / la del que huye el mundanal ruido / y sigue la escondida / senda por donde han ido / los pocos sabios que en el mundo han sido!" ("Retired Life": How tranquil is the life / Of he who, shunning the vain world's uproar, / follows the hidden path, of yore / Chosen by the few who conned true wisdom's lore!: Luis de León, *Poesías orginales de Fray Luis de León*).

6. William Shakespeare, *King Lear*, act 4, scene 1, "Edgar. [aside] And worse I may be yet. The worst is not / So long as we can say 'This is the worst.'"

7. Ernest Renan, *History of the People of Israel*.

8. In reference to George Santayana's well-known dictum: "Progress, far from consisting in change, depends on retentiveness. When change is absolute there remains no being to improve and no direction is set for possible improvement: and when experience is not retained, as among savages, infancy is perpetual. Those who cannot remember the past are condemned to repeat it" (*The Life of Reason*); and to the ranchera "En el último trago" (On the Last Drink) by José Alfredo Jiménez: "Nada me han enseñado los años / siempre caigo en los mismos errores / otra vez a brindar con extraños / y a llorar por los mismos dolores" (Time has taught me nothing / I always make the same mistakes / Once more drinking with strangers / and crying over the same sorrows).

9. Carl G. Hempel, "The Function of General Laws in History."

Chapter 2. Poetry and History

1. Readers interested in the change of metaphors in Spanish history can start with Javier Varela's *La novela de España*.

Chapter 3. The Historical Imagination

1. I owe this revelation to a stroll through Jerusalem with colleague and friend Jan Szeminski.

Chapter 6. Self-History and Autobiography

The subhead "Only Turkeys—and Suspicions—Die on the Eve" on page 130 is a take on the Mexican saying "Sólo los guajolotes se mueren a la víspera" (Only turkeys die on the eve).

1. Heirs of a group of French immigrants (from Barcelonnette) to Mexico who made a fortune in the nineteenth-century textile industry.

Chapter 7. Six Life Stories by Heart

1. In Mexican popular cultures these winds get into people's bodies.

2. "Well, sure, I wanted to go back to La Piedrita [La Piedad], but, no, even when they threw out so many Mexicans [1930s] my husband lost his bakery's customers and then, well, the little ones were born here and here they grew up, and, well, when we had money to go back we weren't healthy enough to make the trip, and so our memories gathered around us here, and here we stayed."

3. "Lordy! I was so much in love with your great granddaddy, it's not that he was handsome, but could he ever sing, with so much feeling . . . Ay, that Agapito, he was a devil! How he made me blush with those songs, 'Perjura' and 'Viejo Amor' [which went] 'an old love is never forgotten, never left behind' . . . Let's don't talk about him, little girl, anymore, it makes my soul melt."

4. "I came here fleeing the war in La Piedad, when the federal army killed one of my uncles, and the parish priest introduced me to a man who took people to Texas. When I got here I kept on playing guitar and learned to be a baker. When I came to Chicago to work in the packing plant, I realized that the whole thing was pretty ugly: blacks didn't like us, Poles even less, because they said we broke the strike; I didn't like the way things were at all, and since I already knew how to play the guitar and make bread, I went to see a compatriot who worked in the bakery of one of those strange Germans, they say they're Jews, and I worked

there until my friend and I saw that there were a lot of folks who wanted their *cemas de Numarán* [typical breads from Numarán, Mexico], the ones that are real crumbly, so at night we started baking bread in the little apartment we had, and in the mornings we sold it to our countrymen. Then I sent money for my wife to come, I taught her the job and just like that, with her and other women friends, we made bread at home to sell."

5. "My *comadre* Leonor, who'd been in Chicago for some time, sent a letter saying that there were lots of Polish blondes there, and that Agapito hadn't neglected them, that the son of the butcher from the San Francisco barrio had already had a child with one of those Polacks, so I came to Chicago, yes, to get what was mine."

6. Corrido transcribed in volume 1 of Paul S. Taylor, *Mexican Labor in the United States* (Berkeley: University of California Press, 1928–1934): "What's the point in knowing my trade / Since there are a lot of bakers / And while I'm making two rolls / They're turning out more than a million // There are some darker than tar / but they say they are Anglos / They're covered in flour up to the neck / And they use petticoats for pants // A lot of my fellow countrymen don't want to talk / About what their mammas taught them / And they go around saying they're Hispanic / and denying the national flag."

7. "Ay, child, what can I tell you, I'm from La Piedrita [La Piedad], and at night my mind goes back there and during the day I erase everything and I'm here, well, you don't forget the attachments formed when you were small, but when I go to La Piedad I don't find myself there, everything has changed so much, and one is the collection of memories of the ones you love, child of the Lord, and my loved ones are here, little one, look, you're here, right?"

8. "Ay, no, little one, what would we be doing now in that town? Being maids for the Álvares, like my mother? People with no car and no house, with no education? Not at all, little one, everything from there stayed with me like prayers, pure reciting of memories but . . . well, we're here together and well . . . Thank you, Señor de San Francisco! Thank you, Señor de la Piedad!"

9. Joan Maragall, "Oda a Espanya," in *Obra poética*.

10. Màrius Torres, "La reducció poètica," in *Poesies*.

Chapter 8. Polyglotism and Monolingualism

1. For further elaboration of this Catalan term, see chapter 10.

Chapter 9. *Amar queriendo como en otro tiempo*

1. This is a paraphrase of the very famous Cuban tune "A llorar a Papa Montero" (Crying for Papa Montero) by Eliseo Grenet, popularized by Cuban singer-composer María Teresa Vera in the late 1920s.

2. The title of this chapter is very difficult to translate, something like: "To love being in love as they did in another time." From the poem "Tiempo" by Mexican poet Renato Leduc. The poem became very popular in 1970s Mexico when put to music and sung by Mexican singers José José and Marco Antonio Muñiz.

3. Unless otherwise indicated, the quotations refer to titles or lyrics of boleros.

4. The subhead for this section is an allusion to the poem "Vivo sin vivir en mi" (I live without living in myself) by the Spanish mystic Saint Teresa of Ávila: "I live without living in myself / and so high the life I hope for / that I die because I don't die."

Chapter 10. Wicked Tongue (Extracts)

1. Here Don Ignacio seems to be quoting Alfonso Reyes's "La Habana" (included in *Antología*). For the Cuban song about "Papa Montero," see chapter 9.

2. Here Don Ignacio makes use of the famous Cuban danzón "Fefita" (early twentieth century).

3. Don Ignacio seems to be referring to Fernando Pessoa, *A educação do estóico*.

4. Here Don Ignacio is using a Mexicanism: to make one's own little hole in order to live and hallow.

5. Chueca is one of Madrid's hip barrios; Coyoacán is an old village near Mexico City that is now one of the megalopolis's hip barrios.

6. *Lunfardo* was a dialect spoken in Buenos Aires.

7. Don Ignacio clearly was fascinated with vulgar Mexican expressions. This one is particularly so, something like "Don't believe it, mister, the sphincter for shitting squeezes better."

8. Don Ignacio is referring to Ramiro de Maeztu, a Spanish conservative Catholic writer and representative in Parliament during Spain's Second Republic, who was assassinated in Madrid in 1936, during the Republican, anarchist, and Communist uprisings after the coup d'état of July 1936.

9. Don Ignacio is quoting Manuel António Pires's poem "Aos meus livros": "And we only know / we'll die alone / (at least we'll escape from the neighbors' pity)" (in *Poesía, saudade da prosa*).

10. Here Don Ignacio recalls Jorge de Sena's *O reino da estupidez*—to live, even in ignorance, at the end is hard, and it's not even a matter of choice. To love reading, that would be difficult—but it doesn't damage anyone.

11. Don Ignacio is referring to C. Mendès, *Monstres parisiens*.

12. Don Ignacio refers to Francisco de Quevedo's satirical poem, mocking Góngora, meaning where there was hair, in the skull: "Calvo que no quiere encabellarse" (A bald guy who doesn't want to grow hair).

13. Again, Don Ignacio recalling Quevedo's poem, meaning something like "my head has become my butt."

14. "*Epilogue* of the times / *storehouse* of wrinkles / archive of the ages / and *workshop* of skills." Don Ignacio seems to be alluding to a ballad by Tirso de Molina entitled "A una vieja habladora que callando registraba a un galán lo que le pasaba con su dama desde su casa" (To a talkative old woman, who, falling silent, took note from her house for a beau of what his lady was doing).

15. "The national palace, / formerly viceregal, / and the federal congress / general commissary / the presidential salon / general treasury / and the general archive." I found this poem quoted by Don Ignacio in Telésforo Ruiz, *Apuntes poéticos*.

16. "Since today the soul is contraband / and the positive reigns / there's nothing left but the archive / for he who is growing old."

17. "People who are called subaltern classes": a reference to Antonio Gramsci's notion of subalterns in the song "Jo vinc d'un silence" by Raimon, Valencian singer-composer, popular in the 1960s and 1970s.

18. "Clear mirror of souls / feared by the enemies / Granada's strong wall / mirror of the militia / archive in which my hope / lives, and all of my contentment, / cause of all of my anxieties." Don Ignacio copies part of one of the old popular ballads known as "Romances de Abenamar."

19. Don Ignacio paraphrases the poem "Finjamos que soy feliz" (Let's pretend that I'm happy) by Sor Juana Inés de la Cruz.

20. Here Don Ignacio changes his tune and alludes to the Mexican bolero "Basura," which was very famous in the 1940s, sung by Trio Los Panchos.

21. "Canción del deshojamiento de las palabras" (Song about pulling the petals off words) by the Spanish poet Luis Rosales.

BIBLIOGRAPHY

As always, I have avoided bibliographic onanism. Every essay is the result of readings or it is not. Not all these essays, however, are susceptible to a precise bibliography. Here are the minimum references.

Abelove, Henry, ed. *Visions of History*. New York: Pantheon Books, 1983.

Acosta, José de. *Historia natural y moral de las Indias: en que se tratan las cosas notables del cielo, y elementos, metales, plantas y animales dellas y los ritos y ceremonias, leyes y govierno y guerras de los indios* (1590). Mexico City: Fondo de Cultura Económica, 1940.

Adams, Henry. *The Education of Henry Adams*. Blacksburg, VA: Wilder, 2008.

Agulhon, Maurice, and Pierre Nora, eds. *Essais d'égo-histoire*. Paris: Gallimard, 1987.

Alatorre, Antonio. *Cuatro ensayos sobre arte poética*. Mexico City: El Colegio de México, 2007.

———. *Los 1001 años de la lengua española*. Mexico City: Fondo de Cultura Económica, 2002.

Ankersmit, Frank R. *Sublime Historical Experience*. Stanford, CA: Stanford University Press, 2005.

Aristotle. *The Poetics of Aristotle*. Edited with critical notes and a translation by S. H. Butcher. London: Macmillan, 1907.

Aron, Raymond. *Mémoires*. Paris: Julliard, 1983.

———. "The Philosophy of History." In Marvin Farber, ed., *Philosophic Thought in France and the United States*, 301–320. Albany: State University of New York Press, 1968.

Auden, Wystan Hugh. *Homage to Clio*. New York: Random House, 1960.

Auerbach, Erich. "Vico's Contribution to Literary Criticism." In *Time, History, and Literature: Selected Essays*, 3–10. Princeton, NJ: Princeton University Press, 2014.

Augustine, Saint, Bishop of Hippo. *Confessions and Enchiridion*. Trans. Albert C. Outler. London: SCM Press, 1955.

Aurell, Jaume. *Theoretical Perspectives on Historians' Autobiographies: From Documentation to Intervention*. New York: Routledge, 2016.

Bartra, Roger. *Antropología del cerebro: la conciencia y los sistemas simbólicos.* Mexico City: Fondo de Cultura Económica/Valencia, Spain: Pre-Textos, 2010.

———. *La jaula de la melancolía: identidad y metamorfosis del mexicano.* Mexico City: Grijalbo, 1987.

———. *La sangre y la tinta: ensayos sobre la condición postmexicana.* Mexico City: Océano, 1999.

Bayart, Jean-François. *Les études postcoloniales, un carnaval académique.* Paris: Éditions Karthala, 2010.

Becker, Carl L. *Detachment and the Writing of History: Essays and Letters.* Ithaca, NY: Cornell University Press, 1958.

Benedetto, Antonio di. *Zama.* Buenos Aires: Centro Editor de América Latina, 1967.

Benjamin, Walter. *Illuminations.* Ed. and with an introd. by Hannah Arendt. Translated by Harry Zohn. New York: Harcourt, Brace & World, 1968.

Berkhofer, Robert F. *Beyond the Great Story: History as Text and Discourse.* Cambridge, MA: Harvard University Press, 1997.

Berlin, Isaiah. *Vico and Herder: Two Studies in the History of Ideas.* New York: Viking Press, 1976.

Black, Max. *Models and Metaphors: Studies in Language and Philosophy.* Ithaca, NY: Cornell University Press, 1962.

———. *Perplexities.* Ithaca, NY: Cornell University Press, 1990.

Bloch, Marc. *Apologie pour l'histoire ou métier d'historien.* Paris: Librairie Armand Colin, 1949.

———. *L'Étrange défaite: témoignage écrit en 1940.* Paris: Gallimard, 1990.

Bloom, Harold. *The Anxiety of Influence: A Theory of Poetry.* New York: Oxford University Press, 1973.

Blumenberg, Hans. *Paradigmen zu einer Metaphorologie.* Frankfurt am Main: Suhrkamp, 1998.

Borges, Jorge Luis. *El aleph.* Buenos Aires: Emecé, 1962.

———. *Ficciones.* Buenos Aires: Emecé, 1944.

———. "The Golem." Trans. Frank Thomas Smith. *Southern Cross Review* 94 (May–June 2014). Available at https://southerncrossreview.org/94/golem-borges-eng.htm.

Boswell, James. *The Life of Samuel Johnson* (1791). New York: Garden City Books, 1945.

Bouhours, Dominique. *La manière de bien penser dans les ouvrages d'esprit: dialogues.* Paris: Chez la Veuve de Sébastien Mabre-Cramoisy, 1687.

Brading, David A. *The Origins of Mexican Nationalism.* Cambridge, UK: University of Cambridge, Centre of Latin American Studies, 1985.

Braudel, Fernand. *Écrits sur l'histoire.* Paris: Flammarion, 1969.

Browning, Robert. *Sordello.* Ed. Rev. Arthur J. Whyte. London: J. M. Dent & Sons, 1913.

Buarque de Holanda, Sérgio. *Sérgio Buarque de Holanda: escritos coligidos*. Ed. Marcos Costa. 2 vols. São Paulo: Unesp-Fundação Perseu Abramo, 2011.

Byrne, Ruth M. J. *The Rational Imagination. How People Create Alternatives to Reality*. Cambridge, MA: MIT Press, 2005.

Campolla Nuñez, Guillermo. "El amor es un tóxico." *Revista Mexicana de Ciencias Médicas y Biológicas* (February 1944): 16–25.

Canetti, Elias. *Auto de fe*. Prologue by Mario Vargas Llosa. Trans. Juan José del Solar. Barcelona: Círculo de Lectores, 1994.

Carlyle, Thomas. "On History" and "On History Again." In Thomas Carlyle, *Historical Essays*, 3–13, 15–22. Berkeley: University of California Press, 2002.

Carpentier, Alejo. *El siglo de las luces*. Barcelona: Seix Barral, 1981.

Carr, E. H. *What Is History?* New York: Knopf, 1962.

Castilla del Pino, Carlos. *Pretérito imperfecto*. Barcelona: Tusquets, 1997.

Castro, Américo. *La realidad histórica de España*. Mexico City: Editorial Porrúa, 1966.

Celan, Paul. *Selected Poems and Prose of Paul Celan*. Trans. John Felstiner. New York: W. W. Norton, 2001.

Chacón, Dulce. *La voz dormida*. Madrid: Alfaguara, 2002.

Chatterjee, Partha. *A Possible India: Essays in Political Criticism*. New Delhi/New York: Oxford University Press, 1997.

Chaudri, Nirad C. *The Autobiography of an Unknown Indian*. New York: Macmillan, 1951.

Clendinnen, Inga. *Agamemnon's Kiss: Selected Essays*. Melbourne: Text Publishing Company, 2006.

———. *Ambivalent Conquests: Maya and Spaniard in Yucatan, 1517–1570*. Cambridge: Cambridge University Press, 1987.

———. *Tiger's Eye: A Memoir*. Melbourne: Text Publishing, 2001.

Cobarrubias Orozco, Sebastián de. *Tesoro de la lengua castellana o española* (1611). Available at http://fondosdigitales.us.es/fondos/libros/765/16/tesoro-de-la-lengua-castellana-o-espanola/.

Cochrane, Peter. "Exploring the Historical Imagination." *Griffith Review* 31 (February 2011). Available at https://griffithreview.com/articles/exploring-the-historical-imagination/.

Collingwood, R. G. *An Autobiography*. Oxford: Oxford University Press, 1939.

———. *Essays in the Philosophy of History*. Austin: University of Texas Press, 1965.

———. *The Idea of History*. Oxford: Clarendon Press, 1946.

Connolly, Cyril. *Enemies of Promise*. London: G. Routledge & Sons, 1938.

Cooper, Frederick. *Colonialism in Question: Theory, Knowledge, History*. Berkeley: University of California Press, 2005.

Corti, Egon Caesar, Conte. *Maximilian und Charlotte von Mexiko*. Leipzig: Amalthea-Verlag, 1924.

Cosío Villegas, Daniel. *Memorias*. Mexico City: Joaquín Mortiz, 1976.

———. *Un tramo de mi vida*. Mexico City: Fondo de Cultura Económica, 1997.

Cosío Villegas, Daniel, Francisco R. Calderón, Luis González y González, Moisés González Navarro, and Emma Cosío Villegas. *Historia moderna de México*. 5 vols. Mexico City: Hermes, 1955–1972.

Croce, Benedetto. *The Defence of Poetry: Variations on the Theme of Shelley*. Philip Maurice Deneke Lecture Delivered at Lady Margaret Hall, Oxford, on October 17, 1933. Oxford: Clarendon Press, 1933.

———. *La filosofia di Giambattista Vico*. Bari, Italy: Laterza, 1933. Translated as *The Philosophy of Giambattista Vico* by R. G. Collingwood. New York: Russell & Russell, 1964.

———. "L'autobiografia come storia e la storia come autobiografía." In *Filosofia, poesía, storia*. 480–482. Milan: R. Ricciardi, 1951.

———. *Memorie della mia vita: appunti che sono stati adoprati e sostituiti dal "Contributo alla critica di me stesso."* Naples: Istituto Italiano per gli Studi Storici, 1966.

———. *Teoria e storia della storiografia*. 2nd ed. Bari, Italy: G. Laterza, 1920.

———. *Una pagina sconosciuta degli ultimi mesi della vita di Hegel*. Bari, Italy: Laterza, 1950.

Cunqueiro, Álvaro. *Papeles que fueron vidas*. Barcelona: Tusquets, 1994.

———. *Viajes imaginarios y reales*. Barcelona: Tusquets, 1986.

Danesi, Marcel. *Vico, Metaphor, and the Origin of Language*. Bloomington: Indiana University Press, 1993.

Darnton, Robert. *The Case for Books: Past, Present, Future*. New York, PublicAffairs, 2009.

Dray, William H. *History as Re-Enactment: R. G. Collingwood's Idea of History*. Oxford: Clarendon Press/Oxford University Press, 1995.

———. *On History and Philosophers of History*. Leiden, NY: Brill, 1989.

Droysen, Johann Gustav. *Outline of the Principles of History*. Trans. E. Benjamin Andrews. Boston: Ginn, 1897.

Du Bois, W. E. B. *The Souls of Black Folk* (1903). New York: Modern Library, 2003.

Duby, Georges. *Art et societé au Moyen Âge*. Paris: Éditions du Seuil, 1997.

During, Simon, ed. *The Cultural Studies Reader*. London/New York: Routledge, 1999.

Ellmann, Richard. *Oscar Wilde at Oxford*. Washington, DC: Library of Congress, 1984.

Escalante Gonzalbo, Fernando. *A la sombra de los libros: lectura, mercado y vida pública*. Mexico City: El Colegio de México, 2007.

Fabre, Luis Felipe. *La sodomía en la Nueva España*. Valencia, Spain: Pre-Textos, 2010.

Fasolt, Constantin. *The Limits of History*. Chicago: University of Chicago Press, 2004.

Fausto, Boris. *Memórias de um historiador de domingo*. São Paulo: Companhia das Letras, 2010.

Feijóo, Benito Jerónimo. *Teatro crítico: ensayos filosóficos* (1748). Introduction and selection of texts by Eduardo Subirats. Barcelona: Anthropos, 1985.

Ferguson, Niall. *Civilization: The West and the Rest*. New York: Penguin Press, 2011.

———, ed. *Virtual History: Alternatives and Counterfactuals*. London: Papermac, 1998.

Fernández de Oviedo y Valdés, Gonzalo. *Historia general y natural de las Indias, islas y tierrafirme del mar océano, por el capitán Gonzalo Fernández de Oviedo y Valdés, primer cronista del Nuevo Mundo* (1526). Madrid: Impr. de la Real Academia de la Historia, 1851–1855.

Fitzpatrick, Sheila. *A Spy in the Archives: A Memoir of Cold War Russia*. London/New York: I. B. Tauris & Company, 2015.

Florescano, Enrique. *Imágenes de la patria a través de los siglos*. Mexico City: Taurus, 2005.

———. *Memoria mexicana: ensayo sobre la reconstrucción del pasado, época prehispánica–1821*. Mexico City: Joaquín Mortiz, 1987.

Foucault, Michel. *Oeuvres*. Ed. Frédéric Gros. 2 vols. Paris: Gallimard, 2015.

Gadamer, Hans-Georg. *Von der Wahrheit des Wortes*. Vol. 8 of *Gesammelten Werke*. Tübingen: Mohr, 1993.

García, Genaro. *Crónica oficial de las fiestas del primer centenario de la Independencia de México* (1910). Mexico City: Centro de Estudios de Historia de México Condumex, 1991.

García Icazbalceta, Joaquín. *Don fray Juan de Zumárraga, primer obispo y arzobispo de México*. Mexico City: Andrade y Morales, 1881.

Gay, Peter. *Savage Reprisals: Bleak House, Madame Bovary, Buddenbrooks*. New York/London: W. W. Norton & Company, 2003.

Gellner, Ernest. *Nations and Nationalism*. Ithaca, NY: Cornell University Press, 2008.

Giannetti, Eduardo da Fonseca. *A ilusão da alma*. São Paulo: Companhia das Letras, 2011.

Gibbon, Edward. *The Decline and Fall of the Roman Empire*. Harmondsworth, UK: Penguin, 1983.

Gibson, Mary Ellis. *The Autobiography of Edward Gibbon*. London: Dent; New York: Dutton, 1911.

———. *History and the Prism of Art: Browning's Poetic Experiments*. Columbus: Ohio State University Press, 1987.

Ginzburg, Carlo. *Il filo e le tracce: vero falso finto*. Milan: Feltrinelli, 2015.

———. *Il formaggio e i vermi: il cosmo di un mugnaio del '500*. Turin, Italy: Einaudi, 1976.

———. *No Island Is an Island*. Trans. J. Tedeschi. New York: Columbia University Press, 2000.

———. *Occhiacci di legno: nove riflessioni sulla distanza*. 2nd ed. Milan: Feltrinelli, 1998.

———. "Our Words and Theirs: A Reflection on the Historian's Craft, Today." In Susanna Fellman and Marjatta Rahikainen, eds., *Historical Knowledge: In Quest of Theory, Method and Evidence*, 97–119. Cambridge: Cambridge Scholars Publishing, 2012.

González y González, Luis. *El oficio de historiar*. Zamora, Mexico: Colegio de Michoacán, 1988.

———. *Pueblo en vilo*. Mexico City: El Colegio de México, 1969.

Grafton, Anthony. *What Was History?: The Art of History in Early Modern Europe*. Cambridge: Cambridge University Press, 2007.

Guerrero, Sergio. Collection of Poems. Unpublished MS.

———. "The Other Side of the Lighthouse" (1990). Unpublished MS.

Gutiérrez Nájera, Manuel. *Manuel Gutiérrez Nájera*. Ed. R. Pérez Gay. Mexico City: Cal y Arena,1996.

Guzmán, Martín Luis. *Memorias de Pancho Villa* (1951). Mexico City: Porrúa, 1984.

Haber, Stephen, ed. *Crony Capitalism and Economic Growth in Latin America: Theory and Evidence*. Stanford, CA: Hoover Institution Press, 2002.

Hahn, Óscar. *Archivo expiatorio: poesías completas, 1961–2009*. Madrid: Visor Libros, 2009.

Halperín Donghi, Tulio. *Son memorias*. Buenos Aires: Siglo XXI, 2008.

Hamnett, Brian. *The Historical Novel in Nineteenth-Century Europe: Representations of Reality in History and Fiction*. Oxford: Oxford University Press, 2011.

Hardman, Martha James, Lucy Therina Briggs, Nora Clearman, Laura Martin, Juana Vázquez, and Juan de Dios Yapita. *Aymara: compendio de estructura fonológica y gramatical*. La Paz: Instituto de Lengua y Cultura Aymara/Gainesville, FL: Aymara Foundation, 1988.

Hartog, François. *Régimes d'historicité: présentisme et expériences du temps*. Paris: Seuil, 2003.

Haslam, Jonathan. *The Vices of Integrity: E. H. Carr, 1892–1982*. London: Verso, 1999.

Hazlitt, William. *Table Talk*. London: J. M. Dent/New York: E .P. Dutton, 1960.

Heidegger, Martin. "The Origin of the Work of Art." In *Poetry, Language, Thought*, 15–86. Trans. Albert Hofstadter. New York: Harper & Row, 1971.

Heine, Heinrich. *Deutschland, ein Wintermärchen*. Göttingen: Niedersachs Wallstein, 2018.

Hempel, Carl G. "The Function of General Laws in History." *Journal of Philosophy* 39, no. 2 (Jan. 15, 1942): 35–48.

Higham, John. *History: Professional Scholarship in America*. New York: Harper & Row, 1973.

Hobsbawm, Eric J. *Interesting Times: A Twentieth-Century Life*. New York: Pantheon Books, 2002.

———. *Nations and Nationalism since 1780: Programme, Myth, Reality*. Cambridge: Cambridge University Press, 2004.

Hofstadter, Richard. *The Age of Reform: From Bryan to F. D. R.* New York: Vintage Books, 1955.

———. *The Paranoid Style in American Politics and Other Essays*. Chicago: University of Chicago Press, 1979.

Howe, Susan. *The Quarry* (1974). New York: New Directions, 2015.

Howson, Gerald. *Arms for Spain: The Untold Story of the Spanish Civil War*. New York: St. Martin's Press, 1999.

Huizinga, Johan. *El concepto de la historia*. Trans. Wenceslao Roces. Mexico City: Fondo de Cultura Económica, 1946.

———. *Homo Ludens*. Trans. Eugenio Ímaz. Mexico City: Fondo de Cultura Económica, 1943.

———. "The Task of Cultural History." In *Men and Ideas*, trans. James S. Holmes and Hans van Marle, 17–76. New York: Meridian Books, 1959.

———. *The Waning of the Middle Ages: A Study of the Forms of Life, Thought and Art in France and the Netherlands in the XIVth Century*. Trans. F. Hopman. London: E. Arnold & Company, 1924.

Humboldt, Wilhelm von. *Humanist without Portfolio: An Anthology of the Writings of Wilhelm von Humboldt*. Ed. and trans. Marianne Cowan. Detroit: Wayne State University Press, 1963.

———. "On the Historian's Task." In *History and Theory* 6, no. 1 (1967): 57–71.

Huntington, Samuel P. *Who Are We?: The Challenges to America's National Identity*. New York: Simon & Schuster, 2004.

James, Henry. *The Question of Our Speech: The Lesson of Balzac: Two Lectures*. Boston: Houghton Mifflin Company, 1905.

James, William. *The Letters of William James*. Boston: Atlantic Monthly Press, 1920.

Johns, Adrian. *The Nature of the Book: Print and Knowledge in the Making*. Chicago: University of Chicago Press, 1998.

Júdice, Nuno. *Antología de la poesía portuguesa cotemporánea*. Mexico City: Aldus, 2007.

Judt, Tony. *The Memory Chalet*. New York: Penguin, 2010.

Kandel, Eric R. *In Search of Memory: The Emergence of a New Science of Mind*. New York: W. W. Norton & Company, 2006.

Katz, Friedrich. *The Life and Times of Pancho Villa*. Stanford, CA: Stanford University Press, 1998.

———. *Nuevos ensayos mexicanos*. Mexico City: Era, 2006.

———. *The Secret War in Mexico: Europe, the United States, and the Mexican Revolution*. Chicago: University of Chicago Press, 1983.

Kayser, Wolfgang. *Das Sprachliche Kunstwerk*. Bern, Switzerland: Franke Verlag, 1968.

Kelley, Donald R. "*Historia Integra*: François Baudouin and his Conception of History." *Journal of the History of Ideas* 25, no. 1 (January–March 1964): 35–54.

Keynes, John Maynard. *The Economic Consequences of the Peace*. New York: Harcourt, Brace and Howe, 1920.

Kilito, Abdelfattah. *L'Auteur et ses doublés: essai sur la culture arabe classique*. Paris: Éditions du Seuil, 1985.

Kittay, Eve Feder. *Metaphor: Its Cognitive Force and Linguistic Structure*. Oxford: Oxford University Press, 1987.

Klein, Kerwin Lee. *From History to Theory*. Berkeley: University of California Press, 2011.

Knight, Alan. *Repensar la Revolución Mexicana*. 2 vols. Trad. Silvia L. Cuesy. Mexico City: El Colegio de México, 1913.

Kocka, Jürgen. *Sozialgeschichte: Begriff, Entwicklung, Probleme*. Göttingen: Vandenhoek & Ruprecht, 1977.

Koselleck, Reinhart, Otto Brunner, and Werner Conze. *Geschichtliche Grundbegriffe: Historisches Lexikon zur politisch-sozialen Sprache in Deutschland*. 8 vols. Stuttgart: Klett-Cotta, 1972–1997.

Kracauer, Siegfried. *History: The Last Things before the Last*. New York: Oxford University Press, 1969.

Krauze, Enrique. *Biografía del poder*. Mexico City: Tusquets, 2012.

Kunitz, Stanley. "An Interview with Stanley Kunitz." *Iowa Review* 5, no. 2 (Spring 1974): 76–85.

Lakoff, George, and Mark Johnson. *Metaphors We Live by*. Chicago: University of Chicago Press, 1980.

———. *Philosophy in the Flesh: The Embodied Mind and Its Challenge to Western Thought*. New York: Basic Books, 1999.

Langer, Susanne K. *Philosophy in a New Key: A Study in the Symbolism of Reason, Rite, and Art*. Cambridge, MA: Harvard University Press, 1957.

León, Luis de. *Poesías orginales de Fray Luis de León, revisadas por Don Federico de Onís*. San José, Costa Rica: García Monge, 1920.

Lerner, Gerda. *Fireweed: A Political Autobiography*. Philadelphia: Temple University Press, 2003.

Levi-Montalcini, Rita. *Elogio dell'imperfezione*. Milan: Baldini & Castoldi, 1990.

Lida, Raimundo. *Belleza, arte y poesía en la estética de Santayana y otros estudios*. Mexico City: El Colegio de México, 2014.

Lilla, Mark. *G. B. Vico: The Making of an Anti-Modern*. Cambridge, MA: Harvard University Press, 1993.

Lockhart, James. *The Nahuas after the Conquest: A Social and Cultural History of the Indians of Central Mexico, Sixteenth through Eighteenth Centuries*. Stanford, CA: Stanford University Press, 1994.

López Alonso, Moramay. *Measuring Up: A History of Living Standards in Mexico, 1850–1950*. Stanford, CA: Stanford University Press, 2012.

Lordat, Jacques. *Exposition de la doctrine médicale de P.-J. Barthez et mémoires sur la vie de ce médecin*. Paris: Gabon, 1818.

Lowenthal, David. *The Past Is a Foreign Country*. Cambridge: Cambridge University Press, 1999.

MacCormack, Sabine. *On the Wings of Time: Rome, the Incas, Spain, and Peru*. Princeton, NJ: Princeton University Press, 2006.

Machado, Antonio. *Poesías completas*. Buenos Aires: Espasa Calpe, 1940.

Machado de Assis, Joaquim Maria. *Contos*. Rio de Janeiro: Agir, 1963.

———. *Memórias póstumas de Brás Cubas*. Rio de Janeiro: Record, 1968.

Magris, Claudio. *Itaca e oltre*. Milan: Garzanti, 1982.

Mandelstam, Osip. "The Word and Culture." In *Complete Critical Prose*, trans. Jane Gary Harris and Constance Link, 112–116. Ann Arbor, MI: Ardis, 1979.

Manzoni, Alessandro. *On the Historical Novel*. Translated with an introduction by Sandra Bermann. Lincoln: University of Nebraska Press, 1984.

Maragall, Joan. *Obra poética: versión bilingüe*. Madrid: Castalia, 1984.

Marquard, Odo. *Felicidad en la infelicidad: reflexiones filosóficas*. Trans. N. Espinosa. Buenos Aires: Katz, 2006.

———. *In Defense of the Accidental*. Trans. Robert M. Wallace. New York: Oxford University Press, 1991.

———. *Schwierigkeiten mit der Geschichtsphilosophie*. Frankfurt am Main: Suhrkamp, 1973.

Martínez, José Luis. *Nezahualcóyotl, vida y obra*. Mexico City: Fondo de Cultura Económica, 2006.

Martínez Baca, Francisco. *Los tatuajes: estudio psicológico y médico-legal en delincuentes y militares*. Mexico City: Tipografía de la Oficina Impresora del Timbre, 1899.

Marx, Karl. *The Eighteenth Brumaire of Louis Bonaparte* (1852). Available at https://www.marxists.org/archive/marx/works/1852/18th-brumaire/.

Matute, Álvaro. *Lorenzo Boturini y el pensamiento histórico de Vico*. Mexico City: Universidad Nacional Autónoma de México, Instituto de Investigaciones Históricas, 1976.

Meier, Christian. *From Athens to Auschwitz: The Uses of History*. Trans. Deborah Lucas Schneider. Cambridge, MA: Harvard University Press, 2005.

Mencken, H. L. *The American Language: An Inquiry into the Development of English in the United States* (1919). New York: Alfred. K. Knopf, 2006.

Mendès, Catulle. *Monstres parisiens*. 2nd ed. Paris: E. Dentu, 1882.

Menéndez Pelayo, Marcelino. *Historia de los heterodoxos españoles*. 2 vols. Madrid: Biblioteca de Autores Cristianos, 2000.

Ménendez Pidal, Ramón. *Estudios sobre el Romancero*. Madrid: Espasa-Calpe, 1973.

Merleau-Ponty, Maurice. *La prose du monde*. Paris: Gallimard, 1969.

———. *The World of Perception* (a translation of *Causeries 1948*). New York: Routledge, 2004.

Meschonnic, Henri. *Célébration de la poésie*. Lagrasse, France: Verdier, 2001.

Meyer, Jean. *La cristiada*. 2 v. Mexico City: Siglo XXI, 1976.

———. *Le livre de mon père ou une suite européenne*. Mexico City: private edition, 2014.

———. *Rusia y sus imperios, 1894–1991*. Mexico City: Centro de Investigación y Docencia Económicas/Fondo de Cultura Económica, 1997.

———. *Yo, el francés: La intervención en primera persona, biografías y crónicas*. Mexico City: Tusquets, 2002.

Meyer, Jean, ed. *Egohistorias: El amor a Clío*. Mexico City: Centre d'Études Mexicaines et Centraméricaines, 1993.

Michaëlis de Vasconcellos, Carolina. *Cancioneiro da ajuda, edicão critica e commentada por Carolina Michaëlis de Vasconcellos*. 2 vols. Halle a.S., Germany: M. Niemeyer, 1904.

Mills, C. Wright. *The Sociological Imagination*. New York/Oxford: University Press, 1959.

Mink, Louis O. *Mind, History, and Dialectic: The Philosophy of R. G. Collingwood*. Bloomington: Indiana University Press, 1969.

Modell, Arnold H. *Imagination and the Meaningful Brain*. Cambridge, MA: MIT Press, 2003.

Momigliano, Arnaldo. *Essays in Ancient and Modern Historiography*. Middletown, CT: Wesleyan University Press, 1975.

Monk, Ray. *Ludwig Wittgenstein: The Duty of Genius*. New York: Penguin Books, 1991.

Mooney, Michael. *Vico in the Tradition of Rhetoric*. Princeton, NJ: Princeton University Press, 1985.

Moradiellos, Enrique. *Don Juan Negrín*. Barcelona: Península, 2006.

Muñoz, Rafael F. *Santa Anna: el dictador resplandeciente* (1938). Mexico City, Fondo de Cultura Económica, 2011.

Musil, Robert. *Der Mann ohne Eigenschaften: Roman*. Hamburg: Rowohlt, 1960. Translated by Eithne Wilkins and Ernst Kaiser as *The Man without Qualities*. London: Picador, 1979.

Nicholson, Harold. *Some People*. London: Faber & Faber, 1927.

Nossack, Hans Erich. *Der Untergang*. Frankfurt am Main: Suhrkamp, 1950. Translated as *The End: Hamburg 1943* by Joel Agee. Chicago: University of Chicago Press, 2004.

Novick, Peter. *That Noble Dream: The Objectivity Question and the American Historical Profession*. Cambridge: Cambridge University Press, 1993.

O'Gorman, Edmundo. *Crisis y porvenir de la ciencia histórica*. Mexico City: Impr. Universitaria, 1947.

———. *The Invention of America: An Inquiry into the Historical Nature of the New World and the Meaning of Its History*. Bloomington: Indiana University Press, 1961.

———. *México: El trauma de su historia*. Mexico City: Universidad Nacional Autónoma de México, 1977.

———. "Prólogo a la *Historia natural y moral de las Indias*" (1940), "Prólogo a los *Sucesos y diálogo de la Nueva España* de Gonzalo Fernández de Oviedo y Valdés" (1946), and "El caso México" (1944). In *Imprevisibles historias*. Mexico City: Fondo de Cultura Económica, 2009.

Ortega y Gasset, José. *España invertebrada*. Madrid: Espasa-Calpe, 1921.

Ozick, Cynthia. *Metaphor & Memory: Essays*. New York: Knopf, 1989.

Pascal, Blaise. *Pensées*. Paris: Pocket, 2003.

Paso, Fernando del. *Noticias del imperio*. Mexico City: Diana, 1987.

Paz, Octavio. *El arco y la lira*. Mexico City: Fondo de Cultura Económica, 1956. Translated by Ruth L. C. Simms as *The Bow and the Lyre: The Poem, the Poetic Revelation, Poetry and History*. Austin: University of Texas Press, 1973.

———. "Hablo de la ciudad." *Vuelta* 118 (September 1986): 8.

Peguy, Charles. *Clio: dialogue de l'histoire et de l'âme païenne* (1917). Paris: Gallimard, 1932.

Penna, Sandro. *Tutte le poesie*. Milan: Garzanti, 1970.

Pérez Galdós, Benito. *Episodios nacionales*. 3 vols. Barcelona: Galaxia Gutemberg, 2008.

Pessoa, Fernando. *A educação do estóico*. Lisbon: Assirio & Alvim, 1999.

———. *A língua portuguesa*. Ed. Luisa Medeiros. Lisbon: Assírio & Alvim, 1997.

Pinker, Steven. *The Better Angels of Our Nature: Why Violence Has Declined*. New York: Viking, 2011.

Pires, Manuel António. *Poesía, saudade da prosa: una antologia pessoal*. Lisbon: Assirio & Alvim, 2011.

Popkin, Jeremy D. *History, Historians, and Autobiography*. Chicago: University of Chicago Press, 2005.

Portugal, Homero de. *El declamador sin maestro: más de 100 poesías para declamar*. 11th ed. Mexico City: Lux, 1940.

Prieto, Guillermo. *La musa callejera*. Mexico City: Tipografía Literaria de Filomeno Mata, 1883.

———. *Memorias de mis tiempos*. Paris/Mexico City: Vda. de C. Bouret, 1906.

Proust, Marcel. *Swann's Way*. Trans. Lydia Davis. New York: Viking, 2003.

Ramón y Cajal, Santiago. *Recuerdos de mi vida: historia de mi labor científica*. Barcelona: Alianza, 2008.

Ranke, Leopold von. *The Theory and Practice of History*. Introduction by Georg G. Iggers. Trans. Wilma A. Iggers. London/New York: Routledge, 2011.

Rao, Velcheru Narayana, and David Shulman, eds. and trans. *Classical Telugu Poetry: An Anthology*. New Delhi/New York: Oxford University Press, 2002.

Rao, Velcheru Narayana, David Shulman, and Sanjay Subrahmanyam. *Textures of Time: Writing History in South India, 1600–1800*. Delhi: Permanent Black, 2001.

Real Academia de la Lengua Española. *Diccionario de la lengua española*. Available at http://www.rae.es.

Renan, Ernest. *History of the People of Israel*. Vol. 1. Boston: Robert Brothers, 1896.

———. *Oeuvres complètes de Ernest Renan*. Vols. 6 and 10. Ed. Henriette Psichari. Paris: Calmann-Lévy, 1947–1961.

———. *Recollections of My Youth*. Trans. C. B. Pitman. New York: G. P. Putnam's Sons, 1883.

Renard, Jules. *Journal*. Paris: Gallimard, 1955.

Reyes, Alfonso. *Antología: prosa, teatro, poesía*. Mexico City: Fondo de Cultura Económica, 2014.

———. *La X en la frente: textos sobre México*. Mexico City: UNAM, 1993.

———. *Visión de Anáhuac*. Monterrey, Mexico: Gobierno del Estado de Nuevo León, 1993.

Ricoer, Paul. *Memory, History, Forgetting*. Trans. Kathleen Blamey and David Pellauer. Chicago: University of Chicago Press, 2004.

Romancero español y morisco. Valencia: Prometeo, n.d.

Rorty, Richard. *Philosophy and Social Hope*. New York: Penguin Books, 1999.

———, ed. *The Linguistic Turn*. Chicago: University of Chicago Press, 1967.

Rorty, Richard, J. B. Schneewind, and Quentin Skinner, eds. *Philosophy in History: Essays on the Historiography of Philosophy*. New York: Cambridge University Press, 1984.

Ruiz, Telésforo. *Apuntes poéticos*. Mexico City: Murguía, 1866.

Ryan, Kay. *The Best of It: New and Selected Poems*. New York: Grove Press, 2010.

Sacks, Oliver. *The Man Who Mistook His Wife for a Hat and Other Clinical Tales*. New York: Summit Books, 1985.

———. *The Mind's Eye*. New York: Alfred A. Knopf, 2010.

———. *On the Move: A Life*. New York: Vintage Books, 2015.

Sacks, Sheldon, ed. *On Metaphor*. Chicago: University of Chicago Press, 1979.

Sánchez-Albornoz, Claudio. *Con un pie en el estribo*. Madrid: Revista de Occidente, 1974.

———. *España: un enigmo histórico*. 2 vols. Buenos Aires: Editorial Sudamericana, 1954.

Sánchez Albornoz, Nicolás. *Cárceles y exilios*. Barcelona: Anagrama, 2012.

Santayana, George. *Character and Opinion in the United States: With Reminiscences of William James and Josiah Royce and Academic Life in America*. New York: C. Scribner's Sons, 1920.

———. *The Last Puritan*. New York: Scribner, 1937.

———. *The Letters of George Santayana*. Ed. and introduction by William G. Holzberger. Vol. 5, Book 6. Cambridge, MA: MIT Press 2004.

———. *The Life of Reason*. Vol. 1. New York: C. Scribner's Sons, 1905.

———. *Persons and Places: The Background of My Life*. 2 vols. New York: Scribner, 1947.

———. *The Philosophy of Santayana: Selections from All the Works of George Santayana*. New York: Scribner, 1953.

———. *Scepticism and Animal Faith: Introduction to a System of Philosophy*. New York: C. Scribner's Sons, 1929.

———. *Soliloquies in England and Later Soliloquies*. New York: C. Scribner's Sons, 1922.

Santos, Wanderley Guilherme dos. *Acervo de maldizer*. Rio de Janeiro: Rocco, 2008.

———. *Discurso sobre o objeto: uma poética do social*. São Paulo: Companhia das Letras, 1990.

Sapir, Edward. *Language: An Introduction to the Study of Speech*. New York: Harcourt, 1949.

Sarmiento, Domingo Faustino. *Facundo: civilización y barbarie* (1845). Caracas, Venezuela: Biblioteca Ayacucho, 1985.

Schwob, Marcel. *Vies imaginaire*. Paris: G. Charpentier & E. Fasquelle, 1896.

Seghers, Anna. *Anna Seghers: Briefe, 1924–1952*. Berlin: Aufbau Verlag, 2008.

———. *Transit* (1948). Trans. M. B. Dembo. New York: New York Review of Books, 2013.

Semprún, Jorge. *L'Écriture ou la vie*. Paris: Gallimard, 1994.

Sena, Jorge de. *O reino da estupidez*. 2 vols. Lisbon: Moraes, 1978–1979.

Sergi, Giuseppe. *Antidoti all'abuso della storia*. Naples: Ligouri Editore, 2010.

Sevilla Fernández, José Manuel. "La presencia de Giambattista Vico en la cultura española (II. Notas sobre su tratamiento y estudio durante el siglo XX hasta la década de los '70)." *Cuadernos sobre Vico* 1 (1991): 97–132.

Sewell, William. *Logics of History: Social Theory and Social Transformation*. Chicago: University of Chicago Press, 2005.

Sidney, Philip. *An Apology for Poetry* (1583). Ed. Geoffrey Shepherd. London: T. Nelson, 1965.

Sierra, Justo, ed. *México: su evolución social*. 3 vols. Mexico City: J. Ballescá y Compañía, 1900–1902.

Skinner, Quentin. "The Idea of Negative Liberty: Philosophical and Historical Perspectives." In Richard Rorty, J. B. Schneewind, and Quentin Skinner, eds., *Philosophy in History*, 193–221. Cambridge, UK: Cambridge University Press, 1984.

Sloterdijk, Peter. *Critique of Cynical Reason*. Trans. Michael Eldred. Foreword by Andreas Huyssen. Minneapolis: University of Minnesota Press, 1987.

Stangl, Anne. *Der allgemeine deutsche Sprachverein*. Vienna: Selbstverlag, 1915.

Steedman, Carolyn. *Strange Dislocations: Childhood and the Idea of Human Interiority, 1780–1930*. Cambridge, MA: Harvard University Press, 1998.

Steinberg, Leo. "The Eye Is Part of the Mind." In *Other Criteria*, 289–306. Chicago: University of Chicago Press, 1972.

Stoler, Ann Laura. *Along the Archival Grain: Epistemic Anxieties and Colonial Common Sense*. Princeton, NJ: Princeton University Press, 2009.

Stone, Lawrence. *The Past and the Present*. Boston: Routledge & Kegan Paul, 1981.

Subrahmanyam, Sanjay. *Explorations in Connected History*. New Delhi: Oxford University Press, 2005.

———. *Penumbral Visions: Making Polities in Early Modern South India*. Ann Arbor: University of Michigan Press, 2001.

Tenorio, Martha Lilia. "Más inquisiciones: Borges y su concepto de la metáfora." *Iberoamericana* 17, nos. 3 and 4 (1993): 20–37.

Thompson, E. P. *Making History: Writings on History and Culture*. New York: New Press, 1994.

———. *The Poverty of Theory & Other Essays.* New York: Monthly Review Press, 1978.

Toews, John E. *Becoming Historical: Cultural Reformation and Public Memory in Early Nineteenth-Century Berlin.* Cambridge: Cambridge University Press, 2004.

———. "Stories of Difference and Identity: New Historicism in Literature and History." *Monatshefte* 84, no. 2 (Summer 1992): 193–210.

Tononi, G., and G. M. Edelman. "Consciousness and Complexity." *Science* 282 (1998): 1846–1851.

Torres, Màrius. *Poesies.* Barcelona: Ariel, 1953.

Trevor-Roper, H. R. *History & Imagination.* Oxford/New York: Oxford University Press/ Clarendon Press, 1980.

Turner, Frederick Jackson. *The Frontier in American History* (1893). Available at http://xroads.virginia.edu/~HYPER/TURNER/.

Unamuno, Miguel de. *En torno al casticismo.* Barcelona: A. Calderón & S. Valentí Camp, 1902.

Vaihinger, Hans. *The Philosophy of "As If": A System of the Theoretical, Practical and Religious Fictions of Mankind.* Trans. C. K. Ogden. London: Routledge & Kegan Paul, 1935.

Valcárcel, Luis E. *Memorias.* Lima, Peru: Instituto de Estudios Peruanos, 1981.

Valente, José Ángel. *Entrada en material.* Madrid: Cátedra, 1985.

———. *La memoria y los signos.* Madrid: Ediciones de la Revista de Occidente, 1966.

———. *Las palabras de la tribu.* Barcelona: Tusquets, 1994.

Valéry, Paul. *The Art of Poetry.* Edited by Jackson Mathews, Trans. Denise Folliot. Bollingen Series 45, Vol. 7. Princeton, NJ: Princeton University Press, 1989.

———. *Regards sur le monde actuel et autres essais.* Paris: Gallimard, 1945.

Vallejo, César. *Los heraldos negros.* Madrid: Anaya & Mario Muchnik/Málaga: Ayuntamiento de Málaga, 1992.

Varela, Javier. *La novela de España: los intelectuales y el problema español.* Madrid: Taurus, 1999.

Vasconcelos, José. *Ulises criollo.* Madrid: Fondo de Cultura Económica, 2000.

Venturi, Franco. "Un vichiano tra Messico e Spagna: Lorenzo Boturini Benaduci." *Rivista Storica Italiana* 4 (1975): 770–784.

Vicens Vives, Jaume. *Aproximaciones a la historia de España.* Barcelona: Universidad de Barcelona, 1952.

Vico, Giambattista. *The Autobiography of Giambattista Vico.* Trans. M. A. Fisch and T. G. Bergin. Ithaca, NY: Cornell University Press, 1944.

———. *Principios de una ciencia nueva: en torno a la naturaleza común de las naciones.* Trans. Josep Carner. 2 vols. Mexico City: El Colegio de México, 1941. Translated by Thomas Goddard Bergin and Max Harold Fisch as *The New Science of Giambattista Vico.* Ithaca, NY: Cornell University Press, 1948.

Villacorta Macho, María Consuelo. "Creando memoria: Pedro López de Ayala y Lope

García de Salazar." In Jon Andoni Fernández de Larrea and José Ramón Diaz de Durana, *Memoria e historia: utilización política en la corona de Castilla al final de la Edad Media*, 59–76. Madrid: Silex, 2010.

Vitale, Ida. *Poesía reunida: (1949-2015)*. Barcelona: Tusquets, 2017.

Vivas, Eliseo. *Creation and Discovery: Essays in Criticism and Aesthetics*. New York: Noonday Press, 1955.

———. *Vivas as Critic: Essays in Poetics and Criticism*. Ed. Hugh Mercer Curtler. Troy, NY: Whitston Publishing Company, 1982.

Wang, Hui. *China's New Order*. Trans. Theodore Huters. Cambridge, MA: Harvard University Press, 2003.

Weiner, Jonathan. *Time, Love, Memory*. New York: Vintage Books, 2000.

Weinrich, Harald. *Leteo: arte y crítica del olvido*. Trans. Carlos Fortea. Madrid: Siruela, 1997.

———. *On Borrowed Time: The Art and Economy of Living with Deadlines*. Trans. Steven Rendall. Chicago: Chicago University Press, 2008.

White, Hayden. "The Burden of History" (1966). In *Tropics of Discourse: Essays in Cultural Criticism*, 27–51. Baltimore: Johns Hopkins University Press, 1978.

———. *The Content of the Form: Narrative Discourse and Historical Representation*. Baltimore: Johns Hopkins University Press, 1987.

———. *Metahistory: The Historical Imagination in Nineteenth-Century Europe*. Baltimore: Johns Hopkins University Press, 1973.

Whitman, Walt. *An American Primer* (1904). Ed. Horace Traubel. Rpt. Stevens Point, Wisconsin: Holy Cow! Press, 1987.

Williams, Tennesee. *Collected Stories*. Introduction by Gore Vidal. New York: New Directions, 1985.

Wittgenstein, Ludwig. *Philosophical Remarks*. Trans. R. Hargreaves and R. White. Chicago: University of Chicago Press, 1980.

Womack, John. *Zapata and the Mexican Revolution*. New York: Vintage Books, 1970.

Woolf, Virginia. *Collected Essays*. Vol. 4: *1925-1928*. London: Hogarth Press, 1967.

———. *The Common Reader: First Series*. New York: Harcourt, Brace & Company, 1953.

———. *The Diary of Virginia Woolf*. New York: Harcourt Brace Jovanovich, 1977.

———. *Moments of Being: Unpublished Autobiographical Writings*. New York: Harcourt Brace Jovanovich, 1976.

———. *Orlando: A Biography* (1928). Oxford: Oxford University Press, 2008.

———. "Sketch of the Past." Woolf Online Project (manuscript). Available at https://goo.gl/ZwTaK2.

Wordsworth, William. "At Rome--Regrets--In Allusion to Niebuhr and Other Modern Historians." In *The Complete Poetical Works*, 754. London: Macmillan & Company, 1888.

Yates, Frances A. *The Art of Memory*. Chicago: University of Chicago Press, 1966.

Yourcenar, Marguerite. *The Abyss (L'oeuvre au noir)*. Trans. Grace Frick. New York: Farrar, Straus & Giroux, 1976.

Zaid, Gabriel. *Cómo leer en bicicleta: problemas de la cultura y el poder en México*. Mexico City: Joaquín Mortiz, 1975.

———. *Leer poesía*. Mexico City: Joaquín Mortiz, 1972.

———. *Los demasiados libros* (1972). Barcelona: Anagrama, 1996.

Zambrano, María. *Filosofía y poesía*. Mexico City: Fondo de Cultura Económica, 1987.

———. *Hacia un saber sobre el alma*. Madrid: Alianza, 1987.

———. *Los sueños y el tiempo*. Madrid: Siruela, 1992.

Zweig, Stefan. *Die Welt von Gestern: Erinnerungen eines Europäers*. Düsseldorf, Germany: Artemis & Winkler Verlag, 2002.